The Mallet of Loving Correction

THIS SPECIAL SIGNED EDITION
IS LIMITED TO
1000 NUMBERED COPIES.

THIS IS COPY 675.

The Mallet of Loving Correction

Selected Writings from Whatever, 2008–2012

John Scalzi

Subterranean Press 2013

First Edition

ISBN
978-1-59606-579-6

Subterranean Press
PO Box 190106
Burton, MI 48519

www.subterraneanpress.com

Dedication

This book is dedicated to Kate Baker, friend and occasional wielder of the Mallet. Thank you for being both.

This book is also dedicated to those who comment on Whatever. May you never be malleted, but if you are, may you take your correction in the loving manner with which it is offered.

Author's Introduction

Oh, look, here we are again.

First, explanations and context, for the one or two of you who need it. This book is a collection of entries from my blog, Whatever, covering the timeframe from June 2008 through November 2012 (it would have gone through to December 2012, but I slacked off that month and didn't write anything on the blog that month I thought worthy of inclusion). This timeframe covers two presidential elections, several generations of electronics, the rise of Twitter and Facebook, multiple waves of Internet craziness, the advance of same-sex marriage as a civil right, and, personally speaking, the publication of several books, the winning of a few awards for writing (including a Hugo for this book's predecessor, *Your Hate Mail Will Be Graded*) and my tenure as the president of the Science Fiction and Fantasy Writers of America. It's been a busy few years all around.

All the entries here were originally published on my blog, which—I am very happy to say—has a large and vibrantly argumentative collection of commenters. All of these entries had comments attached to them once they were published; some had hundreds of comments as the regular visitors argued back and forth with each other. This was particularly the case with the political posts, as you might imagine, but any topic is fair game for an argument. One of the things I am happy about is that, unlike all too many sites, the comments on my site are usually worth reading. This is an artifact of Whatever building a retinue of smart, engaged readers over the decade and a half it's been around. I'm delighted they show up; I'm equally delighted that they stick around.

It's also an artifact of me having a comment moderation policy, in which I keep the conversation on topic, warn people when they are being rude to other commenters or employing cheap rhetorical tricks, and expunge the comments that are obnoxious, lazy or trollish. At some point during the last several years, I began calling the latter "malleting," and created a metaphorical instrument for the purpose: The Mallet of Loving Correction. It is this mallet from which this collection takes its title.

(And yes, now I have in my possession a physical Mallet of Loving Correction, given to me as a gift. It is very large and has on its head a quote from me, which reads "I don't love you any less for being so WRONG on the Internet." Yeah, that about sums it up.)

This book is scheduled for release on September 13, 2013—the fifteenth anniversary of the debut of Whatever. It's strange for me to think that I have been writing Whatever for as long as I have. Even now, more than a decade into the 21st Century, blogs don't have a sterling reputation for being serious writing (a fact I suspect is at least partially related to the word "blog" itself, which sounds more like a fungal infection than a repository for prose), and I imagine there might still be people who wonder why I bother writing it, especially when I could be writing other things, like more novels and books, or other sorts of pay copy.

One answer is, well, I do those things *anyway*—writing the blog doesn't hurt that. A second answer is that writing on Whatever lets me write what I want, when I want, how I want, which is the sort of freedom of expression that I value as a person. A third answer is that the blog reaches tens of thousands of people a day, hundreds of thousands a month and millions in the course of a year. That's an audience any writer would love to have, and I have it. I think I'll keep it for a while longer, thanks.

There's one more reason. In a very real sense, Whatever is my life's work; it's fifteen years (so far) of me thinking about what's going on in my life and in my world. I have no illusions that when I roll off from this rock future generations will note or care about my existence, save possibly for a few academics scrounging for a thesis subject or some descendants curious about that writer in their family timeline. But it matters to me to note my time and my place in it. In this regard Whatever has an audience of one. This is me, remembering in real time.

I hope you enjoy this particular set of memories.

John Scalzi
December 27, 2012

A Note on the Organization of This Book

The Mallet of Loving Correction covers four and a half years of writing but is not arranged chronologically, because one, that's boring, and two, there are times where I would write on one general subject for a few weeks, and having one piece after another on the same subject is also boring.

So, instead, this book is arranged (mostly) alphabetically, by title of entry. I say mostly because there are a few entries that I've moved out of alphabetical sequence because I wanted to. I trust this will not make your OCD explode.

Although the book is not arranged chronologically, every entry does have its publication date prominently noted, so—for example—you'll be able to tell whether I'm talking about the 2008 US presidential election, or the 2012 US presidential election.

Some entries are slightly edited from the version that appeared on Whatever to reflect the fact that they're being presented in a book, not on a Web site. So hyperlinks have been removed and some text changed to give the context that the hyperlinks used to provide. Aside from that and copyediting, however, the content of the entries is unchanged, so you will see me being wildly incorrect on several matters of speculation and opinion, and possibly also on a few matters of actual fact. That's writing in the moment for you. Wheee!

—JS

10 Things to Remember About Authors

Feb
26
2009

Because it appears someone needs to say these things out loud, some thoughts, for the consideration of readers, about authors, particularly novelists. Warning: This is long.

1. Authors aren't machines: Which is to say, we do not reliably and through a purely mechanical process extrude Novel-Length Textual Product with Extra Added Plot and Character Flavors™ on a predictable schedule. Like all things that live, we do our thing imprecisely. Sometimes the novels come out regularly and uniformly; sometimes they don't. Sometimes the novels conform to our own expectations of what they should be; sometimes they come out malformed and need to be fixed before they can be sent out into the world. Sometimes they just don't work at all and have to be tossed. Sometimes production is easy, sometimes it's not.

Certainly many authors *strive* for predictable process, which is why so many of them block out a regular amount of time every day, and try to bang out a regular number of words a day. But working at a regular pace and time and with a regular amount of output *does not mean* that any individual novel will thereby come out on a predictable schedule. Some of those 500 or 1,000 daily words will be unusable; some of those will be spent rewriting other words; some of those words will be so great that it takes the novel in a new direction that the author has to follow to see where it leads, to the exclusion of finishing the novel on a schedule. Predictable process in this case does not necessarily lead to predictable output.

Corollary to the above:

2. Authors are human: Our brains, the organ we use to create our novels, are touchy and imprecise things. They get bored. They get confused. They lose track of plot and narrative threads. They think too much about some things, and not nearly enough about others. They are sometimes ambitious beyond their actual grasp. They are likewise sometimes tremendously poor estimators of their own capacity. Our brains, in short, are a hindrance as much as a help to us—as they are for all humans.

And like all humans, we authors are a vain and rationalizing group, wanting to look good to others and rationalizing when we do not perform to our own expectations or the expectations of others—and often doing a *better* job of rationalizing our failures than others, because, after all, we're pretty good with that fiction thing, and what is rationalization but self-serving fiction? Like all humans we screw up and succeed in nearly equal measure, and hope merely that the screw-ups are smaller overall than the successes. As a class of human, we are not notably different than any other class of human, in terms of performance and behavior. Wish we were better (and more attractive!), but we're not.

Because of the above, the next point naturally follows:

3. Authors have lives: Writing is not all we do. Many of us conned other people into becoming spouses or otherwise being significant others and are thus obliged to spend time interacting with them in a manner that hopefully fosters their inclination to continue said intimate relationship. Some of us, as a consequence of above, might have spawned and are thus obliged to contribute in ways material, intellectual and spiritual, to the development of such offspring. Some of us have even managed to create and maintain familiar association with others in a phenomenon known as "friendship"—which also requires tending.

Beyond these things, we authors also have some required and desired physical and mental activities. We need to eat, sleep, poop, (somewhat more rarely) exercise and (even more rarely, alas) get laid. We may also choose to pursue activities that have no immediate profitable purpose but which refresh our brains through amusement: Watching TV, playing sports, arguing with people about absolutely pointless things online, collecting stamps, traveling, attending conventions or conferences, staring at pictures of other nekkid people, and so on and so forth. Likewise, there are some things we would prefer not to do but have to anyway, like take out the trash, do the laundry, pay the bills, call up publishers/editors and ask where our damn money is, be civil to people we don't like but have some reason not to say "kindly piss off, would you?" to, attend meetings or therapy, and so on. While none of these things is directly related to writing, it's likely without doing them, our interest and/or capacity for writing might be in some way compromised.

And beyond these things are the "Life is a drunk driver and you're the poor bastard pedestrian what just stepped into the crosswalk" items: Someone we love dies. Our day job disappears from under us. We get a divorce. We or someone we know develops a dependency. We get sick (and, if you're a writer in the US, as a freelance person, likely have no health insurance). Not only does this kick us in the ass because we're human, it kicks us in the ass because it's hard to be creative/funny/interesting/engaged in writing when your world is falling apart around you. This isn't asking for an extra dollop of sympathy. It's pointing out that being creative often works best in congenial surroundings.

Following all that:

4. Authors frequently won't tell you about the details of their lives: Which is to say sometimes when you're wondering why that favorite author of yours is late with a book you're expecting, you won't get an explanation that, say, someone close to her is suffering from severe depression and she's spending her time tending to them, or, say, that he's decided that what he's written is crap and he can't in good conscience inflict it on his readers, or, say, that he's spent the last nine months playing World of Warcraft and has now totally leveled out all his characters, which is good, but didn't do any writing, which is, well, bad. And why won't you get an explanation? Simple: *Because it's none of your damn business.*

No, really, it's not. Perhaps you think it is, but you're wrong about that. Just as the particulars of your own life need not be discussed with anyone else not actively involved in it, so too are the particulars of an author's life beyond your purview, unless the author chooses to share them with you (meaning, most likely, sharing with the public in a general sense). And even then you probably shouldn't expect a full accounting of details, because authors, even the ones with blogs and active public presences, quite naturally decide where their public sphere ends and their private sphere begins.

And no, being a fan of an author's books or series doesn't count as being actively involved in that author's life. You are actively involved with his or her *books;* that's not even close to the same thing. Following the author's blog/Twitter/Facebook page and even commenting there doesn't get you into their lives either. As personable as an author can be, live, online or in his or her writing, *personable* is not the same as *personal*. Authors are under no obligation to keep you informed about things in their lives. It's nice if they do, but it's not required. Frankly, it shouldn't necessarily be *expected*.

Intimately tied into this: Authors frequently won't tell you the details of their business lives, either, for much the same reasons.

This is related to the following:

5. Authors do many things for many reasons: Let's say your favorite author, rather than working on a novel you want him to release, instead decides to edit an anthology. You ask: What is this idjit thinking? I and many other fans are waiting for that novel! He could make so much more money by putting that novel out! What on earth could possibly motivate such a bonehead maneuver?

Off the top of my head, here are some reasons:

a) The author was contractually obliged to edit the anthology before he signed for the novel you're waiting for.

b) The author has painted himself into a corner with the novel and needs time to think it through, and while doing that wants to keep himself busy and getting paid.

c) The author is bored writing the novel and needs to do something else, otherwise the completed novel will suck.

d) The author is using his name and influence to help out some fellow writers by editing an anthology, which will allow him to help their careers and throw some money their way.

e) The author is curious about this whole editing thing and wants to see what it's like.

Or: some combination of two or more of the above reasons, or perhaps none of those reasons at all. Point is, what the author does and why he or she does it might not make sense to you, but makes perfect sense to the author. Why the disparity in opinion? Because you're not the author, and *per* point 4, you're likely not get a full explanation of his or her reasoning.

6. One author ≠ another author: Now, perhaps one of your favorite authors jams out a readable novel every six months (or every nine months, or every year, whatever). If she can do that, why can't this other author whose books you love do the same thing? Simple: Because they're two entirely different people. They don't have the same writing habits, the same writing process, the same life circumstances, the same business circumstances or even, likely, the same career goals and aspirations. They produce similar consumer objects (i.e., novels), but everything else is likely quite different.

Now, one thing to keep in mind here is that the publishing world, in general, tries to select for the writers who can produce good, competent prose on a more-or-less predictable schedule, because people follow authors and want more from their favorites, and publishing wants that pipeline filled. One side effect of this, naturally, is that bookstores are filled with authors who produce good, competent prose on a more-or-less predictable schedule. *It does not mean*, however, that every author *does* work this way, or *can* work this way, or *should* work this way if the quality of their work suffers because of it. The business practices and tendencies of the publishing industry, and the type of writer those practices and tendencies favor, shouldn't be used by fans as an argument against the writer whose own schedule does not conform to them. Because, among other things:

7. One novel ≠ another novel: Even the novelists skilled at churning out prose fast enough to make their publishers happy have wide variances in the time it takes to finish one book and another. One novel might take five weeks to finish, another could take five months, or five years—or it might never get finished. Past performance is not a guarantee of future results.

Why the variance? Because some novels are harder than others, and because one's life is never the same one novel-writing time to the next. A novel that might take an author three months to finish when nothing is distracting her might take her two years if she's getting a divorce and trying to get her life back together. A novel that she blocked out six months to write might take two months if it suddenly all comes together in her head, and she races to get it on the page before she forgets how all the puzzle pieces fit together. The kicker is as a reader you might not be able to tell a five-week novel from a five-year novel; process doesn't work that way.

This variance takes place not only from novel to novel but sometimes also within a series; very frequently the first few books of a series are kicked out in rapid order while the final books take longer. This is sometimes an artifact of the series' world becoming more complex and the author having to keep track of more things; sometimes it might be an artifact of the author deciding not to rush; sometimes it's an artifact of the author getting hit by a car. Beyond this there's another salient fact:

8. Authors and their circumstances change over time: It may be the author who earlier in her career could bat out three novels in a year finds she's only capable of one a year now, or vice-versa. It could be an author plans to write a whole lot of books now in order to build the sort of name that allows her to write at a more leisurely pace in the future. It could be that an author who has built her name writing in one genre gets bored with that genre and wants to write something else entirely. It could be an author decides that being an author is too much damn work for not nearly enough money and decides to do something else with her life. It could be that an author becomes so famous that she decides she no longer needs to be edited, even when she does. It could be whatever creative spark that animated an author to literary heights abandons her and everything else she does from that point is merely competent at best. It could be an author just stops caring—or decides to care about something so intently it colors everything she writes.

Authors change because they are people, and people change, even the ones who hardly seem to change at all (if nothing else, they get older). Most of this change from the reader point of view happens offstage, because your primary experience with the author is their books, but you'll notice the change nonetheless. Expecting authors to stay constant, in terms of output, quality or novelty, is not necessarily the most realistic thing a reader can do, unless they genuinely feel they are exactly as they were five, ten, twenty or thirty years ago. In which case they might want to get a second opinion from someone a little less subjective.

When we talk of an author's circumstances changing over time, incidentally, here is something else to remember:

9. Authors' careers (and choices therein) are not always entirely under their control: An author can write a fantastic book no one ever reads because the publisher goes under before the book is published, or decides to promote another book more avidly, or because the book comes out the same day as a blockbuster hits and it gets swamped. An author can write two books in what becomes your favorite series only to be told by the publisher that they're not selling, so the series is canceled. An author can write good books that sell well and still get dropped because the multinational his publisher is part of is trimming costs and his next book didn't get its contract written up in time. Conversely, an author could write something he believes is a silly, pointless trifle, have it become unspeakably huge, and find himself with the really interesting position of being able to become *really rich and famous*...if he just keeps batting out more novels about something he doesn't actually care about all that much, which will consume the biggest portion of his creative life.

Lots of stuff that happens in the careers of authors happens *to* them, with the author then maneuvering either to take advantage of it or to get out of its path of destruction. And while I pointed out events specific to an author above, sometimes it's industry-wide events that happen, like a massive change in how books get distributed, or one of the big bookselling chains going under, or it's global events, like recessions, wars or just some really big, stupid *fad*. Authors are subject to the same chain-yanks and unexpected events as everyone else; the difference is that these will have an effect on the books you were hoping to read. Sometimes there's not much we can do about it. Sorry.

What does this lead up to? Simply this:

10. Keep all of the above in mind the next time you go snarking off on your favorite author for not jumping through your hoops. I'm not saying *don't* snark; that would be like telling the tide not to come in, and besides, I'm the last person to tell people not to snark. I am saying to be aware that behind the books you read is a single person who is trying to bring you something worth reading, while also dealing with all the same basic crap you have to deal with, plus some extra crap that is specific to his or her chosen field.

Unlike in a lot of creative fields, we don't get to farm out some or all of the creative work to someone else; we've got to deal with it ourselves. It's a fair amount of work, particularly if you're one of those authors who wants his or her readers to feel like they've gotten value for their money. Yes, some writers are lazy; yes, some are inveterate fiddlers who don't know when something is done; yes, some writers are just basically screwed up, or hostile, or stoned or whatever. *Most* of them are trying to do a good job for you and get you something you'll be glad to have read.

So, a small request. Before you lump an author who is not performing to your immediate expectations into the "slacktastic asstard" category, won't you at least consider some of the above points? Just consider them, is all I'm asking. I don't think it's too much to ask, especially regarding someone you're hoping will give you something good, and who, most likely, is hoping to do the same thing.

15 Years

Jun
17
2010

Yesterday was the 17th anniversary of the first date between Krissy and myself, the day before that the 16th anniversary of my marriage proposal, and today, as it happens, is the 15th anniversary of our wedding. Yes, that's right, we have a three-day anniversary festival every year. It makes anniversaries easier to remember, if nothing else.

If you've been reading along for the last couple of days, you've probably gotten the (correct) intimation that even after fifteen (or sixteen, or seventeen) years, I am still insensibly in love with my wife and just about unbearably happy to be married to her every day. This is, of course, entirely true. What this elides, however—what this sort of lightly skips over—is that this happiness does not just exist; it has to be created and built and maintained. Six years ago, when I was giving marriage advice to others, I wrote: "Marriage is work. It never stops being work. It never *should*." This is something I still think is true. Human relationships are highly entropic; you have to keep putting energy into them or they fall apart. Marriages are especially entropic because they operate at such a high level of commitment, and yet ironically I think lots of people assume that once achieved, a marriage takes care of itself.

It doesn't. But marriage isn't an object or a thing or a pet with opposable thumbs and the ability to open Tupperware to feed itself while you're out doing something else. It's a system, a process, a relationship. It's not solid state; it's got lots of moving parts. You have to tend to it or it jams up and stops functioning. So: Marriage is work. It never stops being work. It never should.

Work is not a bad thing, mind you. Work can be joyful and pleasurable and a thing which illuminates and gives meaning to every corner of your life. Work can be a very good thing. What makes it work is simply that has to be done.

I'm not going to give you a list of "work tips" because I think a) that'd be a little smug of me and b) different marriages are made up of different people and what works for us isn't necessarily going to work for them. But there is one thing Krissy and I do which I think does have universal application, so allow me to recommend it to you. And it is:

Krissy and I say "I love you" to each other. A lot. As in, it's typically the first thing we say to each other in the morning, and the last thing we say to each other in the evening, and the thing that gets worked into the conversation during the rest of the day. We say it because we mean it, and we often also say it because we mean something else by it. Depending on context, "I love you" means "I love you," or "I need your help with this thing I'm doing" or "I can't believe this is the fourth time I've asked you to take out the trash" or "thank you" or "I miss you" or "I am saying these words to remind myself that I do in fact love you because right now what I really want to do is SMOTHER YOU TO DEATH WITH THIS PILLOW" or "You should get me ice cream" or "You are a good parent" or "Damn you are HAWT" or any number of other things.

And you ask, why don't you just say *those* things instead of "I love you"? For one reason, because generally speaking we could say those things to just about anyone (when, you know, *appropriate*), but "I love you" is reserved away for the two of us, so it's a reminder of what we mean to each other. For another reason, in those times that we're frustrated or exasperated or angry or tired, it lets the other of us know that even though we *are* frustrated or exasperated or angry or tired, that doesn't change the fact that we love them. For another reason, as long as you mean it, saying or hearing those words never gets old. For another reason, saying the words gives you an opportunity to actually remember that you *do* love the other person—it's another opportunity to cherish them in your heart, even (especially) when it's an "I love you" of the "take out the trash, already" variety. And for a final reason, hey, you know what? We just plain *like* saying it to each other, and that's all the excuse we need.

Saying "I love you" isn't in itself a sufficient act of marriage work; words have to be backed up by deeds. Even so, I think saying "I love you" can be both performative and sustaining, the mortar between the bricks in the edifice of a married life. I'd say without hesitation that each of us telling the other that we love them, as often as we tell each other, has mattered to our marriage. It seems a simple and maybe even silly thing, but, I don't know. If you're too complex and serious to tell your spouse that you love them, early and often, I wish you joy in your marriage nonetheless. It works for us, we'll keep doing it, and I recommend it to everyone, for every day of their marriage and life together.

In fact, go do it now. If you're married (and even if you're not), seek out that person whom you love and who loves you, and tell them that you love them. Pretty sure they'll be happy that you said it. Which will make you happy. Which will make Krissy and me happy, on this our 15th wedding anniversary.

25 Geeks NOT to Follow on Twitter

May
15
2009

Since I was on a list of the 100 geeks to follow on Twitter, I thought it would be appropriate to give a little attention to the other side of that particular equation.

The 25 Geeks NOT to Follow on Twitter

1. @DrunkenStalker
2. @MoroseOldBoyfriend
3. @IHeartBoogers
4. @AynRandBoyToy
5. @EnterTheBasement
6. @Cats6Catboxes0
7. @BobaFart
8. @IDontBlink
9. @BathingInMayo
10. @MyVoicesSayKill
11. @BrowncoatBrownshirt
12. @OneShower1985
13. @MyEyesYrBoobs
14. @USENETsMostWanted
15. @MomSezImSocialized
16. @LiveLongAndPerspire
17. @JobsGatesSlashFan
18. @ThatSmellIsMe
19. @SpksOnlyElvish

20. @WhatzNMyColon

21. @OwnzAZune

22. @CuddlePileReviewer

23. @MuggleMugger

24. @PolyDesperate

25. @2Girls1Tweet

AGNOSTICISM WITHOUT PAIN

Feb
8
2012

Slate (reprinting from the *Financial Times*) has a story on how difficult it is to be an atheist in the United States. I read the piece with the same attitude that I have regarding most pieces about how difficult it is to be atheist/agnostic in the US, which is with a mild sense of dissonance. I have been the sort of agnostic that shorthands into "atheist" for all of my thinking life, and I haven't made any secret of my lack of faith. The negative consequences for such a lifestyle choice, so far, at least, have been pretty minimal and indeed close to non-existent. I'm not saying *other* agnostics and atheists have not suffered negative consequences for their lack of belief; I'm sure they have. What I'm saying is that I haven't, and it's mildly curious to me why I have not.

Naturally, I have theories.

The first and most obvious: I am white, male, heterosexually paired, educated and financially well-off—i.e., the advantages I have are substantial and immediately apparent in our culture, so that even if being agnostic somehow offers a disadvantage, it's swamped out by other factors. I have privilege in ridiculous amounts and I know it.

Second, neither in my social nor in my work life is being an agnostic a penalty. I write for a living; the writing I do is consumed by a class of people (science fiction and fantasy readers) who generally are not only *not* scandalized by my agnosticism, but might be mildly surprised if I *did* have strong religious beliefs. Likewise, my social peers are currently other writers and people who tend toward professions where a lack of strong religious belief is not a problem (science and tech-related fields, with some overlap in creative professions). So again, my lack of faith is really not a penalty.

(One interesting wrinkle on this: I live in a rural, conservative community and have for more than a decade. Rural conservative communities are just the sort of place where atheists and agnostics aren't supposed to fit in. But in eleven years living here I can't remember it ever being an issue. I suspect one reason for this is that many of folks here are from churches which have an active policy of tolerance and an emphasis on one's good works. I suspect that another reason is that people here know I'm a writer and just assume writers are odd ducks anyway.)

Third, as far as being agnostic goes, while I'm perfectly open about it, I'm not aggressively so, nor am I generally antagonistic toward the concept of faith. I'm perfectly happy for others to have faith, and generally speaking I don't take offense at the display of faith around me, or stand against it so long as that expression of faith does not encroach on my own rights and prerogatives. If having faith and/or being religious gives you joy, then have it and be it; for myself, I'll pass, thanks. I think it also helps that, from my own personal interest, I know a fair amount about a number of faiths and can speak with at least passing knowledge about them (and am often curious about the things I don't know). People with faith assume those without it have no knowledge, interest or respect for faith. If you let them know you do, in my experience a lot of suspicion goes away.

Fourth, I've been lucky. I grew up without a religious background, so I didn't have to rebel against it. My education was at schools that actively encouraged pluralism and tolerance for faith, including the absence of faith—I was on my high school's "Faith Gang" as a representative of secular humanism, for example. I've gotten through life largely surrounded by tolerant people, both of faith and without it, which allowed me to develop my own views on faith without undue defensiveness or division. Not everyone has that.

Add it all up and you get an agnostic experience without ostracism or penalty, at least so far. I am led to believe that my lack of faith will keep me from being President of the United States, but inasmuch as that's not actually a life goal for me (and Krissy wouldn't let me anyway), this is not a huge setback. Otherwise, essentially, it's not been a problem for me. I wish others who choose not to believe were as fortunate as I have been.

All The Many Ways Amazon So Very Failed the Weekend

Feb
1
2010

(At the end of January 2010, Amazon and Macmillan, one of the major US publishers, had a disagreement about book pricing which ended up with Amazon removing all Macmillan books from its site for several days – without letting anyone know what was happening. This was written in the immediate aftermath of that – JS)

Leaving aside the moral, philosophical, cultural and financial implications of this weekend's Amazon/Macmillan slapfight and What It All Means for book readers and the future of the publishing industry, in one very real sense the whole thing was an exercise in public communications, a process by which two very large companies made a case for themselves in the public arena. And in this respect, we can say this much without qualification: oh, sweet Jesus, did Amazon ever hump the bunk.

How did it do so? I'm glad you asked! Let us count the ways.

1. The Stealth Delisting. Look: Wiping out roughly a sixth of your own bookstore product inventory, even temporarily, is one hell of a dramatic statement. If Amazon had given it any sort of rational or at least *tactical* thought, they could have played it up for all it was worth, starting with strategically-placed rumors to trusted, sympathetic media about the behind-the-scenes struggle with Macmillan, which would build to a more-in-sorrow-than-in-anger corporate decision to put Amazon shoppers first and to stand up to Macmillan, followed by the announcement of a public deadline for the delisting of Macmillan product to highlight the struggle, with a notation that all orders placed before that deadline would of course be honored (hint, hint), and so on. Basically, all sorts of public gamesmanship designed to put the pressure on Macmillan and to make it look like the bad guy. And in the meantime the media would be all abuzz with What It All Means. What drama! What excitement! What *corporate theater.* Amazon could have spun this its way for a week.

But no. Instead, we got the Foot-Stompingly Petulant Friday Night Massacre: One minute the books were there, the next they weren't. And everyone was left going "huh?" Was it a hardware glitch? Was it a software bug? Was it a terrorist act in which renegade Amish attacked Amazon's server farm and poured jugs of hard cider into the machines, shorting out the ones holding Macmillan's vasty inventory? No! It was one corporate entity having a big fat hissy fit at another corporate entity, and everyone had to figure out what the hell was going on over the weekend from bits and pieces that they found on the Internet, which was not easy to do. Which may have been Amazon's plan all along: Kill every sixth book on your site, hope no one notices! Well played, Amazon, well played *indeed.*

2. Amazon Lost the Authors. Hey, you want to know how to piss off an author? It's easy: Keep people from buying their books. You want to know how to *really* piss them off? Keep people from buying their books for reasons *that have nothing to do with them.* And you know how to make them absolutely *incandescent with rage*? Keep people from buying their books for reasons that have nothing to do with them, and keep it a *surprise* until it happens. Which, as it happens, is exactly what Amazon did. As a result: Angry, angry authors. Oh so *very* angry.

Amazon apparently forgot that when it moved against Macmillan, it also moved against Macmillan's authors. Macmillan may be a faceless, soulless baby-consuming corporate entity with no feelings or emotions, but *authors* have both of those, and are also twitchy neurotic messes who obsess about their sales, a fact which Amazon should be well aware of because we check our Amazon numbers four hundred times a day, and a one-star Amazon review causes us to crush up six Zoloft and snort them into our nasal cavities, because waiting for the pills to digest would *just take too long*.

These are the people Amazon pissed off. Which was not a smart thing, because as we all know, the salient feature of writers is that they *write*. And they did, about this, all weekend long. And not just Macmillan's authors, but other authors as well, who reasonably feared that their corporate parent might be the next victim of Amazon's foot-stompery. Which brings us to the next point:

3. Amazon Lost the Author's Fans. The interesting thing about the fans of authors: They feel somewhat connected *to* their favorite authors. So when their favorite authors kvetched on their blogs and Facebook pages and Twitter feeds about the screwing Amazon was giving them, what did many of these fans do? They *also* kvetched on their blogs and Facebook pages and Twitter feeds. So in pissing off a myriad of authors, Amazon also pissed off an exponential number of book readers, many of whom followed their favorite authors' leads in complaining about Amazon, and who themselves were read and followed by an exponential number of others. Even on a weekend, the traditional slow time for the Internets, that's a lot of pissed-off people.

So, two and a half days of the Internet being angry at Amazon. To be sure, there were people taking the side of Amazon, too. But those people lacked the social cohesion of an aggrieved class (writers) backed up by a mass of supporters—not to mention the relatively high profile of these writers online, which, if you were a journalist looking for reaction quotes while on deadline, made them the go-to sources.

Could Amazon have come out and given its side of the story? Sure, but it didn't—not soon enough. First it let angry authors define the event, and then it let someone else, rather more damaging to them than the authors.

4. Amazon Let Macmillan Strike First in the Press Release War. Both Macmillan and Amazon took their time making statements, but Macmillan did its first, and when it did, it didn't bother with any ol' flack to make a statement—no, to underscore the significance of the event, it trotted out its CEO, John Sargent, who outlined in a calm and businesslike letter to his underlings (but presented as a paid ad in Publishers Lunch) the causes of the incident, as he saw them, and the issues at stake. The letter took time to praise Amazon but also did some interesting rhetorical heavy lifting—for example, labeling Amazon a "customer" of Macmillan rather than a "partner," which is a fun corporate way of jamming Amazon into an ecological niche it probably would prefer not to be in.

Bloggers and journalists updated their posts and stories to include Sargent's letter, launching another round of discussion and criticism online, largely at Amazon's expense—not only because Macmillan was now shaping the rhetoric of the discussion, but because Amazon remained silent, offering no official version of the events for another full day. And when it did:

5. Amazon Flubbed Its Own Response. When Amazon responded, it was not via a letter or comment from Jeff Bezos, or some other major Amazon executive, or the head of Amazon's publicity and marketing department, or even Amazon's winter PR intern—no, Amazon's initial reponse was an Amazon forum post from "The Amazon Kindle Team." Which is to say, an unsigned comment from unspecified people, not in senior management, tucked away in a backwater of the Amazon site.

And not only a forum comment, but a mystifyingly silly one: the bit in the comment about Amazon having no choice but to back down in the fight because "Macmillan has a monopoly over their own titles" was roundly mocked by authors, some of whom immediately started agitating against Amazon's "monopoly" of the Kindle, or noted how terrible it was that Nabisco had a "monopoly" on Oreos.

Think on this for a minute, won't you. Think about the disparity of corporate responses here. Macmillan issued a detailed statement from its CEO discussing the event and his company's reasons and rationales for acting as it did. Amazon issued an unsigned forum comment written by someone who is apparently a little shaky on Macmillan's relationship to its own product. Now, which of these two corporate responses seems most appropriate, given the gravity of the situation? Which of these responses appears to be the work of a company that understands what it's doing on a corporate level and why? Which of these responses, in short, appears to be the work of *actual adults*?

But enough fiddling with all this inside pool! In the real world, no one actually gives a good healthy squirt about points one through five. So let's trot out the real, *actual* stupid thing Amazon did:

6. Amazon Destroyed Its Own Consumer Experience, Without Explanation, For Several Days.

Note to Amazon: Real people *do not give a shit* about your fight with Macmillan. Real people want to *buy* things. When your store takes them to a product page on which they cannot buy the thing on the page, they will not say to themselves, "Hmm, I wonder if Amazon is having a behind-the-scenes struggle with the publisher of this title, of which this is the fallout. I shall sympathize with them in this byzantine struggle of corporate titans." What they will say is "why can't I buy this fucking book?" Because, you know, they are *there* to buy that fucking book. And when you don't let them *buy* that fucking book, they aren't going to blame Macmillan. They are going to blame you.

Honestly, now, Amazon: Even if your weekends are slower sales times than your weekdays, how many times over the weekend was a customer not able to buy something they wanted to buy from Amazon? I'm guessing a lot. Do you think *any* of the frustration, irritation and anger for that is going to accrue to Macmillan? Seriously? Because, remember, you didn't actually *tell the public* why you were doing what you were doing for two whole days, and when you did, you buried the explanation *down a hole*, where no normal person would find it. Do you think all of your customers read author blogs and Twitter feeds? Do you think they are imbued with some sort of corporate Spidey-sense that lets them know when you and a publisher are going after each other with hammers?

No, you silly, silly people! When they can't buy something on Amazon, what they will think is *Amazon is broken*. And they would be right. It was. Because you broke it. Intentionally. For days.

(Oh, and: don't *even* try the "they could buy from third party vendors" line with me. If you really believed people *would,* you wouldn't have left it as an option.)

And *all* of this is why a final, ironic bit of Amazon fail will come to pass:

7. Because of the Idiotic Events of This Weekend, People Will Just Want an iPad Even More.

Again, Amazon: Well played. Well played *indeed.*

Amanda Palmer, Kickstarter, and Everything

May
3
2012

Today's question from the mailbag:

Any thoughts on the success of Amanda Palmer's Kickstarter drive?

Unsurprisingly, I have several.

First, as background: Musician, creative person and delightfully weird human being Amanda Palmer put up a Kickstarter page to fund/sell her upcoming musical album, her first full-length production in a few years. She had a goal of raising $100,000 in a month; she raised that sum in something like seven hours, and three days in, she's at (checks, it's 10:20am as I write this line) $439,481. That's pretty excellent [Note: she eventually raised over one million dollars].

Needless to say this has people saying this is proof Kickstarter is the solution to everything/doing everything one's self is the solution to everything/eliminate the middleman, preferably with a shotgun/and so on. On the flip side, Palmer herself has noted detractors, including people who seem to believe Kickstarter is nothing more than high tech begging or panhandling.

So, with that as the background, my thoughts, in no particular order.

1. I think it's fantastic for Amanda Palmer. I say that as a fan of her work, solo and as part of Dresden Dolls, as an admirer of her creative drive and willingness to put in the actual work of maintaining a career, and as someone who has a friend married to her, who she makes ridiculously happy as far as I can tell. As a creative person, it's both gratifying and humbling when people step up and support you—with money! Of all things!—so the fact she's received so much support from her fans is just wonderful. The fact that Kickstarter, as an entity, has made it easier for her and other creative people to fund their projects, is also great, and one of the true benefits of the Internet age.

2. This is a decade in the making. I went back through Whatever to find the first time I made note of something Palmer did; the answer was November 2004, when I put in a link to the song "Coin Operated Boy" by her former band Dresden Dolls. That's seven and a half years ago; the band was active for a few years before then.

Between then and now most of what I know about Palmer is her working her ass off: Making music, playing that music, going off and making more, and building both awareness and a fan base. She left her music label a few years ago and has been putting out music independently since then; she's presumably learned a thing or two about the mechanisms of DIY art during that time—and in that time *she's trained her fans* in the fine art of supporting a truly indie musician (or at the very least, a truly indie Amanda Palmer). This is *hugely* important.

All of which is to say that like so many overnight successes, this isn't. It's the result of someone working for a very long time to get themselves into a position to make the most of this particular kind of opportunity. Complementary to this:

3. Palmer has an awesome network. She's got hundreds of thousands of fans to whom she talks every day via Twitter and other social media, most of whom are rooting for her success. She has friends and loved ones with similar or greater fan reach (even accounting for overlap), who are happy to promote her and her works. Basically, when something happens in the world of Amanda Palmer, it's entirely possible for more than a million people to become aware of it almost immediately.

Again, this doesn't happen overnight. Those friends and loved ones are collected through a lifetime; those fans are created through work, music and touring. Is Palmer using them to promote herself? I suppose she is, but I think it's probably more accurate to say that those people are willingly choosing to be part of her messaging system. I've retweeted stuff from her before, not because I felt obliged but because I like being a participant in her success. I retweet other news from friends and people whose work I admire for much the same reason.

You can buy Twitter followers (if you're willing to spend money stupidly), but you can't buy a living network of people who are invested in you as a person and/or a creator. You have to earn that through work, and by being a person worth friendship.

4. Palmer doesn't get to keep all that money. Leaving aside taxes (duh), Palmer has to pay production costs, musician fees, tour and travel expenses and all other costs incurred in the rather elaborate tiers of stuff she's offering to supporters. A fair amount of that money will go out of the door again. Which is, of course, what happens when one is running a small business, which is precisely what Palmer is doing here.

One of my major concerns about Kickstarter projects in a general sense is that I often wonder how many of the projects actually end up in the black for their creators. This is particularly the case when it comes to writers, artists and musicians, who are famously complete shit at working through their finances anyway, but who are also, through Kickstarter tiers and through encountering production costs that were previously handled by other people, wading into financial waters they often know next to nothing about. I wonder if people understand that Kickstarter isn't a magical ATM but a storefront, and that they are committing to running this store—production and fulfillment both—for the duration. I expect a lot of Kickstarters ultimately end up in the red because the people running them haven't built out a business plan, and have no idea what they're getting into.

I expect that Palmer may be one of the exceptions—precisely *because* she went DIY a few years ago and has had time to learn the ropes and to have some real-world, practical experience with what everything she does (and has proposed doing) costs in a financial sense. That said, I would love to know what sort of margins she's working with here, particularly with some of her more elaborate tiers. I have reasonable confidence she'll end this adventure of hers in the black, but I think everyone boggled by the money she's raised might eventually be surprised how much of it she won't get to keep.

5. Palmer has made some big commitments. For example, she's sold 25 house parties at $5,000 a pop, which she expects to be able to fulfill in the next 12 to 18 months. So, that's essentially 25 other tour dates for her on top of everything else she has to do. Yes, I know, $5k for showing up with a ukulele and hanging out at someone's house for four hours doesn't strike most people as hard work (heck, pay me $5k, I'll totally pop by with *my* ukulele!). But you know what? Spending four hours being *on* in front of strangers—and formally performing for one of those hours—*is* actually work. I know because that's what I do when I tour for my books. Palmer has other events listed which require more than just her showing up with a winsome stringed instrument, which aside from the financial considerations is more time/energy/effort/planning for her. I get tired just looking at everything she's promised to backers.

(This is why, incidentally, people accusing her of "online panhandling" are trolling jackasses. Palmer doesn't have a hand out for charity—she's offering specific goods and services when you set down your coin. You know exactly what you're getting, and what she's committing to. Again, this is a small business, and one with a detailed menu.)

In sum: It's awesome that Palmer's Kickstarter has done so well—but look at what it's entailed. It's entailed time, effort, planning and work both backward *and* forward in time. That currently $439,000 isn't a windfall for her; it's a marker of what all that commitment to the work has earned.

If you're one of the people looking at her Kickstarter money with stars in your eyes and awesome plans of your own in your head, ask yourself first: Have *you* put in the time? Earned the credibility? Scoped out the financial balance sheet? Made the commitment to fulfill every single thing you have promised?

Palmer has. If you haven't—on *any* of this—be aware that your results, shall we say, may vary.

And Now, An Incredibly Long and Detailed Assessment of My Own Last Decade, With Footnotes and Annotations Where Desirable, and Such Digressions As Will Elucidate the Subject in a Manner Amusing to All, Not Sparing Heart-Tugging Anecdotes When Appropriate, Phrased in the Vernacular of Our Times

Dec
31
2009

Oh, well, you know. It was *okay*, I guess.

Backscattering and Groping

Nov
16
2010

Been asked for my opinion on the new and egregiously invasive TSA scans. Well, I think two separate things.

One: On a personal level, I don't really give a crap about whether the full-body backscatter thingamajig makes me look like a naked mannequin and some poor bastard TSA person might have a glimpse at my virtual backscattered junk. One reason for this is that I'm pretty confident my own fake-nude snapshot will get deleted as soon as it's called up; even with my recent loss of 20 pounds, I don't exactly have a body that calls for the "save" button, and I'm not nearly famous enough for such a picture to be of interest on the IntarWeebs.

And even if I *were*, you know what? Like I care. Let's remember that I regularly post hideous pictures of myself on the Internet because it amuses me to do so. So it's not as if I'm brimming over with concern about looking *bad*. I'm not going to *volunteer* a picture of my naked, increasingly middle-aged body—I think too much of you for that—but on the other hand if some pervert at the TSA were to upload it and it were identifiably me, I wouldn't lose a whole lot of sleep over it either. *Yes*, I would say, *that is a very naked, plastic-y, gray version of my own shapely self. You enjoy that.*

Likewise, I'm not going to particularly care about close body search by the unfortunate TSA apparatchik who will will have to run his hand up to my groin area. I don't flatter myself that the fellow will get that much enjoyment out of it, and while I don't thrill to the idea of being groped in an airport for security purposes, the actual physical act doesn't bother me much, either. Basically I would have to keep myself from smirking as *Boom-chika-bow-ow* went through my head as I was being patted down, but really, that's pretty much it. So, yes. Not nearly outraged enough about either on a personal level to have either stop me from getting on a flight.

Two: My complete personal indifference is *entirely separate* from the larger philosophical question of whether these additional invasive steps are actually necessary, or whether I, as an average-looking middle-aged white man with apparently a high tolerance for official invasions of my personal space, am likely to have the same backscatter/TSA body grope experience as, say, a young woman or a swarthy-looking fellow with a beard. I suspect rather strongly that in both cases the answer is *no,* and both of these in themselves are perfectly sufficient reasons for other people to be annoyed and to protest and to engage in civil disobedience regarding these things. Although speaking selfishly I hope that if they do, that they are *behind* me in the security line. Because, hey, the reason I am at the airport is to catch my plane.

My understanding is that there is a movement underfoot to have 11/24/10 as "opt-out day," in which people intend to refuse the body scan at airports on one of the busiest flying days of the year, thus likely slowing down the flying experience even more on what is likely to be an aggravating flying day for just about everyone. As noted, philosophically I have little disagreement with the protest; on a practical level I'm happy that the only travel I have planned for the Thanksgiving holiday is going down the road to the in-laws. Protests are often like that.

As an aside, one thing I occasionally see people asking is why the US (and Canada) can't run airports more like Israel does. I don't pretend to know enough to give a genuinely sufficient answer to this, but I will hypothesize that one reason may be that the Israeli way is possibly not scalable from a small, militarized country of seven and a half million to a large and largely civilian country with 40 times the population. Israel has 11 airports (two international and nine domestic); the US has 376 which have regularly scheduled airline service. This isn't to suggest the US couldn't do its airport security better or less invasively. Just that I don't know if we could do it like Israel.

Being Fictional

Jan
30
2011

The other day in the Whateverettes sidebar I linked to Elizabeth Bear's discussion about being fictional—or, less pithily, her dealing with that fact that lots of people who read her books and/or her blog have an image of her in her head which is a construct, based on that writing, which may or may not have much to do with who she actually is. The number of people carrying a fictional version of her around in their head is smaller than the number of people who have a fictional version of, say, Angelina Jolie or Barack Obama in their head, but it's a large enough number of people that she does have to deal with it.

And it's a weird thing to deal with. As eBear notes:

> *Sometimes, it's a little like dealing with 5,000 high school crushes. Sometimes it's like dealing with 5,000 high school enemies. Sometimes, I learn things about myself I did not know from my Wikipedia page.*

I understand where eBear's coming from, because she and I have essentially the same level of micro-celebrity, and with the same subset of people—which is to say it's difficult to imagine people who know of me not knowing who she is, and vice-versa. And I think she's essentially correct when she notes that the fictional version people have of you in their heads is more about them than it is about you; everything gets filtered through their brain and how people fill in the blanks is by sticking in bits based on their own experiences, sometimes from others but mostly from themselves.

This fictional version of you is additionally compounded by the fact that, if you're a writer, the version of you they're building from isn't the *experience* of you (as in, you're someone they know in real life), but from the fiction you write and/or the public persona you project, either in writing (in blogs and articles) or in public events, such as conventions or other appearances. The fiction one writes may or may not track at all to one's real-world personality or inclinations, and while one's public persona probably does have something to do with the private person, it's very likely to be a distorted version, with some aspects of one's personality amped up for public consumption and other aspects tamped down or possibly even hidden completely.

All of which is to say these fictional versions of one's self are to one's actual self as grape soda is to a grape—artificial and often so completely different that it's often difficult to see the straight-line connection between the two.

And this is why I personally find them fascinating, especially—since I am both an egotist *and* a narcissist—when they involve me. I like going out onto the Web and discovering these strange, doppelganger versions of me, and also the people who speak so authoritatively about the sort of person these doppelgangers are. Occasionally those doppelgangers are better, more clever people that I am in real life, and occasionally they're complete jackasses. Sometimes they're people I'd like to meet; often they're people I would avoid at parties. Their life and career details are generally similar to but not precisely my own, and it's interesting to see how those variations have spun their lives off of mine, and what conclusions people have made about them based on those variations.

What do I do about these fictional versions of me out there? Generally speaking, nothing, because there's nothing to be done about them. When one is in the (mostly) happy position of having more people know of you than you can personally know, an abundance of fictional versions of you is part of the territory. I can't make a deep and personal two-way connection with everyone who reads my books or this blog, and I can't demand that people don't make assumptions about who I am from what they read or hear (well, I *could*, but then part of their data set when they think about me would be that I was both paranoid and completely unrealistic). Generally I try not to do things in public which would encourage people to think I'm a unremitting prick, but I would try to do that even if I didn't have the level of micro-fame I have. And of course some people think I'm an unremitting prick *anyway*.

But you do try not to worry about it. Teresa Nielsen Hayden, who is often a font of wisdom on many fronts, has a useful standard response for dealing with people who confuse their fictional construct of someone with that actual person, which I will paraphrase thusly: "I am not responsible for actions of the imaginary version of me you have inside your head." This is an important thing for people to remember, when they get to the point where more people know them than they know.

Personally, I'm less interested in the fictional versions of me that are out there than I am about the moment where people first ever meet me—either in my real-life "I'm actually standing in front of you" version or the first time they read one of my books or come to this site. I always wonder what that's like for people, and what impression they come away with. There's no way to ask them as they're having it, and I always wonder about it (I could when they were *actually* meeting me, I suppose, but it would be both meta and obnoxious: "Hey! You're meeting me now! How is it for you?"). I'm not worried about the fictional versions they construct from that point, but I always hope the first time they "meet" me it goes well.

Beyond Awards

Sep
17
2009

By now the whole Kayne West/Taylor Swift moment at the MTV Video Music Awards has reached its equilibrium, so there's nothing really much to say about that hasn't been said by everyone else, up to and including the president. But I would like to point out something that's been overlooked in this whole silly thing, which is that Beyoncé Knowles, in the gracious act of ceding her spotlight to Swift after winning the Video of the Year award, also brought home a point regarding the value and purpose of awards in general (and certainly, of the VMAs in particular).

Bluntly put, Beyoncé, with seven Grammys, nine VMAs and (currently) seventy other awards of various stripes (not counting the ones she was given as part of Destiny's Child), is largely beyond most awards at this point; that VMA is just another piece of hardware to stack somewhere. It's not to say she probably doesn't enjoy winning, because it's always nice to win something. But I bet you that had the award gone elsewhere, she'd have spent about a tenth of a second lamenting the fact, if that. Swift, on the other hand, is near the beginning of her career and outside the genre of country music hasn't gotten many awards; this was her first VMA. It's important, at this point, in the mainstreaming of her professional career, and in personal terms, it was probably pretty cool to a nineteen-year-old girl.

Beyoncé's ceding of her award time to Swift wasn't only a nice thing to do, it was also a recognition that the award means more, and is more important, to someone like Swift than someone like her. So not only did Beyoncé do the *right* thing—allow Swift the moment she had been deprived by a jackass—she also rather accurately established her place in the food chain (i.e., *way* up at the top) and did it in the savviest, least diva-like way possible.

Not in a *calculated* way, to be sure; I think she felt bad for Swift and genuinely wanted to give her the moment that was taken from her. But it's also true Beyoncé's actions at the moment were far more memorable than either the award she won or any acceptance speech she could have made. For Beyoncé, being seen as gracious and giving is in fact the actual prize for her. She's smart to recognize the fact.

Bill James' Pop Fly

Apr
3
2011

Baseball analyst Bill James asks over at *Slate*: Why is America better at producing athletes than writers? His argument is that as a society the United States does a much better job of identifying and encouraging athletic talent than it does, say, writing talent; as an opening argument in this he notes:

> *The population of Topeka, Kan., today is roughly the same as the population of London in the time of Shakespeare, and the population of Kansas now is not that much lower than the population of England at that time. London at the time of Shakespeare had not only Shakespeare—whoever he was—but also Christopher Marlowe, Francis Bacon, Ben Jonson, and various other men of letters who are still read today. I doubt that Topeka today has quite the same collection of distinguished writers.*

Well, come on, Bill James. I know you're smarter than that. The only thing London of the late 16th Century and Topeka of the early 21st have in common is population. One was the impressively growing capital of an emerging world power, to which men of intellect were migrating (including Shakespeare and Marlowe, born as they were in Stratford and Cambridge, respectively), while the other is a state capital whose population has expanded roughly two percent in forty years, and whose potentially great writers are likely to migrate to centers of employment for writing—New York and Los Angeles, primarily—for the same reason Shakespeare and Marlowe found it congenial to hie to London for *their* work: Because that's where the action is. In all, this is a spectacularly crap comparison.

The rest of James' article isn't much better, because it proceeds on a thesis that is shaky to begin with, i.e., that America's better at developing athletes than it is writers. My first question here is: by what metric? Are we talking about people working professionally in both fields? Because you know what, the Bureau of Labor Statistics says that as of May 2009, we've got 43,390 professional writers in the United States—"writers" in this case being those who "originate and prepare written material, such as scripts, stories, advertisements, and other material" and excluding those writers primarily working in public relations (of which there are 242,670) and technical writing (of which there are 46,270).

Meanwhile, also according to the BLS, as of 2008, there were about 16,500 professional athletes in the United States. So one could say that the United States develops two and a half times more professional writers than it does professional athletes. And while those pro athletes get paid more ($79,500 on average, compared to a mean of $64,500 for pro writers), it's not *that* much more, and writers on average can do their jobs at a professional level longer than pro athletes. Yes, the top athletes can earn a tremendous amount of money, but then, so can the top writers.

James also flubs the argument in other ways. For example, this bit:

> *The average city the size of Topeka produces a major league player every 10 or 15 years. If we did the same things for young writers, every city would produce a Shakespeare or a Dickens or at least a Graham Greene every 10 or 15 years.*

To which I respond: Really, Bill James? *Any* major league baseball player is equivalent to Shakespeare, Dickens, or Graham Greene? We're seriously arguing that, say, Pedro Feliz is of the same existential value to our culture as the fellow who wrote *The Third Man, The Quiet American* and *The End of the Affair,* much less the fellows who wrote *Hamlet* or *Great Expectations*? I'm going to go ahead and express *doubt* at that contention.

What I expect would be rather more accurate to say is that if a city the size of Topeka produces a major league player every 10 or 15 years, it should also produce an author whose work is picked up by a major publishing house; let's say one of the "big six". Is that possible? Sure it is. You don't even have to get up to the size of Topeka. Claremont, California has a population of about 35,000; it's the place I generally give as my hometown because I went to high school there. So did Mark McGwire, although not at the same school. He and I are six years apart in age. My first book with a major publisher was in 2000 (Rough Guides is part of Penguin); his last game was in 2001.

It's true he started working in MLB before I started being an author, but this isn't entirely surprising, and looking at the contracted and proposed work I have in front of me, it seems entirely possible my career with major publishers will last as long as his did with the MLB. My career accomplishments to date are not as impressive as his, to be sure; but then I didn't take any steroids, either. But whether his career and mine are *directly* equivalent isn't the point; what is the point is that both he and I have played in our respective field's equivalent of "The Show." It's a simple game: You write the book, you print the book, you sell the book. I'm just here to help the publishing house, and God willing, everything will work out.

That's one concrete yet anecdotal example, but it can be repeated over and over. There are a lot of writers who get published by major publishers; there are lots of others who are published by small presses (to continue the (inexact) metaphor, they're minor league but still pro) and still others who write professionally but work in other fields entirely (they're playing football or hockey). We don't lack for writers writing on an equivalent level to playing in a major league sport. They're not all superstars, but they're not all superstars in the major leagues, either. Both fields have a lot of journeymen. There are worse things to be.

James makes another error in his next sentence:

> *Instead, we tell the young writers that they should work on their craft for 20 or 25 years, get to be really, really good—among the best in the world—and then we'll give them a little bit of recognition.*

We don't tell writers to work on their craft for a long time because only then will we give them recognition; we tell them to work on their craft for a long time because generally speaking it takes a long time to "compete" at a pro level when it comes to writing, and particularly in fiction. Writing is not like athletics; there's not an inherent competitive premium on youth. There are brilliant and/or financially successful novelists and storytellers under the age of 25, to be sure; they are as rare, however, as the major league player who is still at the top of the game in his or her 40s. Currently the top ten novels in the US (according to Bookscan) are written by people whose ages range from 39 to 83. It's both an older and wider range of ages than you'd see for the top level of success in athletics.

The irony here is that James' larger point—let's celebrate and cultivate writing and writers in our culture like we celebrate and cultivate athletes—is not one I am in disagreement with in the slightest. I would love for schools and universities and our culture to make a fuss over and invest resources in their budding writers as they do with their athletes. I'd like for them to do the same with their budding actors, musicians, scientists and artists, too, while we're at it. Where James and I disagree—ironically—is in how James jiggles his stats here to make his point. James is stacking his deck to raise the stakes, and in doing so he undercuts his actual argument. He's not doing his Topeka Shakespeare any favors.

A Bitter November

Nov
29
2010

Me (going into the kitchen and finding someone going through the fridge): Who's there?

Strange Yet Oddly Familiar Person: It's *me*, you idiot.

Me (peering to get a better look):...November? Is that you? What are you doing here?

November: Eating some of your leftovers. (Holds up Tupperware) Mind if I finish off your cranberry sauce?

Me: No, that's fine. What I meant to say is that I thought you had already left.

November: What's the date?

Me: Uh...November 29.

November: Right. I still have today and tomorrow, you know.

Me: I suppose you do.

November: Damn *right* I do. I have thirty days. Every year. It's not like I'm *February*. (Sits, sullenly, to eat his leftovers.)

Me: I know. It's just that after Thanksgiving, it feels like November should be over, you know?

November (bitterly): You think I don't *know* that? You think I don't know that as soon as people wrap foil over the turkey pickings and shove them in the ice box, they start looking at me like I missed some sort of important social clue? They start looking at the closet my jacket is in and then down at their wrists as if to say, *whoa, look at the time.*

Me: I'm sure they don't mean anything by it.

November: And nobody actually wears wristwatches anymore! They all get their time from their cell phones. That's what makes it *extra demeaning.*

Me: I don't think everyone wants you out the door on Thursday evening. There's Black Friday, after all.

November (rolls eyes): Oh, *right.* The "traditional start of holiday retail." *Holiday retail,* dude. "Holiday" is just *code,* you know. For *December.*

Me: Code?

November: Friggin' December, man. He was always pushy, you know. Always so *entitled.* Mr. "Oh, I have *two* major religious holidays every year." Yeah, well, you know what? This year, I had Diwali. Okay? *That's* a festival of lights, too. A billion people celebrate it. And that's just the Hindus! I'm not even counting the Jains or the Sihks!

Me: I think that those cranberries might have fermented on you.

November: Don't patronize *me,* buddy. All I'm saying is December is not *all that. I've* got election day. *I've* got Veteran's Day. I've got Thanksgiving. I'm the All-American month.

Me (as my cell phone buzzes): Hold on, I'm getting a text.

November: Who is it?

Me: It's July. The text says, "I felt a great disturbance in the Force, as if November was whining about something and was suddenly silenced BY AMERICA'S BIRTHDAY."

November (holds up hands): You see? You see what I have to put up with?

(DOOR OPENS. DECEMBER bustles through, carrying packages)

December: Oh, man! You wouldn't believe what kind of madness is out there in the stores these days. People are really getting into the holiday—Oh. November. Sorry, I didn't see you there.

November: Of course you didn't. God forbid you should acknowledge my *existence*, December.

December (to me): Did I come at a bad time?

Me: We're having a bit of a moment, yes.

December: I can come back.

November: Yeah, in *three days*, you usurping bastard!

December: I'll just go now. (December leaves)

November: That's right! Go! And take your crappy Christmas carols with you! (Breaks down weeping)

Me: Aw, come on, November. Don't be like that.

November: I just want people to appreciate me, okay? For my entire stay. Is that too much to ask?

Me: No, I suppose it isn't. I'm sorry, November. It was wrong of me.

November (sniffling): It's all right. I know you weren't trying to offend me. Anyway. I'll just be going now. (Gets up)

Me: No, November. Sit down. Please. You can stay if you want.

November: Yeah? Really?

Me: Of course you can. You can even help me with some stuff around the house, if you want.

November (narrows eyes): You're about to put up Christmas decorations, aren't you.

Me (guiltily): Of course not.

A Boy's Own Genre, or Not

Oct
13
2009

Another thing for people to please stop sending to me: a recent and fairly random blog post in a purported online magazine, the premise of which essentially boils down to: "Science Fiction is by boys and for boys and now girls are ruining it for anyone with testicles, except the gays, who are just like girls anyway (and whose testicles frighten me)." I'm not going to link to it, as abject misogynist stupidity should not be rewarded with links. You can track it down on your own if you like.

Nevertheless, two general points to make here.

1. Verily I say unto thee that thanks to Mary Wollstonecraft Shelley, mother of Frankenstein, science fiction is *founded on girl cooties,* so anyone dumb enough to whine about those awful women ruining SF for boys really does need to STFU and take his ignorant ass back to his snug little wank hole;

2. What? An insecure male nerd threatened by the idea that women exist for reasons other than the dispensing of sandwiches and topical applications of boobilies, mewling on the Internet about how girls are *icky*? That's unpossible!

At this late date, when one of these quailing wonders appears, stuttering petulantly that women are unfit to touch the genre he's already claimed with his smudgy, sticky fingerprints, the thing to do is not to solemnly intone about how far science fiction has yet to go. Science fiction *does* have a distance to go, but these fellows aren't interested in taking the journey, and I don't want to have to rideshare with them anyway. So the thing to do is to *point and laugh.*

Well, *actually,* the thing to do is trap such creatures in a dork snare (cunningly baited with Cool Ranch Doritos, Diet Ultra Violet Mountain Dew and a dual monitor rig open to Drunken Stepfather on one screen and Duke Nukem 3D on the other), and then cart them to a special preserve somewhere in Idaho for such as their kind. We'll tell them it's a "freehold"—they'll like that—and that they will be with others of a like mind, and there they will live as *men,* free from the horrible feminizing effects of women and their gonad shriveling *girl rays.* And then we'll tag them with GPS and if they ever try to leave the freehold, we'll have them hunted down by *roller derby teams with spears.* That's really the optimal solution.

But since we can't do *that,* then pointing and laughing will suffice. So, yes: let's all point and laugh at these funny little terrified stupid men, and then ignore them. Because that's what they rate.

Chief Justice Roberts and Political Orthodoxy

Jul
3
2012

It's not an exaggeration to suggest that the Supreme Court holding that the ACA is in fact constitutional (albeit on novel and narrow grounds that no one expected to be used, i.e., the Congress' power to levy taxes) represents the biggest political blow to the current distillation of right-wing ideology that it's had in some time and possibly ever. The blow was made even more psychologically damaging by the fact that it came at the hands of the previously doctrinally reliable Chief Justice John Roberts, who penned the opinion upholding the law, on which he was accompanied by the court's four more left-leaning judges and none of the four right-leaning ones. Roberts, formerly one of the golden boys of the right-wing orthodoxy, has been pushed out of that position with all the force and rage that comes from, well, not being the performing monkey that the current crop of right-wing ideologues thought that they had installed into the Chief Justice position. Roberts, in short, went rogue, and that is unforgivable.

Let's make no mistake about this: the reason that the ACA was driven to the Supreme Court with the alacrity that it was by the right wing was because at the end of the day it fully expected the court to strike it down. As much as right wing politicians like to mewl about activist, unelected judges when they don't get their doctrinal way, they've also spent the last couple of decades doing everything they can to get as many of their doctrinal bedfellows into the judiciary as possible. Nowhere has this been more the case than the current Supreme Court, which some observers judge the most conservative Court since the 1930s.

But more than conservative, the Court is supposed to be *reliable*—that is, adhering to current right-wing orthodoxy regardless of that orthodoxy's relation to classical conservative principles. When the ACA was marched into the Supreme Court, from the right wing point of view it was there to be killed; the legal reasoning of the killing was less important than the 5-4 vote the right wing fully expected it had to exercise its will.

Well, it got a 5-4 vote, all right. It even received what I would consider a classically conservative ruling—is there really an argument that the Congress does *not* have enumerated in its Constitutional rights and duties the ability to levy taxes? What it doesn't have is a victory. And ultimately the reason that it does not have a victory is because the right wing forgot what many orthodoxies forget: That in the end, people aren't machines that do what you want them do when you press the right button. They are human beings, and human beings have (or at the very least have the potential for) agency, i.e., they have their own brains, have their own agendas and can make up their own minds. Which in the end is what Roberts did.

And which, it should be noted, he is supposed to do, Constitutionally speaking. The Founding Fathers, in their wisdom, gave federal judges life tenure. One reason for that was to insulate these judges from the current fashions and passions of the political fray and to give them their own heads about things. Judges are not immune to politics, of course, especially if they want to move up and dream of a Senate confirmation hearing sometime in their future. But it's also equally true that once you've had the confirmation hearing and passed it, you're gone as far as you're going to go. John Roberts is the Chief Justice of the United States. It's a terminal position, employment-wise—which means there's no one who has any lever they can wedge in to get him to move the way they want to. He's on his own recognizance. He has his own head.

Former Bush speechwriter Marc Thiessen recently kvetched in the *Washington Post*, wondering why it is that Republicans are "so bad" at picking Supreme Court justices, i.e., why they drift from their expected positions and start voting in ways that are not doctrinally reliable. Leaving aside the fact that the right wing of the US has shifted itself politically to such an extent that even Ronald Reagan (the real one, not the icon) couldn't pass its current sniff test, the answer is more correctly, why is Thiessen so oblivious that he doesn't understand that the power of political orthodoxy is its ability to force its members to comply—and that the Supreme Court is *designed* to sever its members from such threats of force? That's *why* they drift. And the more strait-jacketed your orthodoxy, the greater the chance of drift. There's no doubt that currently the right wing is about as orthodoxically strait-jacketed as they come.

I don't think there's any question that Roberts is a conservative judge; a look at his track record and even at his ACA write-up makes this abundantly clear. I don't think there's any question that Roberts will continue to be a conservative judge. What the ACA ruling serves notice for, perhaps, is that Roberts is following his own conscience and reasoning regarding what it means to be conservative, rather than taking his cues from the the current right-wing orthodoxy. Ultimately, that's what sending the right wing into their rage about Roberts: That now it's possible he's his own man, not theirs.

Children and Faith

Mar 14 2011

Alphager asks:

As far as I understand from your lent-related post, you are an atheist/agnostic and encourage your daughter to take an interest in religions in general and the christian faiths in particular. Can you explain how that came to be and by which principles (e.g. will you go to church with her? Are you open about your beliefs?) you teach her about religion?

I ask because me and my girlfriend are on the verge of marriage and have been talking a lot about religion and atheism; I'm an atheist and she is the daughter of a protestant pastor. She fears that the question of religious education (or lack thereof) of our (as of yet potential) children could be a major source of conflict.

Well, the reason I encourage her to learn about religion, and Christian faiths in particular, is because the large majority of people on this planet follow a religion of some sort, and here in the United States, the large majority of those who are religious are Christians of one sort or another. I'm an agnostic of the non-wishy-washy sort (i.e., I don't believe in a god nor believe one is required to explain the universe, but I acknowledge I can't prove one doesn't or never did exist) and always have been for as long as I can remember thinking about these things. I don't see being an agnostic meaning one has to be willfully ignorant about religion, nor do

I see my role as an agnostic parent being one where I shield my daughter from the reality that she lives in a religious society.

Where my daughter is on her own journey of discovery regarding faith is not for me to discuss publicly, but I can say that I believe more information is almost always better. So when she wants to know about a particular religion or explore some aspect of faith, I encourage her to do so; when she comes to me with questions about religion, I either answer her questions (being that I know a fair amount about most major religions) or help her find answers. Athena is well aware that I am an agnostic, and what that means, and we've explored that aspect of faith (or lack thereof) as well. I won't tell you what questions she asks about religion, faith, agnosticism and all of that, but I will tell you that she asks good questions, and for my part I answer them as truthfully and as fairly as I can.

There are a number of people who have come to agnosticism or atheism because of conflicts with or disillusionment about religion, and in particular a religion they were born into and grew up in, and others who are agnostic or atheist who feel that religion and the religious impulse must be challenged wherever they find it. For these reasons among others I think people assume those people who aren't religious are naturally antagonistic, to a greater or lesser degree, to those who are. But speaking personally, I don't feel that sort of antagonism; I don't look at those who believe as defective or damaged or somehow lacking. Faith can be a comfort and a place of strength and an impetus for justice in this world, and I'm not sure why in those cases I, as a person without faith, would need to piss all over that.

There are those, of course, who believe their faith (and here in the US, their Christian faith primarily) excuses being bigoted, or cruel, or ignorant, or petty or pitiless, or who use their faith (or the faith of others) to do terrible things and/or to impose their worldly will on others. In my experience, this is less about the teachings of Christ than it is about people being bigoted, cruel, ignorant assholes and then saying Jesus told them to be that way. Well, no, he didn't. These folks are simply looking for an external excuse for their own bad behavior. It's the spiritual equivalent of the dude who goes out on Saturday night, acts like a jackass, gets into a fight or two and wakes up the next morning in a ditch without his pants and then blames it on the Pabst Blue Ribbon. It ain't the beer that's the problem, it's the man behind the can. Likewise, Jesus and his unambiguous message of love and charity toward even the least of us is not responsible for the lout who wraps himself in a cross and preaches a message neatly opposite to Jesus' own. I don't have any problems opposing these people, and letting them know just what bad Christians I think they are. I've don't have any problems pointing out these people to my child, either.

But again, that's not about me as an agnostic opposing those who have faith. It's me as a person who knows the message of Christ pointing out a hypocrite, and me as a person with my own moral, social and political standards countering one whose standards differ. As it happens, I know a reasonable number of people of faith who feel the same way I do, and have many of the same moral, social and political standards as I have. Do I fear them? Discount them? Think them defective? No; I say "I'm glad to know you." We believe many of the same things; that some of their belief comes from the teachings of Jesus, or from Allah by way of Muhammad, or from Buddha, to name just three examples, does not trouble me. Whatever steps we took to get there, we're walking the same path.

As an agnostic, I'm not *afraid* of my child learning about faith and how it's practiced. I think it's necessary, and I think it's valuable. I'm also not afraid that my child might adopt a faith as her own; she may indeed. If I have done my job as a parent, she will have done so from a position of knowledge, and of understanding everything that comes with adhering to a practice of faith—and with the ability to ignore or act against those who would try to use that faith as a lever to get her to do things counter to its teachings.

Likewise, I don't think any agnostic or atheist has much to fear in teaching their children about religion, if they answer their kids' questions truthfully, openly and in the spirit of giving their kids as much information as they can so their children can make their own decisions—which they will anyway, unless you've raised a drone, which is something I think most of us would rather not do. Raising your children to know they can ask things, they will get answers and that they can question *any* belief, religious or otherwise, raises the chance that whatever path they choose regarding faith—including the path that espouses no faith at all—they are on the correct path for them. As a parent, I think that's what you want.

A Couple of Quick and Final Post-Election Notes to Liberals and/or Obama Supporters

Nov
13
2012

As I did offer some notes yesterday to those unhappy with Obama's victory, I figure it might be worth it to give a couple of notes to those who are thrilled about his re-election. Seems fair, etc. So:

1. It's been a week. You can crank back the schadenfreude. Yes, it's time. There's only so much poking of wounded conservatives you can do before you cross the line into just being an asshole about it.

2. Don't get cocky. Obama won by almost exactly the same popular vote margin as George Bush won in 2004. While the point is taken that in presidential elections it's the electoral votes that count, and that getting 271 of those is just as good as getting 400 in terms of job placement, it's worth recognizing that among the citizenry, there's a close-to-even split on how to run this particular railroad. Which dovetails nicely with the next point:

3. The mid-terms elections are out there. And the mid-term elections a) historically tend to favor the non-incumbent presidential party, b) tend to be decided by a smaller, more-committed group of voters. Which is to say: Hey, remember the 2010 elections? Don't think it can't happen again. It can, and it very well may.

4. 2012's electoral coalition isn't automatically permanent. In the short-term? Sure, it'll likely cohere for a couple election cycles at least. But, for example, if the GOP genuinely reaches out to Hispanics—more than the now grossly-obvious rush to embrace immigration reform—I don't think it's impossible that many Hispanics will find elements of the GOP platform attractive. As another example, if same-sex marriage becomes a settled issue in the US, I know enough gays whose economic point of view would make conservatism a congenial intellectual home for them (aside from, you know, the ones who are already there).

5. Don't think the GOP is stupid. Yes, it got its ass handed to it by Obama's high-tech/low-tech combo of exhaustive quant analysis and field operatives knocking on doors. That's going to work once. When 2016 comes around, the GOP will have baked that into their operation, and they'll have some new strategies to try out too. And if whoever is the 2016 Democratic candidate tries to run a 2012 campaign, he or she will get their ass handed to them, too. And in the meantime the GOP is going to do what it does, namely, finding ways to block and frustrate Obama's and the Democrats legislative agenda. They're good at it, too. They own the House of Representatives, remember?

6. Don't think the most reactionary conservatives are actually going to "go Galt." That's just the reactionary conservative version of "moving to Canada." Just as liberals didn't rush the border in 2004, neither are these folks going to crawl into a bunker, or crevasse, or seastead or whatever. They're going to stay where they are, they're eventually going to calm down, and then they're going to get back to what it is they do. This is real world, and it's really hard to flounce out of it.

7. Don't think you know what the future will bring. Hey, around this time 2004, did you think the dude just elected as the junior senator from Illinois would be president? Had you even heard of him? I knew of him very vaguely, mostly because he won his seat against Alan Keyes, who had been recruited when the former Republican candidate fell out because of a sex scandal. Illinois, man.

When he announced his presidential candidacy in February 2007, did anyone think he was going to be anything other than a speedbump for Hillary Clinton? If you think you know how 2016 is going to play out, you may be deluding yourself.

8. Nothing's been decided but who was elected president. I mentioned this last Wednesday, but it bears repeating. Obama's got four more years. Everything else? We'll see. And if you thought you were going to be able to lie back for the next four years, guess again. No one else is taking the time off. The GOP isn't. Almost certainly Obama isn't.

Crimes of Education

Jan 30 2011

I've been getting a lot of e-mail asking for my thoughts about Kelley Williams-Bolar, a woman here in Ohio who was recently sentenced to ten days in prison (of which apparently she served nine) and now has a felony record because she and her father listed the father's residence as the primary residence of her children, in order that the kids could go to school in a better school district. As I understand it, idea here is that because she didn't live in the district and pay taxes there, she committed fraud, although from what I understand the jury wouldn't or couldn't convict on that charge and instead she was found guilty of tampering with court documents. Ironically Ms. Williams-Bolar is not that far off from getting a teaching credential, which she now may not be able to use because she's a felon.

How do I feel about this? Well, I will tell you a true story. When I was in sixth grade, my mother and her then-husband broke up, and in the space of three months I lived in four different houses in three different cities, and in three different school districts. The school district I had been in when this all started had a genuinely excellent "gifted and talented" program, and my teacher at the time, Keith Johnson, was one of those teachers that you're lucky to get once in your entire life. I'd been at the school for a couple of years and I had friends who I still have now. And, not to put too fine a point on it, the breakup of my mother and her husband wasn't exactly out of the blue, and the school and the people who were there who cared about me were an island of stability in a life which was, though no fault of my own, completely messed up.

When my mother left our house and moved, taking me and my sister with her, what she should have done, procedurally speaking, was take me out of that school and put me in a new one, in the city we then lived in. And then two months and two moves later, when we were in a new city and new school district entirely, she should have done it again, giving me three different schools, three sets of schoolmates and three entirely different social situations to adapt to on top of the fact that my family and home life had just been blown up.

She did no such thing. Through four moves, three cities and three school districts I stayed in the same class with the same teacher and the same friends and classmates. How my mother managed to do this is something she would have to tell you, but in point of fact I know that officially—and, I suspect, legally—speaking I was not supposed to have been allowed to stay there. My mother made the decision to do what she thought was better for me rather than what was probably the letter of the law.

Did my mother break the law doing what she did? I don't know, but possibly. Did she break the rules? She certainly did. Did she do the *right* thing? Probably not, from the point of view of the procedures of the school district. From the point of view of what was best for her child: Absolutely. There's really no doubt about that. And if in fact my mother broke the law on my behalf way back when, I can say that doing so made a positive difference at a critical time in my life.

So: How do I feel about Ms. Williams-Bolar? Basically, I think she deserves a prison term and a felony conviction about as much as my mother did, for performing essentially the same actions, thirty years ago.

The Cool Kids Hanging Out

Mar
22
2012

Lance in Huntington Beach asks:

Wil Wheaton just Tweeted Chris Hayes about Rachel Maddow. Why is it that everyone I follow on Twitter, watch on TV or read seems to know one another? Is the world really that small? Does a bit of notoriety buy you immediate acceptance from other notables? Or is there a special club you all belong to and once again, it's me being picked last for dodgeball? Please explain.

First: Dude, it's *totally* you being picked last for dodgeball, man. You're too slow. You keep being taken out first! And your throwing arm? *Sheesh.*

Second: Just because you tweet someone about someone else on Twitter doesn't mean you know them to any significant degree. Twitter just gives one the ability to send a comment to anyone else on Twitter, and if you're following one or both of those people, you'll see the tweet. I could tweet, say, Fred Durst about the Dalai Lama, it doesn't mean I know either of them. Fred Durst could even respond to me (or for that matter, so could the Dalai Lama) and it still wouldn't qualify as "knowing" either of them in any meaningful sense. So that's an important thing to remember about Twitter.

Third: It's not that the world is small, it's that who you are interested in as notables is specialized enough that there's a reasonably good chance they might know each other.

As an example: I am notable, to the extent I am notable, primarily for being a science fiction writer—many of the people who follow me online one way or another (although not all) did so at least initially because they heard of me as a science fiction writer. This means there's a pretty good chance they read science fiction and fantasy and also consider *other* science fiction and fantasy writers as notable to some extent or another.

As a science fiction writer, I attend a reasonable number of conventions, where I've met other science fiction and fantasy writers; I've also been a member of The Science Fiction and Fantasy Writers of America for nearly a decade, and through that I have also had contact with a large number of sf/f writers. Over several years of seeing these folks over and over, some of them have become friends—some of them very good friends—because we have similar life situations, professional concerns, and recreational enthusiasms. Many of the rest of them I've come to know professionally as peers, particularly after I became president of SFWA and these writers became my constituency.

So if you're an sf/f fan for whom these writers are important, and you see me chatting online with my friends who also happen to be sf/f writers, it looks like all the cool kids are hanging out, doing cool kid stuff together online, and so on. And how cool is that? Pretty cool. Of course, if you're *not* an sf/f fan, and you saw me chatting online with my friends who also happen to be sf/f writers, it looks like a middle-aged dude doing a whole lot of procrastination on Twitter with a bunch of other mostly lumpy 30-, 40- and 50-somethings. That is, if you're looking at my Twitter feed at all, and if you're not an sf/f fan, why would you? And thus we learn the truly specialized nature of "notability."

I know sf/f writers because I am an sf/f writer, and this sort of professional association is why (of course) a lot of your favorite actors will know other of your favorite actors, why your favorite musicians will know other of your favorite musicians, why the cool scientists out there seem to know the other cool scientists, and so on. Beyond mere professions, there will be other sorts of situational overlaps. One of the great cultural questions of our time is why do very successful musicians and actors always seem to date other very successful actors or musicians (or supermodels). The answer is, well, who *else* are they going to date? It's not as if someone like George Clooney can put up an OK Cupid profile like a common schmoe. They're going to date other famous people because a) they're the people they know, b) they're the people who understand the life and can (possibly) tolerate all the crap around it. An actor dating a supermodel, or an actress dating a musician, is the famous person equivalent of a corporate VP dating a manager in human resources.

The actual mundane rationales for the surface fabulousness of the famous (or at least notable) aside, there is one advantage to being a notable of any sort, which is that it makes it *slightly* easier to make the acquaintance of the people you nerd out over, because it's possible they already know who you are and may even be fans of your work (or you). And while mutual admiration is not a good foundation to a lifelong friendship, it does make that initial encounter a lot easier, because you each already think positively of the other.

Look, I'm not going to lie: like any other person, "notable" people geek out at getting to meet and hang out with the people they admire. I mean, shit, man: The fact that Robert Silverberg *knows* me? Seems to *tolerate* me? Does not in fact *recoil* when I enter the room? There have to be multiple universes because this one universe *cannot contain all of my squee.* If you have the chance to meet the people you admire, chances are pretty good you're going to take it. If it turns out nothing comes of it, then no harm done. But if it turns out you like each other and become pals? Then you're living the fanboy dream. *Which you never say out loud,* of course. But even so.

And then there's the fact that when you're friends with someone notable, they often have other friends who are notable, who you then get to meet, and thus your network of notable acquaintances grows, simply because your friends have friends, i.e., you meet people like any person meets people, i.e., through your friends.

Now, there's the flip side, which is you meet someone you admire and then find out they're kind of an ass. But I'm delighted to say that at least so far, this has not been my experience. Also, notable or not, you don't want to be That Social Climbing Dick, i.e., the guy who becomes friends with someone and then immediately starts looking to trade up in their friend circle. People aren't stupid and don't like being used. And that, too, is a constant in all human relationships, whether the people in them are "notable" or not.

But basically, Lance, when you see all the folks you consider the "cool kids" talking to each other online, it's that fact that *you* consider them the cool kids that makes it seem like something special. Believe me, they probably thank you for it. But someone else who does not see these people as notable might see it as what it is: a bunch of folks who know each other to varying degrees, doing what people do online—letting each other know they're part of each others' lives. And possibly planning a dodgeball tournament.

The Cubbies Win the Existential Pennant! The Cubbies Win the Existential Pennant!

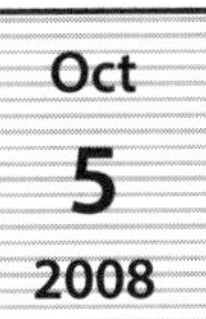

A few days ago someone sent me an e-mail asking me if I was at all concerned that the Chicago Cubs, who finished at the top of the National League, would go all the way to the World Series and win, thus rendering obsolete a comment that one of my characters made in *Old Man's War*, defending the Cubbies despite their then at least two centuries of championship futility. I wrote back and said this was one of those things I really didn't worry about. One reason I didn't worry about it is that there are no explicit dates noted in OMW, so I could just say that those two centuries of futility begin whenever it is the Cubbies win their last one.

But the *other* reason is even simpler, and that is because I firmly believe that the Cubs, when pressed, will always find a way to lose in the clutch. It is their destiny and heavy responsibility to be the sport's designated losers—a destiny they previously shared with the Red Sox, but which they now carry alone, which of course makes it an even heavier responsibility. As I've noted before, if the Cubs were to win, what would they gain? A sports championship, to be sure, but how special can a World Series win actually *be* if even the Florida Marlins have won it? Twice?

But the Cubbies' reign of futility—well, see. What other team could replace them? Among teams who have ever won a World Series, the next longest drought is held by the Cleveland Indians, at an insignificant 60 years. Among those who have never won the World Series, the Texas Rangers are mere pups at 47 years of age. No offense to Indians and

Rangers fans, but the futility of these teams is pedestrian and banal compared to the futility of the Cubs. They are the H0-scale version of existential dread. The Cubbies are the full-sized runaway train, hurtling headlong toward the burned-out bridge over a yawning, bottomless chasm. And the train is filled with adorable *kittens*.

You don't just throw that sort of distinction away on something so obvious and *common* as a World Series championship. They give one of those out every year. The Cubs' streak, on the other hand, is a century in the making. There is nothing else like it in the history of North American professional sports, and it's made even more poignant by the fact that the Cubbies are so often good, as they were this year. They *could* have gone all the way. You could even argue that they *should* have gone all they way. But they didn't. And now they won't. And this is as it should be.

And so when the Cubs were swept in three games by the Los Angeles Dodgers (whose own streak of World Series futility is a mere 20 years long—a pup, as these things go), I was not surprised, and for the sake of Cubs fans, I was somewhat relieved. 'Twere best it was done quickly, and all that; no point dragging those poor men and women through one or two more series just to compound the heartbreak. I understand that Cubs fans may feel differently, of course, but I think they may be too close to the subject.

The fact that I was born and raised in Southern California and am a nominal Dodgers fan has nothing to do with this, either. It could have been any team that stood in the Cubbies' way. And if the Dodgers go all the way, what of it? What's another World Series win to a team that already has six? They have their moment in the sun, and then it's back to the relentless, cyclical grind. Meanwhile, the Cubs, and their streak, continue—a testament to persistence, to futility as Sisyphusian high art: Yea, a statement about the very condition of man. Perhaps a statement best read at a distance, as Cubs' fans might agree. But even so.

I for one admire the Cubs' position in sports and in history, which is why in *Old Man's War* I see their streak continuing well into a third century. World Series wins come and go, but the Cubbies' streak—well. That endures, my friends. That *endures*.

Dateiversary

Jun
16
2010

As constant—nay, *fanatical*—readers of this site, you'll recall how yesterday was the 16th anniversary of me proposing marriage to Krissy. Well, today is the 17th anniversary of the two of us having our first date, which for the record, happened at El Presidente restaurant in Visalia, California, followed by dancing at the Marco Polo bar, which is where we had met three weeks previously (that doesn't count as an official date because she was kind of there with a different date entirely, who she largely abandoned to dance with me, BWA HA HA HAH loser date of Krissy's).

This means, as those of you with *exceptional* math skills have already deduced, that I proposed marriage one day short of a year from our first official date. I chose that date because it was a Wednesday, which meant my newspaper was running my weekly column, and my proposal was the subject of the column. However, I had known for some time that I wanted to marry her. In fact, I had known roughly nine months earlier, because after three months of dating Krissy it was clear that a) there was no way in which she was not awesome, b) there was no way I would ever do any better, mate-wise, than I was doing right that very second, so my task for the next 60 or so years would be not to screw up this relationship.

As any guy who has even the slightest semblance of impulse control will tell you, three months is a pretty quick time for a man to determine that he wants to spend the rest of his life with someone, so about seven years into our marriage, I noted to Krissy with some pride how soon it was that I was convinced that she was the person I wanted to marry.

"Uh-huh," she said, less impressed than I had imagined she would be.

"Well, when did you decide that you wanted to marry *me*?" I asked.

"Our first date," she said.

"AAAAAAAAAAAIIIIIIIEEEEEEEGH," I said, running terrified from the house—or would have had, in fact, I had not been already married to her for seven years at this point and had been almost appallingly happy the whole time. Because you know who knows they want to marry someone after the first date? *Crazy, crazy people,* that's who. And also, apparently, in a data set *completely unattached* to "crazy, crazy people," my wife.

What I actually did say was, "I'm really glad you didn't tell me that at the time."

To which Krissy said, "Of course I didn't tell you. Do you think I'm crazy?"

That statement, or more accurately the strategic intelligence behind it, is part of why we're still married today.

Lest anyone think that Krissy was overstating her position on the matter, my mother-in-law confirmed that when her daughter came through the door after our first date, more or less the first words out of her mouth were "I've met the man I'm going to marry." Which surprised my future mother-in-law, as previous to this her daughter's general opinion of men was, shall we say, not nearly high enough to have marriage be part of it. So I have no reason to doubt that, in fact, Krissy had made the decision that night.

In retrospect, it's a little weird to think that my entire future was falling into place as I obliviously tucked into the El Presidente chimichanga platter, but of course, that's life for you—the most important days of your existence don't always announce themselves in obvious ways. At the time, all I knew was that somehow I had managed to get a date with the single most gorgeous woman I had ever met in my entire life, and I focused on not talking with my mouth full, because I wanted to get to date number two. Well, and I did. And got happily ever after in the bargain.

Which means it was a good first date, seventeen years ago today.

Dear Writer: I'm Sorry, I Don't Have Time to CRUSH YOU

Mar
4
2011

Holly Black—who is *awesome*—has a post on her LiveJournal concerning a recent shibboleth floating about regarding a cabal of young adult authors ("the YA Mafia") who some writers in the field apparently believe will go out of their way to crush under their Doc Martens those writers who would do anything untoward to a member of the YA Mafia, like, say, write something negative about one of their books.

Holly for her part denies the existence of a YA Mafia—but then she would, *wouldn't she*—and also points out that even if such a cabal of writers *did* exist, sniggering nefariously in the shadows, the chance of them actually being able to crush someone else's career is nil, because, honestly, that's not how it works in the real world—not in the least because, as Holly notes: "writers are basically lazy and impractical people. We live in our heads a lot and we can barely get it together to do anything. Seriously, it took me until after 3pm yesterday to get myself a *sandwich*."

First, I want to agree with her wholeheartedly on the lazy thing, because for the last week I've been subsisting on Nature Valley Fruit and Nut Bars, not because I'm in love with their sticky, graintastic goodness but because at this point, the thought of having to shove something into the microwave to *cook* it fills me with such a sense of ennui even just typing those words *makes me tired.*

Second, this wave of anxiety is part of a recurring theme in the write-osphere, in which it is posited that those people with some measure of success actively and jealously guard their perks and privileges against the smudgy others mewling on the other side of the gate, and collude to maintain the status quo, and so on and so forth, back, *back* you mangy animals! Right now this fear is erupting in YA circles, but it's been everywhere else, too. It's not new, and it's not news.

So in the interest of explaining why it's unlikely that any group of successful writers is colluding to keep you down, let me offer up an example of just the sort obnoxious bastard writer who would want to keep the rabble at bay, namely me.

So, hi, I'm your basic reasonably successful author type, and despite being lazy enough to grumble how how *awful* it is that I have to *unwrap* my granola bar before I can *eat* it, my daily schedule is not unpacked. On a daily basis I write a couple thousand words on whatever novel I'm writing, crank out two or three blog posts, check in with SFWA in my capacity as the organization's president and take care of what needs to be addressed that day, do other paid copy not related to novels, take the dog out on at least two walks, answer e-mail and other correspondence, make business-related phone calls to agents, editors and such, spend time with wife, child and pets, occasionally leave the house for errands, read the entire Internet, maybe also some portion of a book, update LiveJournal and Twitter, kill me some zombies, eat, ablute and sleep. That's not on days when I'm traveling, mind you, during which I often do many of these things and also hurl myself across the country at several hundred miles an hour.

That being my schedule, let me ask you: Where do you propose I slide in *fucking with your career*?

Because, I gotta tell you, after everything *else* I do on a daily basis, I don't have a lot of *time* left over to take your dreams, lovingly cradle them in my arms and then just when they feel safe fling them into a pit filled with gasoline and napalm and laugh boisterously while they shrivel and burn. I mean, sure, I *suppose* I could cut back on reading the Internet or headshooting the undead and pencil you in there, but you know, I really do love reading Gizmodo, and those pesky zombies won't kill themselves (again). If I have to choose, I'm going with tech blog reading and Left 4 Dead.

It's nothing personal. It's not like I'm saying that thwarting your career *isn't* important. Indeed, that's just the thing: If I *have* decided that what I really need to do is to block your every entryway into the world of publishing, you better believe *I'm gonna focus.* It's going to be my new hobby to make every single day of your life a *miserable cesspool of unremitting woe.* And that's not something you can just do in five minutes a day, or whatever. No, that shit's hand-crafted and detailed-oriented, and that takes *time.* Lots and lots and lots of time. Nor am I going to farm it out to a posse of lackeys; no, when I come for you and your career, you're going to see me coming from a long way off, and you're going to have lots of time to think about just what I'm going to do to you before I stand in front of you. Giving you lots of time to think about what I'm going to do to you is what makes it *fun.*

But I have to say: unless I've decided to give you that level of personal, *absolutely terrifyingly psychotic* attention, eh, I'm just not going to bother messing with your career. Because, again: who has the time? *I* don't. No one does, except for people who are, in fact, absolutely and terrifyingly psychotic, and very few of them are successful enough at publishing that they are the people these other folks are paranoid about. Even if they were, they wouldn't start a cabal. Terrifying psychotics get along with each other about as well as cats in a bag. It's well-nigh part of the definition of "terrifying psychotics."

Yes: There is the occasional writer who gets their undies all bunched up about a review and then goes on a passive-aggressive public rampage about it. Authors are often neurotic. This should not be news. But what can they really do to you or your career? Short of doing something will get them rightfully thrown into jail, pretty much not a damn thing. Because you know what? *It's not the way it works in the real world.*

Let's go back a couple of paragraphs to where I got all steroid-y about the level of woe I would rain down upon you if I decided to make you my personal project. Sure, I talk a good game up there—I've got a way with words, you know—but in the real world, how would that play out? Let's whip up scenarios, here:

STEROID SCALZI MEETS WITH HIS EDITOR:

Me: There's this writer who I hate with the white-hot intensity of a thousand suns. Never ever publish her. I am Scalzi. You must heed my words.

Editor: Well, I will take that under consideration (makes mental note that I have finally crossed the line from "reasonable human" to "text-extruding asshole who must be managed").

STEROID SCALZI MEETS WITH OTHER WRITERS:

Me: There is a writer whom I wish to destroy. Join me in my quest to smoosh his career like a grape caught under a high school cafeteria table wheel.

Other writers: Send us an e-mail about that (make mental notes to avoid me in the future, because I am clearly a mean drunk).

STEROID SCALZI MEETS WITH A REVIEWER:

Me: If you do not give this writer whom I despise a soul-shriveling review, then never again will I have my publicist send you advance copies of my work. EVER.

Reviewer: I'll remember that (crosses me off the list of people he reviews, reviews someone who is not a dick instead).

STEROID SCALZI COMMUNICATES WITH THE INTERNET:

Me: ARRRGH MINIONS MUST SMASH POOPY WRITER WHO POOPS DO MY BIDDING YOU DARK LOVELIES

Internet: Dude, you're kind of a prick.

And so on. Look, when you're an asshole to people, then other people know it. And while people generally will not stop you from being an asshole, if such is your joy, they're also not going to go out of their way to help you. Humans see assholes as damage and route around them. So much for mafias and cabals.

One final thing to remember is every presumed cabal member is someone who was outside looking in, and probably not as far back as you think. I do like reminding people that my first novel was published in 2005, which was six years ago. Six years is not a lot of time to go from schmooging one's face against the glass of the cabal HQ to being well into the cabal itself. Perhaps it's more accurate to note instead that the idea of a cabal or a mafia is a little silly, and in fact there are just writers. Some of them are nice, some of them are neurotic jackasses, and in all cases the influence they can have on one's career is exponentially smaller than the influence one has on one's own.

DeKloutifying

Nov
14
2011

I got a Klout account a few months ago when it did that promotion of allowing its members to get an early view of the US version of Spotify, and that was reason enough to give it a spin. Well, I still have my Spotify account, but this morning I deleted my Klout account. Part of that was due to the various kvetches I've seen regarding Klout's rather lackadaisical approach to privacy, noted by everyone from Charlie Stross to the *New York Times*, but really, at the end of the day (or the beginning of it, as I deleted the account this morning), I left Klout because I suspect the service is in fact a little bit socially evil.

Klout, for those of you unaware of its existence, purports to provide some general ranking of one's influence on the Internet, across the various social media. The service apparently sucks in data from all the other social media services you belong to which it tracks, throws that into an algorithmic pot, and renders it down to a number between one and one hundred. Then you can look at your score relative to other people's and see where you fit in the grand scheme of influence, at least according to Klout.

Wherein lies a problem: Who made Klout the arbiter of online influence, aside from Klout itself? *I* could rank your influence online, if you like: I'll add your number of Twitter followers to your number of Facebook friends, subtract the number of MySpace friends, laugh and point if you're still on Friendster, take the square root, round up to the nearest integer and add six. That's your Scalzi Number (mine is 172). You're welcome.

Is this number any *less* indicative of your actual online popularity than Klout's score? As far as you know, no. I'm sure Klout has what it considers an excellent rationale for whatever stew of algorithms it uses to assign you a number, but neither you nor I know what it is, or (more importantly) why it's valid as an accurate determiner of your online influence and popularity. As far as any of us know, one's Klout number is determined by college interns, each feverishly rolling a pair of ten-sided dice, and then that number is allowed to oscillate within a random but bounded range every day to give the appearance that something's going on.

However, even if we did know the process Klout uses to determine one's influence, there comes the question of what purpose it serves. It serves Klout's purposes, it seems, in that they have a nice little business quantifying its members' desirability to companies who offer stuff to the members with the implicit agreement that they then talk about it on their social media sites. Good for Klout, and, in the interest of accuracy, I *did* get early access to Spotify out of them, and did write about it, so there you are.

But what purpose does it serve for Klout's members? Aside from the occasional *quid pro quo* freebie, it seems that what Klout exists to do is create status anxiety—to saddle you with a popularity ranking, and then make you feel insecure about it and whether you'll lose that ranking unless you engage in certain activities that aren't necessarily in your interest, but are in Klout's. In other words Klout exists to turn the entire Internet into a high school cafeteria, in which everyone is defined by the table at which they sit. And there you are, standing in the middle of the room with your lunch tray, looking for a seat, hoping to ingratiate yourself with the cool kids, trying desperately not to get funneled to the table in the corner where the kids with scoliosis braces and D&D manuals sit.

This is sad, and possibly evil. It's especially sad and possibly evil because as far as I can see, Klout's business model is to some greater or lesser extent predicated on exploiting that status anxiety. I clicked over to Klout's "perks" section not long ago—"perks" being the freebie things the service wants you to market for them—and rather than being presented with a selection of perks available to me, I was presented a list of perks I *wasn't* qualified for, because apparently I wasn't smart and pretty and popular enough for them, although Klout seemed to suggest that maybe if I did my hair a little differently, or wore some nicer shoes (or dragged more people into their service, making myself more influential in the process) maybe one day I could get the *cool* perks. At which point I decided that Klout was actually being run by *dicks*, and getting let into Spotify a week early—or whatever—wasn't worth being seen with dicks, or supporting that particular business model.

So now I'm out. It was interesting for a while, but ultimately I don't care how influential Klout thinks I am, and I get enough perks in life without Klout's queen bee corporate marketing style. And even if I didn't, I'm more comfortable with who I am and my place in the world (online or otherwise) than Klout needs me to be in order for me to be a useful member for it.

All of which is to say: Bye, Klout. It's not you, it's me. Well, actually, it *is* you. I'm pretty sure I'm too good for you. But, hey: Thanks for the Spotify.

Dude, I Totally Unmarried You Just Now

Jun
20
2008

In his *Chicago Tribune* column yesterday, Eric Zorn notes this interesting bit of "logic" from the same-sex-marriage haters, explaining why all those thousands of same-sex couples who have gotten married in California over the last week aren't *really* married:

> *The Illinois Family Institute's blog refers to the legalization of same-sex nuptials this week in the Golden State as "the California marriage disaster." Such recognitions "do not and cannot exist, no matter what legal document the state issues homosexual couples," writes institute blogger Laurie Higgins. "There is an existential, ontological reality that supersedes the ill-begotten works of man."*

Translation: "They're legally married but I'm in denial, so I'm just going to pretend it didn't happen, like that season on *Dallas*. La la la la la la, I can't see you married homos."

Well, fine. Since apparently it's the *fashion* to deny marriage status to people who are legally married, simply because we don't *like* them and their marriages make us *twitchy*, by the power vested in me by whichever existential and ontological reality conveniently lets me get *away* with it, I hereby declare that marriages which include any of the following never ever *existed:*

1. People who pretend same-sex marriages don't exist.
2. People who drive 55 miles an hour in the far-left lane of the freeway.

3. People who prefer Pepsi to Coke.
4. The craven, toadying yes-men who told George Lucas that, no, really, the fans are gonna *love* Jar-Jar Binks.
5. Anyone ever involved in the production, distribution or sale of acid-washed jeans.
6. Anyone who thinks Dane Cook is funny.
7. Anyone who ever bought a Limp Bizkit album.
8. Anyone who voted for Nader in 2000.
9. Or 2004. Honestly, you people just *suck*.
10. That guy who pushed me down once in 7th grade. Yeah, fuck *you*, Andy Grabowski! All your kids are bastards now!

Do these people's marriages really not exist because I just now wished them away? Yes, exactly to the extent that the marriages of same-sex couples who got married in California no longer exist simply because a bunch of bigots prefer to pretend they don't. Which is to say: No. Because, you see, real, legal, *actual* marriages don't stop existing just because some malign jackass doesn't want to have accept that those marriages are real, and legal, and actual.

However, unlike any marriages on my list, the real, legal and actual same-sex marriages in California *are* in danger of being destroyed by people who aren't actually *in* them. There is no initiative on the California November ballot to "protect" marriage from already-married Creed fans or Pepsi drinkers. There *will* be one to "protect" marriage from already-married same-sex couples.

Which is to say: Isn't it *funny* how some people are going so far out of their way to destroy marriages they say they don't believe actually exist.

Election List I: People/Things I Would Vote For President Before I Would Vote For John McCain

You know, for the last two weeks I've been trying to write a long, cogent piece about who I'm voting for and why, but every time I try I am filled with inchoate rage and just want to kick a puppy or someone who voted for Nader in 2000. So instead I'm going to write a series of short, punchy election lists, which will probably be more amusing and will at the very least keep me from beating on something with a hammer.

And so, to begin:

Election List I: People/Things I Would Vote For President Before I Would Vote For John McCain

1. Barack Obama
2. Bob Barr
3. A large, flat, warm rock
4. Hermann von Googlefleugel, the garden gnome under which I keep my spare house key
5. Arnold Schwarzenegger
6. A kitchen sponge
7. Zamfir, Master of the Pan Flute
8. Chewed gum you find under a desk at the DMV while you take the written part of your driving test
9. Toast!
10. A teratoma that vaguely resembles a pony
11. An incontinent monkey or lemur

12. A large order of McDonald's fries, lightly salted
13. The reanimated corpse of Millard Fillmore
14. A mat of algae
15. A black velvet painting of Wesley Crusher
16. H.R. Pufnstuf
17. A glazed donut
18. That guy on the A train who shouts loudly about his penis from 23rd to Cathedral Parkway
19. A Lite-Brite
20. Fucking Ralph fucking Nader, that goddamned fucking fuck

Election List II: The Verified Miracles of St. Obama

Oct
31
2008

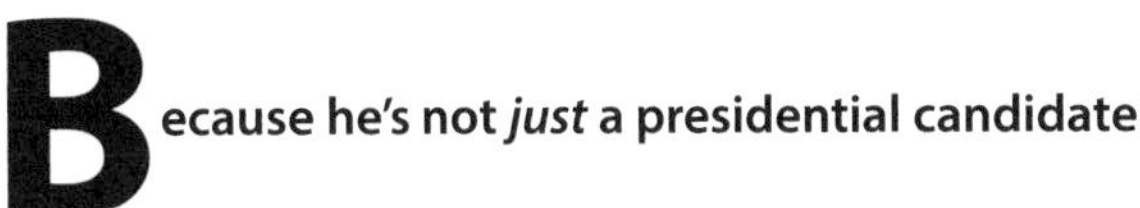

Because he's not *just* a presidential candidate!

Election List II: The Verified Miracles of St. Obama

1. Restored Joe Biden's hairline
2. Not only heals the sick but springs for their co-pay
3. Loaves and fishes for every family making less than $200,000
4. Smells intensely and deliciously of butterscotch
5. Offers hope, and also, Amway
6. That mole on the side of his nose? Made of concentrated *awesome*
7. Every child he hugs on the campaign trail becomes 10% smarter
8. Made Hillary Clinton stump for him
9. Every time he shoots one into the hoop from downtown, an angel gets his wings
10. Is the front-runner for president while being a black man named Barack Obama

Election List III: Things Sarah Palin Has Shot Or Would Shoot From a Helicopter

Oct
31
2008

It's quite a list.

Election List III: Things Sarah Palin Has Shot Or Would Shoot From a Helicopter

1. Wolves
2. Coyotes
3. Arctic foxes
4. Deer
5. Giraffes
6. Tortoises
7. Dolphins
8. Salmon
9. Katie Couric
10. That son of a bitch that divorced her sister
11. Kittens
12. Whoever made that Photoshopped picture of her in a bikini, holding a rifle
13. Owls
14. Baby seals
15. Tina Fey
16. Andrew Sullivan
17. Levi (note to self: Only *wound)*

18. Donkeys

19. Elephants

20. John McCain

Election List IV: The Things I Think About As I Stare At A Picture of Joe Biden

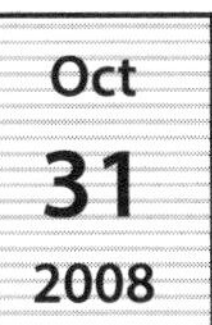

Oct
31
2008

Because I guess I have to write something about him, too.

Election List IV: The Things I Think About As I Stare At A Picture of Joe Biden

1. It looks like doll hair.
2. Men shouldn't botox.
3. I bet Hillary's still really pissed.
4. I think I drove through Delaware once.
5. Yeah, I did. They have a toll road that's, like, a mile long.
6. Seriously, a mile-long toll road? That totally sucks.
7. All my credit card companies are incorporated in Delaware.
8. No, wait, that's South Dakota. Delaware is where all the really big companies incorporate.
9. Like how all those cruise ships are registered in Liberia. Which makes Delaware the Liberia of the US.
10. It still looks like doll hair.

Election List V: The Contents of the Democratic Poll-Watching Kit

Oct
31
2008

or when the Democrats freak out as the polls inevitably tighten.

Election List V: The Contents of the Democratic Poll-Watching Kit

1. Mr. Snuggles, the cuddly Democrat plush bear
2. A dime bag of skunkweed
3. An iPod Nano preloaded with Coltrane, James Taylor and Will.i.am's "Yes We Can" video; also, Peggle
4. John McCain and/or Sarah Palin stress reliever whose eyes pop comically as you squeeze it and shout "you lost Florida!"
5. A special, personalized "don't panic" note from Nate Silver of FiveThirtyEight
6. Tollhouse cookies like the kind the TV you watched during your latchkey kid days told you were like mom used to make
7. Ritalin
8. An autographed photo of Rachel Maddow
9. A game card for the play-at-home version of Congressional Takeover Bingo
10. Suicide Hotline number (in case McCain wins Pennsylvania)

Election List VI: The Contents of the Republican Poll-Watching Kit

Oct
31
2008

It's more compact than the Democrat one.

Election List VI: The Contents of the Republican Poll-Watching Kit

1. A fifth of gin
2. Ambien
3. Sleep mask

Election List VII: Bombshells the McCain Campaign Has Yet to Drop About Barack Obama

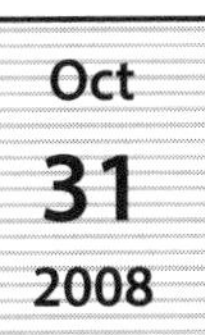

Once these get out, the electoral map will run red!

Election List VII: Bombshells the McCain Campaign Has Yet to Drop About Barack Obama

1. Obama actually 63% black, not 50/50 as previously reported
2. Has not only started measuring the White House drapes, but has already sent them out to be dry cleaned ("to get rid of that horrible Dubya stench")
3. Not just a socialist, but a Fabian
4. Feeds kittens to alligators, and then those alligators to pit bulls, then the pit bulls to sharks
5. Born not in Hawaii but in The Land of the Lost
6. Grandfather actually a Sleestak
7. Is so poor he only owns *one* house
8. While high on poppers, had a threesome with Jeremiah Wright and Rashid Khalidi, while Bill Ayers recorded it on video. The *LA Times* has the tape but won't release it
9. Totally told the McCain campaign that he doesn't actually *like* any of the voters in Pennsylvania or Ohio or Florida or North Carolina or Colorado, and that he's only being

friendly to them for right *now,* but when the election's over, it'll be, like, *yeah,* don't even know who you *are,* so get away from me, *losers.* And that's just not nice

10. Found the change he needed in the campaign bus seat cushions, used it to buy cigarettes

Election List VIII: Instances of "[Name] the [Occupation]" That Have Yet to Be Used By McCain or Palin

This goes out to all the plumbers named Joe out there. I love you, man.

Election List VIII: Instances of "[Name] the [Occupation]" That Have Yet to Be Used By McCain or Palin

1. Brad the Milkman
2. Sid the Deli Owner
3. Bryan the Surly Indie Music Store Clerk
4. Kim the Overnight Wal-Mart Stocker
5. Hakeem the Halal Butcher
6. Aloysius the Chicken Sexer
7. Carol the Humorless, Cavity-Probing TSA Agent
8. Klaus the Eurotrash A&R Man
9. Craig the Porn Reviewer
10. Markos the Blogger
11. Jim the Former Securities Trader, Now Best Buy Appliance Department Sales Trainee
12. Jesus the Lettuce-Picker
13. Ted the Secretly Gay Televangelist
14. Patrica the Humanities Degree Wielding Starbucks Barista
15. Steve the Attack Ad Coordinator
16. Phil the Philatelist
17. Tom the Torturer

18. Sarah the Self-Serving Rogue Campaigner
19. John the Wholly Disappointing Top of the Ticket
20. Barack the President

Election List IX: The Rationales Each Party Will Give If They Lose The Election

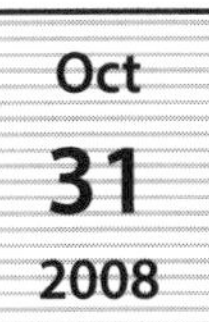

Because it's important to have an excuse.

Election List IX: The Rationales Each Party Will Give If They Lose The Election

Republicans:

1. The black vote
2. Also, the youth vote
3. And the elderly
4. And the Hispanics
5. And the gays and lesbians
6. And the women
7. And the early voters
8. Jesus, who *did* we have voting for us?
9. White dudes with Sarah Palin MILF fantasies? Really, that's it?
10. Give me that gin. And that Ambien.

Democrats:

1. Racism.
2. Diebold.
3. Karl Rove. *Somehow.*

Libertarians

1. Dude, we're *Libertarians.*
2. We never win.
3. We *can't* win.
4. And frankly, if we *did* win, we'd probably all *pee ourselves in terror.*
5. And so would you.
6. Now, let's smoke a bowl and watch some porn.

Election List X: Some of The Horrible Things That Will Happen To You If You Don't Vote

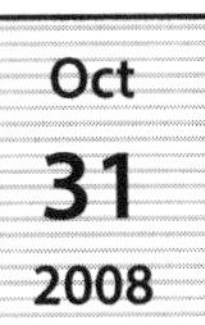

This is all true.

Election List X: Some of The Horrible Things That Will Happen To You If You Don't Vote

1. Your penis will fall off. If you are a woman, you will grow a penis, which will then fall off.
2. Your peers will point and laugh at you more than they already do.
3. You will have to listen to smug voters say "if you didn't vote, you can't complain" for at least two years.
4. You will be consumed by pillbugs whilst you sleep. They will leave behind nothing but your penis, which as you'll recall, has already fallen off.
5. You will smell of sour buttermilk until the next New Hampshire primary.
6. Uncontrolled flatulence.
7. Cars will swerve to hit you, even when you are inside your own home.
8. Your World of Warcraft party will turn on you and smite you mightily.
9. Impotence. And not just because your penis has fallen off.
10. Stairs will rise to trip you.

11. Boils. In Biblical plague amounts.
12. Static cling that no amount of Bounce sheets will ever cure.
13. Your cat will take a dump somewhere in the house that you will never find, and the smell will be carried through the air vents for months, all the while the cat will stare at you with that "you're a real asshole" look they sometimes have. If you do not have a cat, one will be provided for you for the length of time required for it to crap in said undisclosed location.
14. Your credit card will be canceled and your creditors will send someone to repossess your penis. Which has fallen off.
15. Your favorite TV show will be canceled and every time you try to buy the last season on DVD, retailers will be out of stock.
16. Your children will disown you. If you have no children, you will be summarily adopted by a family, and when you attend Thanksgiving at their home, you will be told how disappointed they are in you. For six hours straight. After which they will disown you.
17. Your cabbies will henceforth always take the long route to any destination to which you travel.
18. Zombies, and you without a shotgun.
19. Everyone on your street will win the lottery. You will get a rock.
20. I swear to God, I will learn your address, come to your house, and when you open the door, I will totally kick you in the nads. Which will hurt even more because they're the only reproductive organs you have left. *Because your penis has fallen off.*

I trust now you will be sufficiently motivated to vote.
The election lists are now completed. Thank you for your attention.

Emo: Older Than You Think

Dec
10
2008

It comes as no particular surprise that my writing advice to teens occasionally irritates teenagers, many of whom do not take kindly to someone telling them their writing likely sucks and the only thing for it is to keep at it until it doesn't suck anymore. They also occasionally get annoyed when you suggest to them (as I do in the follow-up to the original article) that the condition of being a teenager now is pretty much the same as it was 20 years ago (or 40 years ago); the trappings may change (iPods instead of Walkmans instead of transistor radios) but the basic concept is pretty much the same, so despite their feelings that ZOMG EVERYTHING IS TOTALLY DIFFERENT NOW, it's really not so much.

This was brought to mind when a teenager, blogging on her own site (no, I'm not linking to it; I don't think this unsuspecting teenage girl needs her site to be overrun by Whateverites, do you?) detailed the various ways she's offended by my advice piece and how it is wrong, and in pointing out how *her* generation of teens is drastically different than any other, asserts (and this is an intentional paraphrase) that when people her parents' age were in school, they didn't have Emos skulking about in the halls.

This made me giggle. I'm old enough to be this girl's dad (or at least her dad's slightly younger brother) and I can assure you that 20+ years ago, we certainly *did* have Emos, i.e., sulky and morose teens scribbling bad poetry into notebooks and retreating into their music because no one understood them and so on. Our Emos listened to British post-punk rather than American post-punk by dint of British post-punk hitting a couple decades earlier, but, otherwise, yeah, pretty much the same concept. We had Bauhaus, they have Fall Out Boy, and both bands just really want to go back in time to the Weimar Republic, what are you going to do. And I'm happy to say the emo-iest folks I knew in high school have acquitted themselves pretty well. Every picture I have of them in the 1984 yearbook is of them dramatically gazing down at their shoes through their hair. I should really dig that yearbook out. It would be instructive.

And of course, *we* didn't invent the dramatically moody young person, either. If you want to take it all the way back, I submit to you that the true Godfather of Emo is not Kurt Cobain or Robert Smith or David Bowie or even Brecht/Weill, but Johann Wolfgang von Goethe, who in 1774 unleashed *The Sorrows of Young Werther* upon the world, with its oh-so-artfully despairing young protagonist doing everything he could to make himself absolutely friggin' miserable, because it was so much more interesting than being happy. The novel helped to kickstart the *Sturm und Drang* movement in German literature and music, and what was the *Sturm und Drang* movement—a movement devoted to wrenching every single possible emotion out of words and music—if not the very proto-est of proto-emo movements?

Sturm und Drang in its turn motivated the Romantic movement, giving us Shelley and Byron and all those other poetic shoe-gazers, and so on and so forth and blah blah blah blah blah until you suddenly find yourself wedged up against the stage at a The Academy Is...concert with a bunch of sixteen-year-old girls screaming their lungs out at William Beckett, who, I gotta admit, has got a whole adorable "Suburban Shelley" look going for him. To be clear, I'm not comparing *The Sorrows of Young Werther* with, say, *Fast Times at Barrington High*; one's a landmark of world literature and the other's a decent album of power pop. I'm just saying you can get from one to the other and recognize them as appealing to more or less the same audience, albeit 234 years apart. So, yeah, Emo's been *around*, folks.

This is not to trivialize this girl's experience of being a teenager, mind you. Being a teenager is powerful thing, because every single damn thing that happens to you happens to you turned up to 11, which is a fundamentally different experience than being an adult, in which most things have happened to you more than once, and you've generally found the volume knob and cranked it down a couple of notches simply to keep yourself sane. And of course her experience of her teenage years *will* be different from anyone else's not in her age cohort; she'll have different music and movies and world events and generational issues and so on. I for one would not wish late 80s hair metal on anyone else; I'm glad no other teenagers will have to take *that* bullet.

But at the end of the day, and when you peel away the effects of one year or another, the teenage experience—the massive highs, the crushing lows, the frustrations and irritations and alienations and deep friendships and crushes and riotously funny moments—is what it is, and remains fairly constant. Put a sixteen-year-old from 1968 in a room with one from '78, '88, '98 and today, and after everyone stops laughing at everyone else's *ridiculous* clothes, I think we'd find they shared a commonality of experience and outlook. And they would all know an "emo" kid, whether they called him emo or not.

The Failure Mode of Clever

Jun
16
2010

So, apropos of nothing in particular, let's say you wish to communicate privately with someone you've not communicated with privately before, for whatever reason you might have. And, wanting to stand out from the crowd, you decide to try to be clever about it, because, hey, you are a clever person, and as far as you know, people seem to like that about you. So you write your clever bit and send it off, safe in the knowledge of your cleverosity, and confident that your various cleverations will make the impression you want to make on the intended cleveree.

Two things here.

1. The effectiveness of clever on other people is highly contingent on outside factors, over which you have no control and of which you may not have any knowledge; i.e., just because you intended to be clever doesn't mean you will be perceived as clever, for all sorts of reasons.

2. The failure mode of clever is "asshole."

Allow me to offer a suggestion. If you are privately communicating with someone for the first time, as a general rule, the best course of action is to be polite and to the point. This is particularly the case if the reason you're communicating with that person is because you are hoping to get them to do something for you, i.e., you're asking for the favor of their time and attention and even possibly their money. That is not a situation in which you want to risk the failure mode of clever.

This is not to say that your cleverness should not eventually come out in your private communication; there's a time for it, and usually that time is after you've established enough rapport with the other person that you know their receptiveness to cleverness in general, and your brand of it in particular. It's "third date" material, as it were, not "first date."

Indeed, the most clever thing you can do with your cleverness is to know when is the right time to use it. When in doubt, don't. And if you're not in doubt, ask yourself if you should be, especially if you're communicating privately with someone for the first time. It's just a suggestion.

A Fan Letter to Certain Conservative Politicians

Oct
25
2012

WARNING: this post is going to be oh-so-very-triggery for victims of rape and sexual assault. I am not kidding.

Dear certain conservative politicians:

Hi! I'm a rapist. I'm one of those men who likes to force myself on women without their consent or desire and then batter them sexually. The details of how I do this are not particularly important at the moment—although I love when you try to make distinctions about "forcible rape" or "legitimate rape" because that gives me *all sorts of wiggle room*—but I will tell you one of the details about *why* I do it: I like to control women and, also and independently, I like to remind them how little control they have. There's just something about making the point to a woman that her consent and her control of her own body is not relevant against the need for a man to possess that body and control it that *just plain gets me off.* A guy's got needs, you know? And my need is for control. Sweet, sweet control.

So I want to take time out of my schedule to thank you for supporting *my* right to control a woman's life, not just when I'm raping her, but for all the rest of her life as well.

Ah, I see by your surprised face that you at the very least *claim* to have no idea what I'm talking about. Well, here's the thing. Every time you say "I oppose a woman's right to abortion, even in cases of rape," what you're *also* saying is "I believe that a man who rapes a woman has more of a right to control a woman's body and life than that woman does."

Oh, look. That surprised face again. All right, then. On the chance that you're *not* giving me that surprised face just for the sake of public appearances, let me explain it to you, because it's important for me that you know *just how much* I appreciate everything you're doing for me.

So, let's say I've raped a woman, as I do, because it's my *thing*. I've had my fun, reminding that woman where she stands on the whole "being able to control things about her life" thing. But wait! There's more. Since I didn't use a condom (maybe I'm confident I can get other people to believe it was consensual, you see, or maybe I just *like it that way*), one thing has led to another and I've gotten this woman pregnant.

Now, remember how I said the thing I really like about raping a woman is the control it gives me over her? Well, getting a woman pregnant is even *better*. Because long after I'm gone, she *still has to deal with me* and what I've done to her. She has to deal with what's happening to her body. She has to deal with doctor visits. She has to deal with the choice whether to have an abortion or not—which means she has to deal with everyone in the country, including *you*, having an opinion about it and giving her crap about it. And if she *does* have an abortion, she has to deal with all the hassle of *that*, too, because folks like you, of course, have gone out of your way to *make* it a hassle, which I appreciate. Thank you.

Every moment of that process, she has to be thinking of me, and how I've forced all of this on her—exercised my ability to bend her life away from what it was to what I've made of it. Me exercising my control.

I gotta tell you, it feels *awesome*.

But! You know what would feel *even more awesome*? The knowledge that, if you get your way and abortion is outlawed even in cases of rape, that my control of her will continue through *all the rest of her life*.

First, because she'll have no legal choice about whether to have the baby I put in her—sorry, dearie, you have no control at all! You have to have it! That's nine months of having your body warp and twist and change because *I* decided that you needed a little lesson on who's actually running the show. That's *sweet*.

Once the baby's born, the woman will have to decide whether to keep it. Here's an interesting fact: Of the women who have gotten pregnant from rape who give birth to that baby, most keep the baby, by a ratio of about five to one. So my ability to change the life of the woman just keeps growing, doesn't it? From the rape, to the nine months of the pregnancy, to the rest of her life dealing with the child I raped into her. Of course, she could put the kid up for adoption, but that's its own bundle of issues, isn't it? And even then, she's dealing with the choices I made for her, when I exercised *my* control over her life.

Best of all, I get to do all that without much consequence! Oh, sure, *theoretically* I can get charged with rape and go to prison for it. But you know what? For every hundred men who rape, only three go to prison. Those are pretty good odds for me, especially since—again!—folks like you like to muddy up the issue saying things like "forcible rape." Keep doing that! It's working out great for me.

As for the kid, well, oddly enough, most women I rape want nothing to do with me afterward, so it's not like I will have to worry about child support or any other sort of responsibility...unless of course I decide that I haven't taught that woman a big enough lesson about who's really in control of her life. Did you know that 31 states in this country don't keep rapists from seeking custody or visitation rights? How great is *that*? That's just one more thing she has to worry about—me crawling out of the woodwork to remind her of what I did, and am continuing to do, to her life.

Look how much control you want to give me over that woman! I really can't thank you enough for it. It warms my heart to know no matter how much I rape, or how many women I impregnate through my non-consensual sexual battery, you have my back, when it comes to reminding every woman I humiliate who is *actually* the boss of her. It's me! It's always been me! You'll make sure it'll always *be* me. You'll see to that.

I am totally voting for you this election.

Yours,

Just Another Rapist.

P.S.: *I love it* when you say that you "stand for innocent life" when it comes to denying abortions in cases of rape! It implicitly suggests that the women I rape are in some way complicit in and guilty of the crimes I commit on top of, and inside of, their bodies! Which works out perfectly for me. Keep it up!

No, seriously, keep it up.

—JAR

Forrest Plumber

Feb
3
2009

Wait, what?

> *Fresh off his stint as a war correspondent in Gaza, Joe the Plumber is now doing political strategy with Republicans.*
>
> *When GOP congressional aides gather Tuesday morning for a meeting of the Conservative Working Group, Samuel Joseph Wurzelbacher—more commonly known as Joe the Plumber—will be their featured guest. This group is an organization of conservative Capitol Hill staffers who meet regularly to chart GOP strategy for the week.*
>
> *Wurzelbacher, who became a household name during the presidential election, will be focusing his talk on the proposed stimulus package. He's apparently not a fan of the economic rescue package, according to members of the group.*

I think it's nice that the GOP has found its new BFF with Joe the Plumber, but if memory serves correctly, every time Mr. Wurzelbacher opens his mouth on the issues of the day, ignorance vomits forth in rushing gouts. I believe the GOP is packaging this as "wisdom from the heartland," but speaking as one in the heartland, dude, it's just ignorance. And what's not ignorance is a GOP talking point, so I expect from the GOP point of view, whatever Joe says is going to be pure gold. *He makes so much sense! He's saying things we've always believed!* Well, yes.

This is not to disparage Mr. Wurzelbacher for being an opportunist, incidentally, and if you are of a mind to, here's a quiz for you:

Hey, you're a bald, chunky, blue-collar nobody from a crappy little midwest town! By chance, you find yourself thrust into the national spotlight and have a chance to do something more interesting with your life than sit in your crappy little midwest town and get balder and chunkier. Do you:

a) Say, "no thanks, I'd rather stay a nobody";

b) Do all the wacky crap everybody asks you to do for as long as you possibly can, because in your heart you know it will never ever get any better than this for you for as long as you might possibly live.

Take your time on that one, people.

So, no: I don't blame Joe the Plumber one bit for taking up the invitation to talk strategy with the GOP, or fly to the mideast, or any other thing he might be offered to do that sounds interesting to him. Dude's living the dream, man. As long as they keep letting him, why shouldn't he. I support Wurzelbacher milking this thing. Good for him. I hope he's having fun. I suspect he is.

The real question is not what Joe's doing, but what the hell the GOP's *thinking*. Maybe they haven't been keeping up with current events, but the last guy who hitched his wagon to Joe the Plumber found that wagon in the ditch. Joe the Plumber is an everyman, perhaps, but he's the sort of everyman who got outvoted by all the *other* sorts of everymen out there, and whose numbers appear to be shrinking as time goes on in any event. Which is to say that it's good for Joe the Plumber that the GOP wants to hear from him; it's probably not so great for the GOP.

Fox News Would Like To Take A Moment To Remind You That the Obamas Are As Black As Satan's Festering, Baby-Eating Soul

Jun 12 2008

Back in the day—you know, when presidential candidates were respectably *white*—news organizations called potential First Ladies "wives." But now that black folks are running, we can get all funky fresh with the lingo, yo. So it's basically *fine* for Fox News to use "Baby Mama" for Michelle Obama, slang that implies a married 44-year-old Princeton-educated lawyer is, to use an Urban Dictionary definition of the term, "some chick you knocked up on accident during a fling who you can't stand but you have to tolerate cuz she got your baby now." Because the Obamas are black! And the blacks, they're all *relaxed* about that shit, yo. Word *up*. And anyway, as the caption clearly indicates, it's not Fox News that's calling Michelle Obama "Baby Mama," it's *outraged liberals*. Fox News is just telling you what those outraged liberals are saying. They didn't *want* to use the term "Baby Mama." But clearly they had no *choice*.

Meanwhile, over at her personal site, Michelle "Fox News' Ethnic Shield" Malkin defends Fox News' use of the "Baby Mama" phrase by essentially making two arguments. First, Michelle Obama once called Barack Obama her "baby's daddy," and as we all know, a married woman factually and correctly calling her husband her child's father is *exactly the same* as a major news organization calling a potential First Lady some chick what got knocked up on a fling. Second, the term "baby-daddy" has gone out into the common culture; heck, even Tom Cruise was called Katie Holmes' baby-daddy, you know, when he impregnated her and she subsequently gave birth while the two were not married, which is *exactly* like what happened between Michelle and Barack Obama, who were married in 1992 and whose first child was born six years later.

So by Malkin's reasoning it's perfectly fine for Fox News to call Michelle Obama the unmarried mother of Barack Obama's children because an *entirely different phrase* has to her mind entered the common culture, and there was this one time that Michelle Obama once uttered something that sounded *like* that entirely different phrase, which is not the phrase that Fox News used. But wait! Malkin also points to someone in her comment thread saying that one time, Michelle Obama actually used the phrase "baby daddy"! No apostrophe! It's in a comment thread, so it *must* be true. Therefore, Michelle Obama apocryphally using a piece of urban slang makes it perfectly okay for Fox News to use an entirely different piece of urban slang. And *that's* why, you see, it won't be a *problem* for Bill O'Reilly to refer to Barack Obama as "my nigga" on the next *O'Reilly Factor.*

It's shit like this that makes a different story on CNN, about whether Barack Obama should be considered black or biracial, an absolute hoot. Here's a quick test on whether Obama should be considered fully black: *Poof!* Barack Obama has been magically transported to a KKK meeting in deepest, whitest Klanistan without his Secret Service detail. There's a rope and a tree nearby. What happens to Obama? If you say, "why, Barack Obama walks out of there alive, of course" then sure, he's biracial. Also, you're a *fucking idiot*. To everybody who cares about Obama's racial identity, either positively or negatively, the man is a black man, married to a black woman, who has black children. Black black *black* black *black* black black *black*.

It sure as hell matters to Fox News, which is why it's dog whistling about Barack so loudly that it's vibrating the windows. Calling Michelle Obama a "baby mama" isn't just Fox News having a happy casual larf; it's using urban slang to **a)** remind you the Obamas are black, **b)** belittle a woman of considerable personal accomplishment, and **c)** frame Barack Obama's relationship to his wife and children in a way that insults him, minimizes his love for and commitment to his family, and reinforces stereotypes about black men. Someone at Fox News just ought to call

Barack Obama "boy" at some point so we can have all the cards right out there on the table.

This will keep happening. Fox News will keep finding ways to remind its viewers that the Obamas are black (and possibly Muslim), Michelle Malkin will continue to make excuses for Fox News' dog-whistling racism that expose the fact that she's about as familiar with logical thinking as a rainbow trout is with knitting, and eventually some portion of the Fox News audience will get to the ballot box in November convinced that they're not really racists, they just know that there's something about that Obama boy they *just don't like*. This is how it will go. Let's not pretend it's not part of equation, this election year.

Friends

Nov
23
2011

My oldest friend who I still know and stay in contact with is Kyle Brodie, whom I met in the second grade. We hit it off on the first day, not in class but on the bus ride home. We started having a conversation and we both found each other so mutually clever that we just knew we were totally going to be best friends. And we were, until he moved away, as people do. But we kept in touch here and there and have genuinely reconnected again in the last couple of years; he's still as clever as ever and I'm delighted that 34 years ago I made the right decision to be his friend (and he to be mine).

The newest friend I have I made this last weekend; it's Adrienne Kress, an author I met at SFContario 2 in Toronto, and much like Kyle in second grade, it was her humor and cleverness in conversation that made me feel like I could have a connection with her, and encouraged me to spend time with her over the course of the convention. It is of course far too early to know if this enjoyment of her company and liking her as a person is going to mean I'll be friends with her as long as I've been with Kyle, and honestly, it would be totally unfair of me (as well as possibly creepy for her) if I had that expectation. And you know what? I don't. We'll see how it goes. But in the meantime, I'll consider her a friend, and happily so.

In between Kyle and Adrienne are some hundreds of people over the course of my life with whom I have been fortunate enough to be friends, to a greater or lesser extent.

"Friend" is an imprecise term, mind you. Classifying someone as a "friend" is a little like classifying them as a "mammal"—it's probably correct but it doesn't actually tell you much. There are all sorts of different types of friends, from the sort of friend barely above the level of casual acquaintance to the sort of friend who, when they call and say "I have a problem, bring a shovel," you bring a shovel and deal with the problem without so much as a second thought. The taxonomy of friendship is exhaustive and even then doesn't take into consideration that nearly all friendships are in motion. Your best friend in sixth grade may be someone to whom you barely speak anymore, for no other reason than life happens. The person with whom you shared mostly only a friendly passing relationship for years may unexpectedly become one of your most important friends. Friends you may see in real life only once a year—if that—may share a bond with you of surprising warmth. Time and circumstance and the fact we are ourselves always changing means our friendships are always changing too. New ones are added. Old ones trail away. Sometimes they return. Sometimes they don't.

It's not easy to define what a "friend" is in any event. There's a joking definition which gets somewhere in the neighborhood: "a friend is someone who knows the real you and likes you anyway." I think it might be more accurate to say that that a friend is someone that helps you to be the person you are, and likes you anyway. But even that doesn't get to it completely. I mean, hell, I have some friends that sometimes I don't even *like* very much. That doesn't stop them from being my friend, and sometimes even some of the best of my friends. It's tempting to throw up one's hands and classify friendship in the same way Potter Stewart defined pornography: Hard to define but you know it when you see it.

Nevertheless, I'll strive for a simple definition. I think at the end of the day, a friend is someone you emotionally want in your life, who wants you emotionally in theirs. Why do you want them in your life, and they in yours, and how much in it for both? That's something for the two of you to work out, and when you can't figure it out, or sometimes you end up wanting different things, that's when the friendship changes or ends. It's also possible that your friendship is not mutually graded: You may feel an intense attachment to a friend who feels less intensely about you, and vice-versa. This can sometimes lead to problems. And finally friendship is two people dealing with each other, and you know how people are. Sometimes no matter how much you want to be friends with someone, or how much other people think you should be friends (or on occasion how much you would like to be friends for the sake of a mutual friend), it just doesn't work. Friendship isn't actually easy. People aren't easy.

But the reward is that you get to have friends. You have the people to whom you may vent, with whom you can laugh, who will support you when you need it and for whom you may be a shelter. People who are, as is often said, the "family of choice"—those with whom you may stand and face what the world sends your way. People who are a part of you, have helped you become you, and who might be a part of who you are moving forward.

I have been genuinely blessed with friendships of all sorts and have been thankful for them all, from the most casual friendships to the ones that have lasted and grown all through my life. For each of these and in their way, I have tried to be a good friend in return, and worry that I haven't been. I can be oddly bad at connection; e-mails slip past me, calls turn into week-long bouts of phone tag, I get wrapped up in my own head and I wander about in otherwise oblivious ways. Even friends who I consider to be best friends I can be out of communication with for months at a time. So I am likewise thankful that when I do once again get in contact, they are gracious to me and still friends. It means a lot to me, more than I can easily express here.

So, my friends: Thank you, each of you and all of you, from the ones I have known all my life to the ones I am just meeting. It's a good life with you in it. I hope your life is better for me being in yours.

Gawker, Reddit, Free Speech and Such

Oct
16
2012

I've been watching with some interest the drama surrounding Gawker writer Adrian Chen revealing Reddit user/celeb/moderator/troll Violentacrez's real life identity (Michael Brutsch), which among other things resulted in Brutsch losing his job, presumably because Brutsch's employer was not 100% comfortable employing someone who spent his days moderating online forums with titles like "Chokeabitch" and bragged about the time his 19-year-old stepdaughter performed oral sex on him. It also resulted in Reddit globally banning links from Gawker (since rescinded, although forum moderators ("subredditors") can choose to block links within their forums—and do), and various bannings due to discussion of the drama.

Wrapped up in all of this are various chest beatings about free speech and whether someone's online anonymity is sacred, even if he is a creep, the culture of Reddit in particular and the Internet in general, and in a larger sense where the rights of one individual—say, a creepy middle-aged dude—begin to impinge on others—say, young women who don't believe that merely being in public is an invitation to be sexually degraded. This is all interesting stuff, to be sure, and naturally I have a few thoughts on these topics. In no particular order:

1. The "free speech" aspect of this is largely nonsense. Reddit is not a public utility or a public square; it's a privately owned space on the Internet. From a legal and (United States) constitutional point of view, people who post on Reddit have no "free speech" privileges; they have what speech privileges Reddit itself chooses to provide them, and to tolerate. Reddit chooses to tolerate creepiness and general obnoxiousness for reasons of its own, in other words, and not because there's a legal or constitutional reason for it.

Personally speaking, when everything is boiled down to the marrow, I think the reason Reddit tolerates the creepy forums has to do with money more than anything else. Reddit allows all those creepy subreddits because its business model is built on memberships and visits, and the dudes who visit these subreddits are almost certainly enthusiastic members and visitors. This is a perfectly valid reason, in the sense of "valid" meaning "allowing people to be creepy isn't inherently illegal, and we make money because of it, so we'll let it happen." But while it makes sense that the folks at Reddit are either actively or passively allowing "we're making money allowing creeps to get their creep on" to be muddled with "we're standing up for the principles of free speech," it doesn't mean anyone else needs be confused by this.

If someone bleats to you about any of this being a "free speech" issue, you can safely mark them as either ignorant or pernicious—probably ignorant, as the understanding of what "free speech" means in a constitutional sense here in the US is, shall we say, *highly constrained* in the general population. Additionally and independently, the sort of person who who says "free speech" when they mean "I like doing creepy things to other people without their consent and you can't stop me so fuck you ha ha ha ha" is pretty clearly a mouth-breathing asshole who in the larger moral landscape deserves a bat across the bridge of the nose and probably knows it. Which is why—unsurprisingly—so many of them choose to be anonymous and/or use pseudonyms on Reddit while they get their creep on.

On the subject of anonymity:

2. Anonymity/pseudonymity is not inherently evil or wrong. Astute observers will note that on Whatever I allow both anonymous and pseudonymous postings, because sometimes you want to say something you wouldn't normally say with your name attached and/or because you have personal/business reasons to want not to have a trail of comments lead back to you. Perfectly reasonable and perfectly acceptable, and as I moderate the site pretty attentively, anyone who decides to use the cloak of anonymity to be an assbag will get their words malleted into oblivion in any event.

It's not anonymity or pseudonymity that's the issue. The issue is people being assholes while anonymous because they don't believe it's ever going to get back to them. This is a separate issue from anonymity/pseudonymity. Someone who is anonymous shouldn't be assumed to be an assbag, any more than someone who uses their real name should be assumed to be a kind and decent human being. In both cases, it's what they say that should be the guide.

However:

3. If at this point in Internet history you think you're really anonymous/pseudonymous on the Internet, or that you have a *right* to anonymity/pseudonymity on the Internet, you're kind of stupid. Yes, *stupid*, and there's no other way to put it. I remember back in 1998 and people with pseudonymous online diaries freaking out because they ranted about a family member or boss online, and then that person found out, and as a result the diarist was fired and/or had very awkward Thanksgivings for several years. And you know what? Even back in 1998, when the Web was still *reasonably* new, while one could be sympathetic, in the back of the head there was always *well, what did you expect?* It's not that hard to find things out. Something will give you away sooner or later. Here in 2012, if you're going to make an argument to me that anonymity truly exists on the Web, I'm going to want you to follow up with an explanation of how the Easter Bunny is riding unicorns on Mars with Kurt Cobain.

I find it difficult to believe that Redditors don't understand that anonymity online is merely a facade; indeed it's probably one of the reasons that revealing the identity of pseudonymous Redditors is looked on as such a huge betrayal. That said, anyone who goes to Reddit and truly believes that a site-standard ethos of "don't reveal our members' identities" fully protects them from being revealed or allows them to revel in obnoxious and/or creepy behavior without fear of discovery, they're kind of dumb. I won't say that they deserve what they get—maybe they do, maybe they don't—but I will say they shouldn't be terribly *surprised*.

Now, you might argue that someone has a right to pseudonymity or anonymity online, and depending on your argument, I might even agree with you (hint: such an argument doesn't involve posting sexualized pictures of minors or the unconsenting). But I would also agree with you that it would be cool if the Mars rover beamed back a picture of Kurt and Peter Cottontail jamming on "Pennyroyal Tea" while their unicorns kept the time on tambourine. Back here in the real world, you should get used to the idea neither is happening soon.

Speaking of the real world:

4. Reddit is not the Internet, the Internet is not Reddit, and in neither place is one obliged to privilege anonymity/pseudonymity. It seems like a lot of the angst emanating from Reddit regarding this event is based on a community standard of not outing anonymous or pseudonymous Reddit users. However, just because something is a community standard does not mean one is obliged to follow it in all ways at all times, and if the "com-munity standard" is doing real harm or is being used as a shield to allow people to act badly without consequence, then it's a reasonable question of whether this "standard" is to be allowed to stand unchallenged.

In any event, an argument that those outside the community are bound to its standards is a tough one to make outside of that community. Am I, John Scalzi, enjoined by Reddit "community standards" on my own site? Not in the least, and if anyone suggested I was, I would point and laugh at them. Am I when I am on Reddit, signed into my Reddit account ("Scalzi," which, I would note, is not particularly anonymous/pseudonymous)? Well, I'm enjoined by the actual rules (seeing as I have no right to free speech as understood by the US Constitution while I am there), and generally would try to abide by established local practices. But there are rules and then there are guidelines, and I don't need to believe that the latter has the force of the former.

In the case of Adrian Chen, the Gawker writer who revealed Violentacrez's real-life identity, I think he's perfectly justified in doing so. Whether certain denizens of Reddit like it or not, Chen was practicing journalism, and writing a story of a figure of note (and of notoriety) on one of the largest and most influential sites on the Internet. They may believe that Mr. Brutsch should have an expectation not to have his real life identity revealed on Gawker, but the question to ask here is "why?" *Why* should that be the expectation? How does an expectation of pseudonymity on a Web site logically extend to an expectation of pseudonymity in the real world? How does one who beats his chest for the right of free speech on a Web site (where in fact he has no free speech rights) and to have that right to free speech include the posting of pictures of women who did not consent to have their pictures taken or posted then turn around and criticize Gawker for pursuing an actually and legitimately constitutionally protected exercise of the free press, involving a man who has no legal or ethical presumption of anonymity or pseudonymity in the real world? How do you square one with the other? Well, you can't, or at least I can't; I have no doubt some of the folks at Reddit can guide that particular camel through the eye of the needle.

But they would be wrong. Mr. Brutsch's actions are newsworthy, and it's neither libel nor defamation for Gawker to correctly attribute his actions to him, whether or not he ever expected them to be attached to his real life identity. If they don't think so, I heartily encourage them to take up a collection for Mr. Brutsch so he can sue Gawker. I know what the result would be, but I think the path to getting there might be instructive to some Redditors.

Or maybe (and hopefully) they already know they don't have a legal or ethical leg to stand on, which is why they eventually fall back on *well, this just isn't done* and then ban Gawker links on Reddit. Which, of course, is their right. That is, so long as the people actually running Reddit believe it is.

GIZMODO AGREES: APPLE FANS ARE STATUS-SEEKING BETA MONKEYS

Jun
9
2009

Thus, its entry today lamenting the fact that with the latest iteration of the Apple product line there is no longer any meaningful technological or design distinction between the expensive, top-level Apple products the hipsters flash about in coffee shops and subways to signal their reproductive fitness, and the plebian-level Apple products common trolls use to sign into MySpace and/or listen to their Nickelback MP3s:

> *A leveling of class distinctions in Apple products is going to sting people who valued the affectation of elitism that came with using Apple's top-of-the-line products. Even subtle differences—like the premium paid for the matte black MacBook over the otherwise identical shiny white one, were signals, beamed out to the others in the coffee shop, declaring who was "da boss." You know, the guys who wore the white earbuds with pride five years ago…*
>
> *Maybe Apple is trying to create good design that works for anyone and everyone. I can respect that. Still, the question remains: Does this make rich people look like poor people, or poor people look like rich people? The privileged must know.*

Gizmodo is getting its snark on, obviously, but it also hit the nail on the head as to why I, at least, have a mild allergic reaction to the Cult of Apple. It's not that Mac laptops and iPhones aren't nice pieces of equipment; they surely are. It's just that they're also the tiny coke spoons of the early 21st century—a bit of déclassé ostentation flashed by people who think they're signaling one thing when they're in fact signaling something else entirely, and that thing is: *I may be an asshole.*

To be sure, the guy with an Android phone and a Toshiba laptop may be no *less* of an asshole. But you're not necessarily going to assume that from his technology alone. This is why I'm always vaguely annoyed when someone smugs at me that I should get a Mac for my next computer: part of my brain goes, *yeah, it's a nice machine, but then I'll be indistinguishable from all those Williamsburg dicks.* Next will be a canvas manbag and chunky square glasses, followed shortly by leaping in front of the G train. Thank you, no.

Yes, yes: Not everyone hoisting a MacBook Pro or soon to be flashing an iPhone 3GS is a vacuous hipster status monkey. But then, not everyone who drove a Trans Am in 1982 was a beefy, mullet-wearing Rush fan, either. Yet when you picture a 1980s Trans Am owner in your mind, is he *not* today's Tom Sawyer? Does he *not* get high on you? Well, see.

A General Observation

Sep
20
2009

The Internet does seem to be full of people whose knowledge of complex concepts appears limited to a dictionary definition.

Some of them seem to be proud of that.

Having Been Poor

Apr
1
2009

writes:

Reading your 'being poor' topic and having been under-monetized at points in my past, I'm wondering how you think that affects/should affect a person's current lifestyle. Could being a packrat be related to that? Habitually looking at the price of everything just another case of OCD? How about being traumatized by the thought of throwing away leftover food?

It's an interesting question. I don't think having been poor at a certain point in one's life *should* have to affect one's lifestyle on a day-to-day basis; having been poor doesn't necessarily have to afflict one with something akin to post-traumatic stress disorder when it comes to money, or have caused lasting damage to one's psyche. I'm aware that sometimes it does, of course. But I'm also aware of people who handle that aspect of their past just fine, and don't let their previous poverty fill them with either shame or apprehension. I'm pretty much in that boat, as far as I can tell: Having been poor when I was younger was not fun, but it's not something I dwell on day to day. I have other things to fill up my time.

That said, speaking on a personal level, I am aware of some behaviors that I suspect have at least something to do with having been poor when I was a kid:

I tend to save a lot more of my income than most people I know, so that if the bottom drops out of my life, I have a cushion. And when I say "I" here, you should understand it to mean "we," as it's actually my wife who handles the family finances. Without going into actual figures, I suspect we save about 20% of our income on a yearly basis; the current national savings rate is about 4% at the moment (and not too long ago was rather a bit under that). Now, one reason that we can do that is that we make a comparatively large amount of income relative to the national average, so doing a large amount of saving does not cut into our spending on essentials or even much on our frivolities. But even when we made substantially less we were saving quite a lot.

I'm notably debt-averse. Having seen first-hand how debt screws with people, neither I nor Krissy has much in the way of consumer debt. I use my Amex for most purchases I make so that I can have a paper trail for my accountant, but the Amex is a charge card, not a credit card, and I have to pay it off every month (Amex keeps trying to enroll me in the program that lets me carry a balance; I keep telling them that's not why I use them). We have Visa cards as well and also use them, but keep the balance on them low enough that we could pay them off at once without making a dent in our savings.

Likewise, we don't get fancy with the debt we do have, namely our mortgages: We have stable, predictable, boring 30-year mortgages on our properties, thus avoiding the drama of ARMs and other dumb ways to finance the place one lives.

I buy for value over flash: I'm not particularly cheap when it comes to high ticket items, but I also have a tendency to buy solidly performing objects over the hottest and coolest thing, partly because I intend to use whatever I'm buying for a fairly long time. This is why, as an example, the average life expectancy for a car in the Scalzi household is 12 years and climbing and why I still use a television I bought in 1991, and also why, when I buy a new computer, I pass the old one down to Athena. It's also why I mildly resent cell phones at this point, since I know the Blackberry Storm I bought last November will have a usable lifespan of about two years, which doesn't fit with my lifestyle choices, those bastards.

Related to the above, while not notably cheap in a day-to-day sense, you're also not going to be seeing me spend conspicuously; my tastes and most of my enthusiasms are notably middle class at best. Part of this is the financial section of my brain asking "why are you spending money on *that?*" and if I can't come up with a good answer for it, I tend not to buy it. Part of it is also a practical aspect of my personality ("what are you going to *do* with that?") that keeps me from collecting things if I don't have a use for them in more than a "gee, that's pretty" aspect.

(This isn't always true, of course: I bought the original artwork for the *Old Man's War* hardcover for about half the advance for the book, primarily because you only have a first novel once, and I wanted a physical commemoration of that. On the other hand, that's also probably the single most expensive thing I have in the house. The thing I spend the most on is books, which drives Krissy a little nuts, because I already have enough of *those*.)

(Related to this: I'm a bit of a packrat, but I don't think it's because I was once poor, it's because **a)** I'm lazy and getting rid of stuff takes time and thought, and **b)** I tend to associate things with events around the time I got them, so it's like getting rid of memories, and I'm a sentimental bastard. I sort of need to get over that; at this point I have more crap than clear memories.)

All of the above can be summed up, I think, as: Don't buy what you can't afford, don't buy what you don't have use for and have enough on hand for when life whacks you upside the head. Which I think in general is good advice for anyone, but in practice tends to be an attitude of people who have experience with poverty one way or another.

(But not the attitude of everyone with experience with poverty, to be sure: there's the flip side of this attitude, in which people who were formerly poor feel the need to show off their new perceived wealth through ostentatious display. I've been fortunate that my showing off gene did not feel the need to express itself that way.)

Note I don't think these attitudes of mine are particularly *virtuous* one way or another; they're simply attitudes that I'm comfortable with and which work for me. But I don't doubt that the reason they are there has something to do with where I have been before in my life, in terms of poverty. There are worse ways for poverty to mark someone, to be sure. In this as well as in other ways, I've been pretty lucky.

Health Care Passage Thoughts

Mar
22
2010

Because the passage of one of the most significant bills in history should not go unnoted here:

I've been silent here about the health care issue since an entry on January 20, primarily because I didn't have a thing to add to it, in particular this portion:

> *...contrary to apparently popular opinion, health care isn't quite dead yet. Now the real interesting thing is to see what the Democrats do next—whether they curl up in a legislative ball, moaning softly, and let their health care initiative die, or whether they double down, locate their gonads and find a way to get it done (there are several ways this can be accomplished).*
>
> *From a purely strategic point of view, I'm not sure why they don't just ram the thing through the House as is, fiddle with it a bit during reconciliation and get to Obama to sign it. To put it bluntly, the Democrats will look better by flipping the GOP the bird and then using the ten months until the 2010 election to get voters back on their side than showing to the voters that despite a large majority in both houses, they collapse like a flan in the cupboard at the first setback. We'll see what happens now, and I suspect what happens in the next week or so will make a significant impact on what happens in November.*

And, well. It took the Democrats several weeks longer to find their gonads than I thought it should have, but then again I thought the health care process should have been accomplished several months ago to begin with, back when they had 60 senators. But the Democrats have an apparent structural problem, which is that when they have everything going their way, a lot of them feel that means they should immediately go another way. It took losing their Senate supermajority and the GOP overwhelming the public discourse on the health care process to get enough Democrats in line, with many I suspect motivated by the simple fear that what the GOP would do to them if health care passed was less painful than what would the GOP would do to them if it failed.

Basically, I find what passes for Democratic legislative strategy absolutely appalling. Decades from now, when they make the ponderous Oscar-bait movie about the struggle for health care (with Jaden Smith as Obama and two-time Academy Award winner Snooki as Speaker Pelosi), it will make for exciting twists and turns in the plot, but out here in the real world, you shouldn't have to let your organization get the crap beat out of it in order to motivate those in it to do the thing everybody knows it wants to get done. What the Democrats have managed to do with health care isn't a Pyrrhic victory—I'll get to that in a moment—but it surely was taking the long way around: over the river, through the woods, down into the landfill, into the abattoir, across a field of rabid, angry badgers. Next time, guys, make it easier on yourselves.

That said, the Democrats were magnificently fortunate that, as incompetent as they are, they are ever-so-slightly less incompetent than the GOP, which by any realistic standard has been handed one of the largest legislative defeats in decades. The GOP was not simply opposed to health care, it was opposed to it in shrill, angry, apocalyptic terms, and saw it not as legislation, or in terms of whether or not health care reform was needed or desirable for Americans, but purely as political strategy, in terms of whether or not it could kneecap Obama and bring itself back into the majority. As such there was no real political or moral philosophy to the GOP's action, it was all short-term tactics, i.e., take an idea a majority of people like (health care reform), lie about its particulars long enough and in a dramatic enough fashion to lower the popularity of the idea, and then bellow in angry tones about how the president and the Democrats are ignoring the will of the people. Then publicly align the party with the loudest and most ignorant segment of your supporters, who are in part loud because you've encouraged them to scream, and ignorant because you and your allies in the media have been feeding them bad information. Whip it all up until health care becomes the single most important issue for both political parties—an all-in, must win, absolutely cannot lose issue.

It's a fine plan—unless you're on the losing side, which the GOP now is. And while the folks in the GOP will be happy to tell you that they are going to ride this baby into majorities come November, they have a very simple problem in that now they're running not against a bill, but a *law*, some of the benefits of which will immediately come into play, and which removed from overheated nonsensical rhetoric are almost certainly going to be popular. In the first year of the bill being signed into law, insurance companies will be barred from dropping people when they get sick. Do GOPers want to come out being for insurers dropping people when they need their health insurance the most? The new law will let parents keep their kids on their insurance until their kids are 26, keeping a large number of otherwise uninsured young adults covered. Do GOPers want to run on depriving millions of young Americans that health care coverage? In this economy? Seniors will get a rebate when they fall into that prescription drug "donut hole," and the law will eventually eliminate that hole entirely. Do GOPers think it'll be smart to tell seniors that closing the "donut hole" is a bad thing?

So this is the GOP's problem going forward: people love to hate "socialism" in the abstract, but they love their benefits once they have them, and now the GOP will have to go from saving people from "socialism" to taking away benefits, and that's a hard row to hoe. I don't credit the Democrats with a surfeit of brains when it comes to tactics, but if the GOP really wants to run on repealing health care law this year or in 2012, even the *Democrats* can manage to point out to millions of voters that this means letting insurers drop you or your children from their rolls and making it harder for seniors to buy the prescription drugs they need to survive. Yes, yes: who's killing grandma *now*?

There's another problem for the GOP. While I think it's likely the Democrats will lose seats this election cycle (as often happens to the party of the president—any president—in mid-term elections), I think the idea that the GOP is going to retake either the House or Senate (or both) is optimistic at best, and the idea that they would be able to retake both with the majorities needed to overcome a presidential veto is the sort of magical thinking that usually indicates either profound chemical imbalances in the brain or really excellent hashish. So Americans will have two and a half years to get used to their new-found health care rights and benefits, most of which in the real world are perfectly sensible, beneficial things, before we all get to vote on who is going to be the next president. Now, perhaps Obama will be voted out of office and perhaps he won't, but if whomever is the GOP candidate in 2012 plans on running on repealing the health care laws, well, you know. Good luck with that. I'm sure Obama would be delighted for them to try.

And yes, what *about* Obama? Well, all he did was manage to do something no other president has managed to do, a thing upon which other presidencies have foundered, against opposition that was total, persistent and fanatical. I wish he had managed to do it sooner and with less damage to his standing, and that his own inexperience and aloofness had not been a proximate cause to its delay, which it was. I wish his allies in the legislature had not been appallingly disorganized; I wish his opponents in the legislature were more interested in the good of the people they represent than in playing tactical games. What's gotten passed isn't 100% of what I would have wanted to have passed, not just for what's in it but also for what's not.

But in the end, it got done. We have health care reform. We have it because Obama decided that it was going to get done, one way or another, and that it was worth risking his presidency over—and worth risking Democratic control of the House and Senate as well. Like the GOP, he went all in, but unlike the GOP, he didn't do it just for tactical advantage or for short term advantage of power and party; he did it because when all and said and done I think he really does believe that health care reform is to the benefit of the American people, and that it in itself was more important than just being president for as long as Constitutionally possible.

To be clear, and contrary to GOP thinking, I think this is the act that will *make* him a two-termer, the poor bastard. But even if by some chance he's one-and-done, I think he can say he did the thing he came to Washington to do, and that he did something that was the right thing to do. As it happens, I agree with him; I think it makes moral, philosophical and economic sense for as many Americans as possible to have access to regular, competent health care. It was a reason I voted for him, and in itself is worth my vote for him.

Mind you, there is more I expect from him before he leaves office, whether that's in 2013 or 2017. The fact he got this done—despite everything—gives me confidence that he'll get those things done too.

He's Not Winning, He's Just Not Losing

Mar
7
2012

Super Tuesday has come and gone and Mitt Romney is doing what Romney apparently does, which is gather delegates to himself in the least impressive way possible. It takes a special presidential candidate to outspend his main rival four to one in Ohio and yet win the state with only a 1% margin—correction, it takes a special candidate to outspend his main rival *who is an unmitigated public bigot* in Ohio and yet win with only a 1% margin—and it appears that Romney is that candidate.

Meanwhile Rick Santorum, the unmitigated public bigot in question, won three states and led in Ohio for a substantial portion of the evening before dropping only a single percentage point behind Romney in the final tally. That's more than enough for him to stay in the race, particularly because the next stretch of primary states are in the South and Midwest, i.e., not Romney's best territory in that they're full of evangelicals and/or blue-collar folks. Looking at the primary calendar, in fact, it's not until April 24 that Romney gets a batch of states that look generally friendly to him—that's the day a bunch of Northeast states vote—and even then Pennsylvania's in there to mess up his math.

My predictions in this primary season have been atrocious, so no one should actually rely on my opinion, but it looks to me like Romney, despite all his cash and the fact that Santorum is objectively terrifying to people outside the Conservabubble, might not actually wrap this up until the whole damn primary season finishes up in June. Santorum is running strong enough to pick up some of the more conservative states, and, hey, who knows, maybe Gingrich will pick up another pity primary or two down there in the South. Or maybe Romney *doesn't* wrap it up at all, and we have that fabled brokered convention that makes all the politinerds squee with delight. And then what? A brokered Romney/Santorum ticket? Man, I get the twitchy giggles just *thinking* about that one.

(Dear GOP: A Romney/Santorum ticket would be like handing Barack Obama the largest, most delicious fruit basket ever created. Delivered by a pony. A sparkly pony. With ribbons in its mane. Named "Buttercup." Just so you know.)

Now, those of you with a sense of memory may point out that Obama didn't wrap up his nomination until June 2008 (and that before then, there were 20 debates between the Democratic candidates, nearly as many as the Republican candidates had this electoral season), and that the partisan rancor between the Obama and Clinton camps was pretty impressive. Didn't stop Obama from taking the White House. This is a fair point. It's also a fair point to note that 2008 was a year with no incumbent in the White House—and that this year the incumbent is reasonably popular and currently benefiting from a (slowly) growing economy. For *this* incumbent, an extended primary season is beneficial, since it keeps his eventual opponent busy beating up and spending money on someone else. And as Santorum is to the right of Romney, it will also make it harder for him to pivot to the center later, to pick up all those independents he'll need to actually win.

It's also fair to note that on the GOP side in 2008, McCain locked up the GOP nomination on March 4. This year's primary calendar wouldn't have made locking up the nomination entirely likely, but there's no reason that by this time someone couldn't have been a prohibitive favorite for the nod. Romney, who was supposed to be, still isn't.

And, I don't know. In a way that's heartening, I suppose. If Romney has shown us anything this year, it's that you can have nearly all the money in the world it's possible to have thrown into your campaign and still be fundamentally unattractive to a large number of the people you need to convince to be the GOP nominee. Money isn't everything in this campaign, although so far it's been just barely enough to keep Romney in the winning column. I do wonder what's going to happen when Romney finally gets to the general election and has an opponent that he *can't* outspend four or five to one, with the hope of eking out another low-single-digit victory.

Actually, I'm lying—I don't really wonder. I in fact have a pretty good guess what's going to happen to him. I don't suspect he's going to like it.

How I Think

Mar
24
2010

DeCadmus asks:

John, I'm consistently impressed with how you break topical issues of the day down into their constituent parts; how you reason and make your points (and take apart others') in your comments. I see some of the same at play in your novels; your storytelling and character building.

I'd like to know ***how*** *you think. Were you taught something particularly useful about reasoning in school? What tools do you leverage to build your citadel of considered opinion and wily discourse?*

Schooling in fact does have something to do with it. In a formal sense, I've noted before that my degree from The University of Chicago is in Philosophy, and specifically it's a degree in Philosophy with Allied Fields, with those allied field being linguistics and philosophy of language. What this means is that I spent a reasonably large amount of time in school (to the extent that I actually attended classes, which is another issue entirely) looking at the how and why of language. If you were to ask me my favorite philosophical treatise—that is, the one I found most interesting in terms of waking up neurons in my brain and making them go "hmmm"—then I would point you in the direction of *How to Do Things With Words*, by J.L. Austin. My own brand of thinking is not precisely a direct line from Austin's writings, but one very important takeaway I got from Austin, and a thing which crystallized that which to that point I had suspected but had not much thought about concretely, is that words themselves are action; they do not simply describe the world but in a very real sense *make* the world. Therefore it makes sense to pay attention to the worlds people are attempting to create in their words.

Less formally, both my high school and my college were argumentative places, and I mean that Socratically; in both places if you lobbed out an opinion during class (or, shit, just laying about in the dorm), you could expect to have to defend that argument. There's an old joke that at the University of Chicago, when someone says "good morning," the appropriate response is "how do you know?" Now, there are ways of doing this wrong; for a while my once and future college girlfriend was dating one of those college conservatives who liked to posit morally appalling things just to get a rise out of people, and would retreat to "I'm just playing devil's advocate" after he pissed people off. I'm pretty sure he ended up being punched in the head, not for being a college conservative (of which Chicago had, oh, just a *few*), but because he was an asshole. But in a larger sense, if you spend years having your statements challenged by teachers, professors and your peers, over time you learn to argue, and you learn how to challenge and take apart poor arguments.

The gist of this is that by both education and by environment and independent of any particular native facility for words, I was sensitized to the power and value of language, reason, rhetoric and logic, and not only regarding how I used each myself, but how they were used *on* me, and especially when they were being used poorly.

Apart from all this, but something that could be used integrally with it, is the fact that both as a younger person and as an adult, I spent and do spend a lot of time observing people. This fact is not immediately obvious if your only interaction with me is here on Whatever, where rhetorically *I* am generally in "let me tell you what I think" mode, but as I'm fond of reminding people, my presentation here on Whatever is performance; it's me, but it's not *all* of me, just the parts best suited for what I want to do here. Out in the real world, I don't spend all my time pontificating. I spend a fair amount of it watching people.

Without getting too much into the drama of it, part of this was due to early circumstance: When you're a small, sensitive kid from a poor and often unstable home environment, you spend a lot of your time looking at who could be trouble and who could be an ally. But, you know, part of it is just *me.* I find people fascinating. I want to know who they are and why they are the way they are. That means you pay attention to them: how they act, how they react, how they interact, and how they do all of that in relation to you, including the words they use with you and on you.

Finally, added to all of this is the simple fact my brain is wired for communication, and writing is my best expression of this fact. I learned early on what writing does for me (both internally and externally) and what it allows me to do for and to others, and *this,* you can be assured, was an interesting thing for me to discover. Now, when I was younger, I was smug and thought the *sheer force of my personal awesomeness* would make everything I wrote brilliant and that everyone would love every bit of it, and this is why I've spent a fair amount of my adult life apologizing to friends from high school and college for foisting my writing on them at every opportunity. Age has taught me about humility and the desirability of editors, but perhaps more charitably it's pointed out to me that paying attention to the rhetorical craft and particulars of my own writing is important if I want to engage and move people.

Having just vomited all that out on you, let me point out that it's not like I wake up each morning and think "today I shall *marshal all that I have learned* of rhetoric and discourse in the service *of justice*" and then leap to the keyboard, fresh to the day's fight. I'm nowhere that worked up about my writing. Like anything, if you do it long enough, you end up just doing it without having to think too much about it. At this point, a lot of it is muscle memory. I mean, I *do* think about my writing, the mechanics and effects thereof, quite a lot. But that's a craftsman considering his tools (or what tools he needs to get and work with to get better), which is usually independent of actually getting in there and doing the work. When it comes time for the typing, what I've learned about how to communicate, argue and reason climbs into the back seat, and the actual act of writing gets into the driver's seat. How I think gives way to what I write.

How to Be a Good Commenter

Sep
18
2012

One of the things I'm proud of at Whatever is that the comment threads are usually actually worth reading, which is not always something you get with a site that has as many readers as this one does. Some of this is down to my moderation of the site, and my frequent malleting of trolls/idiots/assbags, but much of it is also down the generally high standard of commenter here. I do a lot less malleting than I might have to, because the people who frequent here do a fine job at being good commenters.

And I hear you say: Why, I would like to be a good commenter too! Not just here, but in other places where commenting occurs online! Well, of course you do. You're a fine upstanding human being, not some feculent jackass with a keyboard, an internet connection and a blistering sense of personal inferiority that is indistinguishable from common sociopathy.

So for you, I have ten questions to ask yourself before you press the "post comment" button. Yes, ten is a lot. No one said being a good commenter was easy. But the good news is that the more you're a good commenter, the less you'll actually have to think about being one before you type. It becomes a habit, basically. So keep at it.

Here are your questions:

1. Do I actually have anything to say? Meaning, does what you post in the comments boil down to anything other than "yes, this," or "WRONG AGAIN," or even worse, "who cares"? A comment is not meant to be an upvote, downvote or a "like." It's meant to be an addition to, and complementary to (but not necessarily complimentary *of*) the original post. If your comment is not adding value, you need to ask whether you need to write it, and, alternately, why anyone should be bothered to read it. On a personal note, I find these sort of contentless comments especially irritating when the poster is expressing indifference; the sort of twit who goes out of his way to say "::yawn::" in a comment is the sort I want first up against the wall when the revolution comes.

2. Is what I have to say actually *on* topic? What is the subject of the original post? That's also the subject of the comment thread, as is, to some extent, the manner in which the writer approached the subject. If you're dropping in a comment that's *not* about these things, then you're likely working to make the comment thread suck. Likewise, if as a commenter you're responding to a comment from someone else that's not on topic to the original post, you're *also* helping to make the comment thread suck. On a busy blog or site, there will be many opportunities to talk about many different subjects. You don't have to talk about them in the wrong place.

3. Does what I write actually *stay* on topic? As a corollary to point two, if you make a perfunctory wave at the subject and then immediately use it as a jumping-off point for your own particular set of hobby horses, then you're also making the thread suck. This is a prime derailing maneuver, which I like to dub "The Libertarian Dismount," given the frequency with which members of that political tribe employ it—e.g., "It's a shame that so many people are opposed to same-sex marriage, but this is just why government has no place legislating relationships between people, and why in a perfect society government steps away and blah blah blahdee blah blah." If you can't write a comment that isn't ultimately a segue into topics *you* feel are important, ask yourself why everything has to be about you.

4. If I'm making an argument, do I actually know how to make an argument? This I believe: Most people really can't argue their way out of a paper bag. It's not their fault; it's not as if, in the US at least, we spend a lot of time training people in rhetoric. Be that as it may, if you are making an argument in a comment, it will help if the argument you're making is structurally sound. It's not my job to teach you the basics of rhetoric, but I will at the very least note that at Wikipedia there is a fine list of logical fallacies, which I beg you to peruse and consider. I will also say that in my experience the single most common bad argument is the assumption that one's personal experience is universal rather than intensely personal and anecdotal. Sorry, folks: you are probably not actually the living avatar of What Everyone Believes and Knows.

5. If I'm making assertions, can what I say be backed up by actual fact? I know you believe what you believe, and that's nice for you, but if you want *me* or others to believe what you believe, then I'd like to see the data, please. Otherwise I'm just going to assume you are talking out of your ass, and I suspect most other people will make a similar assumption. The nice thing about the Internet is that facts, backed up by trustworthy sources—complete with references and methodologies!—are reasonably easy to find and link to. Wikipedia drives me up a wall sometimes, but the one undeniably good thing it's done is to train a generation of nerds to ask: "[*citation, please*]". As the obvious corollary:

6. If I'm refuting an assertion made by others, can what I say be backed up by fact? Because often comment threads are filled with the sounds of refutation. However, refutation without substantiation is not refutation at all; it's just adding to the noise. Don't add to the noise. Noise is easy. Be better than mere noise.

7. Am I approaching this subject like a thoughtful human being, or like a particularly stupid fan? I originally wrote "stupid sports fan," but that was being unfair to sports fans, who are no more likely to be stupid and irrational about their favorite sports team than gadget fans are to be irrational about their favorite bit of tech or media fans their favorite series of books/shows/movies, or politics fans to be about their favorite ideology. The problem is when these sort of folks descend on a thread and get all rah-rah for their "team," whatever that team is, and things get dreary and sad, fast. Look, everyone has their biases and inclinations and favorites, and that's fine. This doesn't mean you won't come across as a brainless plumper for your side when you, in fact, plump brainlessly for them in a comment. If your comment boils down to "WOOOO GO TEAM [insert person/thing here] HELLS YEAH" then, again, you're the problem with the comment thread, not anyone else.

8. Am I being an asshole to others? Yes, I know you think you're being clever when you are being snide and sarcastic about that other commenter, or about the original poster. I would remind you what the failure mode of clever is. Also, being a complete prick to others in a comment thread is an easy tell to those others that you can't make a sufficient argument on any other ground than personal abuse. Which is not a good thing for you. Now, it's also important to note that not everyone starts off being an asshole to others—commenters can begin responding to each other politely and then as things go on become more and more frustrated and exasperated until one or both (or more! Because comment threads aren't always or even usually one-on-one discussions) go Full Asshole. So it's worth keeping a tab on things. Two things here: One, assume good will on the part of others when talking to them; two, just because the other guy goes Full Asshole doesn't mean you have to follow his shining example.

9. Do I want to have a conversation or do I want to win the thread? Some people have to be right, and can't abide when others don't recognize their fundamental right to be right, and will thus keep making attempts to be right long after it is clear to every other person that the conversation is going nowhere and the remaining participants are simply being tiresome. When you get two or more of those people in the same thread, well, the result can be grim. I'm not saying that you are one of those people who absolutely has to be right, but, right now, I'm thinking of that xkcd cartoon of the guy who won't go to bed *because someone is wrong on the Internet.* Does that cartoon resemble you? Be honest, now. If it does, then there's a pretty good chance you have to be right, and you have to win the comment thread. Which, to be blunt, makes you a bit of a bore to have a conversation with, and means that there's ultimately a really good chance you'll eventually end up being an asshole to someone because you *can't let it go.* Don't be that guy.

10. Do I know when I'm done? I'm not saying you should enter each comment thread with an exit strategy, but on the other hand, it wouldn't hurt. It's okay not to make a lifetime commitment to a comment thread. Likewise: If you're having a conversation in a comment thread that's going nowhere, it's okay to admit it and get out. Letting the other dude have the last word will not mean you have Lost the Internets; really, quite the opposite, in fact. Similarly, if you find a comment thread is making you angry or sick or pissed off, walk away. If you find that the reason you're still in a comment thread is to thump on someone else, go get some air. If the thread has stopped being fun and started to be something like *work*, seriously, man, what the hell are you doing? Go away. It's a *comment thread*. In short, know when to say when, and if you *don't* know, then pick a number of responses that you are going to allow yourself in a thread (five, maybe?) and then stick to it. And finally, if you announce you're leaving a comment thread, leave and don't come back. No one likes a bad faith flouncing.

Got it? Then comment away.

How to Know If You're Cheating

Jun
8
2011

Since it's a topic of discussion these days.

Scenario: You've just done something physically and/or emotionally intimate with another consenting adult human being who is not your spouse/partner.

So, gonna tell your partner?

a) Yes.

b) *Any other response.*

If the answer is "b," then there's a really excellent chance you're cheating.

"Cheating" is not about whether you've physically met someone, whether they're in the same room with you, the levels of dress you or they are wearing, or whether what you're doing with them can be quantified on a baseball diamond. Cheating is allowing another person into a level of intimacy your partner expects to be theirs alone. That level of intimacy is not uniform from person to person. There is no guarantee that your partner's expected level of intimacy will be entirely congenial to you; in that respect what qualifies as "cheating" is not up to you.

Most people get that. Most people also don't want to hurt their partner and/or don't want to get caught doing something they know their partner will consider cheating. Which is why *any other response* than an unqualified "yes" to telling your partner about an intimate encounter with another consenting adult human being is a good first indicator you've just done yourself some cheating.

(If you're having intimate encounters with someone who is not consenting and/or adult and/or a human being, you have other problems as well, which we will not delve into now.)

Note that in my formulation, what anyone else other than your partner thinks is cheating (or not) is immaterial, because those *other* people are not in the same relationship you are with your partner. Friends/family/workmates/strangers may choose to think you're a cheating horndog; they may choose to think your partner is being entirely unreasonable about what constitutes "cheating"; they may think you both are idiots. They can have any opinion they want. They can also go fly a kite. In the end, the opinion you need to be concerned about is your partner's.

If you're not an idiot (or brand new to the relationship), then you probably should have a good idea what constitutes "cheating" in your relationship. If you don't know (and aren't content with being branded an idiot), you should probably ask. It will be a clarifying discussion, if nothing else. If you don't want to ask, a) you're an *idiot,* and b) here's a tip: if you ever find yourself in a situation where you ask yourself, "this thing I'm doing, it doesn't *really* count as cheating, does it?" then the answer is probably "yeah, it does." Because if you have to ask, etc.

You're welcome.

How to Lose the House

Sep
15
2010

Just for *fun*, I'm going to go off on the Democrats today.

Nate Silver over at Five Thirty Eight now estimates that there is a two in three chance that the House will go into Republican hands in the next session, and while my own (rather less statistically robust) estimation is that the odds are less favorable to the Republicans than that, neither is it particularly favorable to the Democrats. I think the House could go either way, and if the Dems do retain the House, it will be by a very thin majority, indeed.

I don't particularly wish for the Republicans to take over the House, although if they do it's not bad for *me*: John Boehner, presumptive House Majority Leader and the orangest man in American politics, happens to represent my district, and given the voter demographics here will do so until there's nothing left of him but a small, russet melanoma. And I'm a well-to-do Caucasian man in any event, the demographic which the GOP is prepared to prop up indefinitely at the expense of all of the rest of you. Sorry about that. But if the GOP *do* take the House, it won't be because Americans actually prefer the current Republican platform, which can be summed up as "let's forget 2008 ever *happened*," but because the Democrats have been so woefully incompetent on so many levels.

Not in passing the legislation they have, which they were in fact elected to do—and if you plan to say in the comments "but Americans didn't want *that* legislation," please jam it back into your insipidly partisan brain hole. Obama was pretty damn clear what his intentions were when he took office, and the American people were on board enough to give his party large majorities in the House and Senate. Where the Democrats have shown complete incompetence is in how they went about their legislative agenda (i.e., like unherdable brain-damaged stoats), and how they've allowed the GOP—and its crazy nephew from the attic, the Tea Party, as well as its bullhorn Fox News—to frame everything they've done as one step short of eviscerating live kittens and feeding noisily on their carcasses on live TV.

Really, this just completely appalls me: That a political party handed one of the largest legislative majorities in decades can do *what it was sent to do by voters* in such a manner that it seems both defensive and apologetic for doing so, and has allowed the party which was swept from power for being to political intelligence what late-era Hapsburgs were to genetic robustness to potentially crawl back into power, not on the strength of its political ideas but on its ability to exploit the Democrats' weaknesses in organization and communication.

And some Democratic partisans will say, but, you don't *understand*. The GOP and all its various offshoots and media abettors, they're just so *mean*. To which I say: Really? This is somehow a surprise? Of course they're mean—they've got nothing else. The GOP has no actual and verifiable legislative plan, nor is it currently smart enough to come up with one. What you're left with when you've got no brain is shaking your fist and yelling at the clouds for being socialist. The GOP can't help themselves doing this any more than they can help themselves thinking that the best way to cure diphtheria is to give a fund manager a tax cut. For god's sake, this has been the GOP strategy since at least 1994, when that bilious creature known as Newt Gingrich erupted out of the back benches with his strategy to turn the word "liberal" into the moral equivalent of "pederast."

Given the paucity of intellect in the GOP, you can't really blame it for running back to this strategy over and over, especially when it works. What you *can* do is blame the Democrats for continuing to fall for this shit, over and over and over again. The reason it works is because the Democrats can't or won't call stupid stupid; they keep trying the "let's be reasonable" thing against people working hard so that the sentence "OBAMA IS A NIGERIAN ISLAMO-SOCIALIST WHO'S GOING TO

MAKE YOU GAY MARRY AN ANCHOR BABY" doesn't strike 20% of Americans as evidence that something in the utterer's brain has just exploded. You can also blame the Democrats for doing a piss-poor job of reminding voters that what they're passing in Congress is what they were sent there to do. And you can also blame them for not doing the one thing the GOP actually does remarkably well, which is keep its caucus in line and on message and voting the same way on the things that actually matter.

And as it happens, I *do* blame the Democrats for this. In a sane world—in a world where the Democrats had enough political acumen that they couldn't only get Congressional majorities when the GOP had screwed things up so badly that even the dimmest of voters could no longer ignore the damage—we wouldn't be talking about the very real likelihood that the GOP, *this* GOP, arguably the least intellectually and legislatively impressive GOP in the history of that august party, might take back the House. That we *are* talking about it really is all down to the Democrats. If they lose the House, it won't be because the GOP deserve to have won it. It'll be because the Democrats simply weren't smart enough to keep it.

That would make them, in fact, stupider than the modern GOP. The mind reels.

I'll Get Back to You When I Get Back To You

Jun
10
2009

Look, a *New York Times* piece on how smartphones have morphed from luxury to necessity, which includes this following observation regarding responding when people e-mail or text you:

> *"The social norm is that you should respond within a couple of hours, if not immediately," said David E. Meyer, a professor of psychology at the University of Michigan. "If you don't, it is assumed you are out to lunch mentally, out of it socially, or don't like the person who sent the e-mail."*

All together, now: Bullshit.

First: If you are the sort of person who believes that all your e-mails/texts must be responded to instantaneously or sooner, you may be a self-absorbed twit. Please entertain the idea that your responder may have a life of his or her own, with priorities which may not conform to yours. Chimpanzees, dogs and certain species of squid have all developed a theory of mind—you can too, if you try. We're all rooting for you out here.

Second: If you're the sort of person who believes that all e-mails/texts must be responded to instantaneously or sooner, that probably means you're ignoring something important right in front of you, like the other person at the table, or traffic on the freeway, or a large dog about to savage you because you're carelessly walking on his lawn. For your own safety and the courtesy of others, please do pay attention to the real world. Just because an e-mail or text wants your attention doesn't mean you're obliged to give it.

Third: Can we all agree that we *don't* want to live in a world where we are obliged to respond to e-mails/text in an unrealistically short period of time, lest we be thought an enormous douchenozzle? I think trying to respond to your e-mails/texts over a course of a day or even two is perfectly reasonable, coupled with the understanding that, in fact, not every e-mail/text requires a response, so you might not get one. If you really need an immediate response, you can ask for one in the e-mail/text—again, with the understanding that a) abusing the "please respond asap" privilege dumps you into the "self-absorbed twit" category, and b) that person may still not respond immediately.

Basically, if we all agree that we can act like people who don't have to be *ZOMG the centaar of Teh Univarse!!!one!!* for every other person and thing, things will be a lot more pleasant overall.

Mind you, even if we *can't* all agree with this, I'm still going to answer my e-mail/texts on *my* own sweet schedule, not anyone else's. Yes, I have a smartphone. And yes, I do in fact answer e-mails and texts with it; it's fun to do so. But the main reason I have the phone is so that if my car flips and I'm pinned under two tons of Honda steel, I can call for help. I may or may not answer texts/e-mails any sooner because I have the phone. Not answering immediately does not mean I don't like you; it means I have my own life and I'm busy with it. If you can't manage to grasp that basic and obvious fact, that goes into the bin marked "your problems," not mine.

Note that this formulation does not apply if you are my wife. If you are my wife, your e-mails and texts are returned immediately. Because I *totally love you,* babe. Everyone else: Eh. I think this is a fair set of priorities, personally.

An Incomplete Guide to Not Creeping

Aug
9
2012

The last couple of months have been a really interesting time for geekdom, as it's had its face rubbed in the fact that there are a lot of creepy assbags among its number, and that geekdom is not always the most welcoming of places for women. Along that line, this e-mail from a con-going guy popped into my queue a few days ago:

> *Any tips on how not to be a creeper? I try not to be, but I don't know that I'm the best judge of that.*

Let's define our terms here. Let's say that for this particular conversation, a "creeper" is someone whose behavior towards someone else makes that other person uncomfortable at least and may possibly make them feel unsafe. A creeper may be of any gender and may creep on any gender, but let's acknowledge that a whole lot of the time it's guys creeping on women. Creeping can happen any place and in any community or grouping of people, but in geekdom we see a lot of it at conventions and other large gatherings.

Let me also note that the reason I stress this is an incomplete guide is because a) there's no way to cover every contingency and b) I'm writing this from the point of view of someone who doesn't get creeped on very much (it almost never happens to me) and when it does happen I am usually in a position, by way of my gender, age, personal temperament and contextual notability, to do something about it. Other people who are creeped on—particularly women—aren't necessarily in the same position. So the advice I give you here is informed by my point of view, not theirs, and as such is almost certainly incomplete (but hopefully not wrong). This is just a start, in other words, and others will have different and probably better perspectives on the subject.

That said, these are the rules that *I* use when I meet people, particularly women, for the first time and/or to whom I find myself attracted in one way or another. Because, yeah, I do meet a lot of people and/or I do find many of the people I know in a casual way to be attractive in one way or another. The very last thing I want is for them to feel that I am a creepy assbag. These are the things I do to avoid coming across as one.

Bear in mind that following these recommendations will *not* make you a good guy. They will just hopefully make you be not so much of a creeper. These are preventative measures, in other words, and should be viewed as such.

Fair enough? Okay, then. Let's start with some biggies.

1. Acknowledge that you are responsible for your own actions. You are (probably) a fully-functioning adult. You probably are able to do all sorts of things on your own—things which require the use of personal judgment. Among those things: How you relate to, and interact with, other human beings, including those who you have some interest in or desire for. Now, it's possible you may also be socially awkward, or have trouble reading other people's emotions or intentions, or whatever. This is your own problem to solve, not anyone else's. It is not an excuse or justification to creep on other people. If you or other people use it that way, you've failed basic human decency.

2. Acknowledge that you don't get to define other people's comfort level with you. Which is to say that you may be trying your hardest to be interesting and engaging and fun to be around—and still come off as a creeper to someone else. Yes, that sucks for you. But you know what? It sucks for *them* even harder, because you're creeping them out and making them profoundly unhappy and uncomfortable. It may not seem fair that "creep" is their assessment of you, but: Surprise! It doesn't matter, and if you try to argue with them (or anyone else) that you're in fact not being a creep and the problem is with them not you, then you go from "creep" to "complete assbag." Sometimes people aren't going to like you or want to be near you. It's just the way it is.

3. Acknowledge that no one's required to inform you that you're creeping (or help you to not be a creeper). It's nice when people let you know when you're going wrong and how. But you know what? That's not their job. It's especially not their job at a convention or some other social gathering, where the reason they are there is to hang out with friends and have fun, and *not* to give some dude an intensive course in how not to make other people intensely uncomfortable with his presence. If you are creeping on other people, they have a perfect right to ignore you, avoid you and shut you out—and not tell you why. Again: you are (probably) a fully-functioning adult. This is something you need to be able to handle on your own.

Shorter version of above: It's on you not to be a creeper and to be aware of how other people respond to you.

Also extremely important:

4. Acknowledge that other people do not exist just for your amusement/interest/desire/use. Yes, I know. You *know* that. But oddly enough, there's a difference between *knowing* it, and actually *believing* it—or understanding what it means in a larger social context. People go to conventions and social gatherings to meet other people, but not necessarily (or even remotely likely) for the purpose of meeting *you*. The woman who is wearing a steampunky corset to a convention is almost certainly wearing it in part to enjoy being seen in it and to have people enjoy seeing her in it—but she's also almost certainly not wearing it *for* you. You are not the person she has been waiting for, the reason she's there, or the purpose for her attendance. When you act like you are, or that she has (or should have) nothing else to do than be the object of your amusement/interest/desire/use, the likelihood that you will come across a complete creeper rises exponentially. It's not an insult for someone else not to want to play that role for you. It's not what they're there for.

So those are some overarching things to incorporate into your thinking. Here are some practical things.

5. Don't touch. Seriously, man. You're not eight, with the need to run your fingers over everything, nor do you lack voluntary control of your muscles. Keep your hands, arms, legs and everything else to yourself. This is not actually difficult. Here's an idea: That person you want to touch? Put *them* in charge of the whole touch experience. That is, let them initiate any physical contact and let them set the pace of that contact when or if they do—and accept that that there's a very *excellent* chance no touch is forthcoming. Do that when you meet them for the first time. Do that after you've met them 25 times. Do it just as a general rule. Also, friendly tip: If you do touch someone and they say "don't touch me," or otherwise make it clear that touching was not something you should have done, the correct response is: "I apologize. I am sorry I made you uncomfortable." Then back the hell off, possibly to the next state over.

6. Give them space. Hey: Hold your arm straight out in front of your body. Where your fingertips are? That's a nice minimum distance for someone you're meeting or don't know particularly well (it's also not a bad distance for people you do know). Getting inside that space generally makes people uncomfortable, and why make people uncomfortable? That's creepy. Also creepy: Sneaking up behind people and getting in close to them, or otherwise getting into their personal space without them being aware of it. If you're in a crowded room and you need to scrunch in, back up when the option becomes available; don't take it as an opportunity to linger inside that personal zone. Speaking of which:

7. Don't box people in. Trapping people in a corner or making it difficult for them to leave without you having the option to block them makes you an assbag. Here's a hint: If you are *actually* interesting to other people, you don't need to box them into a corner.

8. That amusing sexual innuendo? So *not* amusing. If you can't make a conversation without trying to shoehorn suggestive or sexually-related topics into the mix, then you know what? You can't make conversation. Consider also the possibility that playing the sexual innuendo card early and often signals to others in big flashing neon letters that you're likely a tiresome person who brings nothing else to the table. This is another time where an excellent strategy is to let the *other* person be in charge of bringing sexual innuendo to the conversational table, and managing the frequency of its appearance therein.

9. Someone wants to leave? Don't go with them. Which is to say, if they bow out of a conversation with you, say goodbye and let them go. If they leave the room, don't take that as your cue to follow them from a distance and show up wherever it is they are as if it *just happens* you are showing up in the same place. Related to this, if you spend any amount of time positioning yourself to be where that person you are interested in will be, or will walk by, for the purpose of "just happening" to be there when they are, you're probably being creepy as hell. Likewise, if you attach yourself to a group just to be near that person. Dude, it's obvious, and it's squicky.

10. Someone doesn't want you around? Go away. Here are some subtle hints: When you come by they don't make eye contact with you. When they are in a group the group contracts or turns away from you. If you interject in the conversation people avoid following up on what you've said. One of the friends of the person you are interested in interposes themselves between you and that person. And so on. When stuff like that happens, guess what? You're not wanted. When that happens, here's what you do: Go away. Grumble to yourself (and only to yourself) all you like about their discourteousness or whatever. Do it away from them. Remember that you don't get to define other people's comfort level with you. Remember that they're not obliged to inform you about why they don't want you around. Although, for God's sake, if they *do* tell you they don't want you around, *listen to them.*

Again: Not a complete instruction set on how not to be a creeper. But a reasonable start, I think.

In Which I Select a Current GOP Presidential Candidate to Vote For

Nov
11
2011

As most of you are no doubt aware, in 2012, I am about as likely to vote for a GOP candidate for president as I am likely to vomit a Volkswagen Beetle straight out of my esophagus. But if I *had* to vote for a GOP candidate for president, which current GOP candidate would I vote for? Well, I'll tell you, in a list, from least likely to most likely.

9. Michele Bachmann: Look, it's not *just* the eyes. This woman is completely off the beam, blathers idiocies at an appallingly frequent rate and apparently knows about as much about anything outside the closed-loop of Tea Party talking points as the squirrels in my yard, busily gathering nuts for the winter, who I fear would bum-rush Bachmann if she came to my house and carry her away, Veruca Salt-style. Attractive, though, which does nothing to quell my longstanding concern that GOP voters think about potential female presidential candidates the way drunk fraternity brothers think about conquests, i.e., who cares if she's zoned-out as long as she's hot (see: Sarah Palin). In the end it's the complete apparent didactic ignorance she spouts that puts her on the bottom of my list.

8. Rick Santorum: A querulous bigot, with whom I am dismayed to discover I share a birthday. Somewhat more apparently intelligent than Bachmann, but what does that say. If he and Bachmann were the last presidential candidates on Earth, I would vote to return the US to Britain. Fortunately the man has even less chance of being president than Bachmann—indeed, has even less chance of being president than all but one person on this list, I think—and his apparent confusion as to why he's not doing better than he's doing says something about his disconnect from reality.

7. Gary Johnson: Who? I mean, seriously: who? I know he's still running, since his Web site says he is, and he even was at some of the debates, but, dude: You're wasting your time. If all the other GOP candidates were hit by lightning at one of the debates you weren't invited to, you still wouldn't be the GOP presidential candidate; they'd drag Chris Christie kicking and screaming to the Republican National Convention long before they'd even acknowledge you were there. Yes, it sucks; you were by all indications a pretty decent governor. But you had your moment with the "shovel-ready" quip. Maybe you'll make a good Secretary of the Interior or something.

6. Ron Paul: He's certainly a man who sticks to his principles, which is admirable enough when you are one representative out of 435. But I doubt his principles scale, which is to say that if he had the same executive style as his legislative style, he'd veto everything that didn't meet his "it's not in the Constitution!" shtick, which would be just about everything, and thus would run the country into the ground in about six months flat. And I suppose that would be perfectly fine for a lot of the people who would vote for Ron Paul as president. But it wouldn't be fine for me. I think he's best where he is.

5. Herman Cain: He's this cycle's "straight talking no-nonsense CEO from BusinessLand" entry, and in that role he's been facile enough that he appears to have convinced a large number of people that his 9-9-9 tax scheme will somehow benefit them rather than doing what it actually does, which is to give the rich an immense tax break while raising the taxes on a substantial number of working Joes and Janes, so good for him, I guess. On the other hand he's clearly and woefully uninformed on anything that Herman Cain has decided Herman Cain doesn't want to know about, and you know what? All those sexual harassment settlements don't exactly inspire confidence, and that's just about the most polite way I can put that. Andrew Sullivan is of the opinion Cain's not in this to win this, and that he's in it to sell his books and raise his speaking fees. I suspect he may be right.

4. Rick Perry: Aaaaaaaauuugh! Republican Governor of Texas! Run away! Run away! And he's even more what Dubya is than Dubya was: That big smiley good ol' boy thing, with an engine in the brainpan that doesn't exactly run on premium fuel, as evidenced by that absolutely ridiculous "optional tax overhaul" plan he and his brain trust farted out a few weeks ago. Perry started strong in the field but faded once he opened his mouth, which actually makes me think better of potential GOP voters. Ironically, while lots of commentators pinpointed his brain freeze in the most recent debate as the end of his campaign, I had some sympathy for him when it happened, since I'll be introducing people I've known for 30 years to other people and blank on their names. It happens. What he shouldn't have said was that "oops" at the end. *That's* what killed him.

3. Newt Gingrich: I'm just as amazed as anyone that Gingrich lands this high on my list, and it has more to do with this current GOP field being populated by the confounding crew that it is than anything else. Gingrich is a classic politinerd, which is to say he wonks out like no one's business but then when he has to deal with actual live humans he's like a giraffe talking to a fungo; it just doesn't work. His compassion-blindness is what makes him great at the politics of character assassination, but it also means that politicians who understand people can box him into a corner and poke at him until he explodes. Hell, that was one of Bill Clinton's favorite things to do. In a general election, Obama would rope-a-dope him all the merry day long. On the other hand, he does know how Washington works and it's possible if handled properly (i.e., like a fragile ball of thin glass with EXPLODE on the inside) he might be able to govern. I'd actually love to meet and chat with Gingrich; I think as long as he and I never talked politics everything would be fine. But I think having him as president would be a very bad idea, only a slightly better idea than everyone else on the list below him.

2. Mitt Romney: Come now, Republicans: Do any of you really think Romney won't be your eventual candidate? Really? *Really?* I think we all know this is how it's going to go. Yes, Romney is the bland high school treasurer type, the one who carefully crafts his extracurriculars for maximum effect on his college applications, and who spends his time thinking about what to say that will make him popular with the other kids rather than, you know, being *interesting* in his own right. But at the end of the day you've got to beat Obama in a presidential election, which means you have to find some way to appeal to the independent voters—and not only that but the independent voters your Tea Party adventures of 2010 have scared the crap out of. And that's Romney, the Safety Prom Date, the one you pick for the dance because you know he'll show up in a limo, give you a nice dinner, dance with you and then not complain while you mostly hang out with your friends, and then on the way home will refrain from doing anything other than a couple overly polite kisses without tongue and a two-second breast-cupping, mostly for form's sake. No, he's not gay. He wants you to know he *respects* you. Just try not to think of football captain Rick Perry too much as he's doing it, okay? Mmmmm…Rick *Perry.*

Anyway. If he gets elected, I suspect he'll actually be somewhat moderate, for values of moderate that translate to "relative to the modern GOP," which means "far to the right of anywhere Ronald Reagan ever was," but whatever. I mean, he was governor of Massachusetts, for God's sake. He knows something about meeting in the middle. For someone like me, he's workable. But no, I'm not excited about him either.

1. Jon Huntsman: Smart fellow with an eclectic past (played in a rock band *and* was a missionary to Taiwan!) who went on to be an extraordinarily popular two-term governor of Utah, who played to traditional Republican strengths like cutting taxes while at the same time promoting a Federal increase of the minimum wage and signed on to the Western Climate Initiative. Worked for administrations both

Republican and Democratic, and when he was Obama's ambassador of China, got his name blocked on search engines for walking around in street protests, just to, as he said "see what's going on." Has this to say: "To be clear. I believe in evolution and trust scientists on global warming. Call me crazy." Supports civil unions for same-sex couples, which puts him on the same ground as Obama. And so on.

In other words, Huntsman seems to be what I would actually like to see in a GOP candidate—and, indeed in a Democratic candidate as well: A fellow who has particular core values and works toward them but doesn't appear to be a doctrinaire whack-job subscribing to a scorched-earth policy when it comes to working with people of other political views. Huntsman has politics I'm not on board for, such as his stance on abortion, but this is the field I have to work with, and in this field, if I had to vote for someone, this is the guy who gets my vote—and if he became president, he would be someone I would have at least some optimism about.

So where is he in the polls? Pulling down somewhere between 4.5 and six percent, well behind Romney and Cain, the current front runners, and indeed trailing Bachmann, Gingrich and Ron Paul. At least he's ahead of Johnson and Santorum. My support for him tells me I would probably make a terrible modern Republican. But then again, this is something I already knew.

It's Okay Not to Read Me

Jul
2
2012

I noted this briefly on Twitter last night but I think it's worth expanding just a little bit. Last night I read a mostly vaguely negative review of *Redshirts* on a personal blog in which the reviewer basically admitted, in somewhat different words, that they're just not an enthusiast of most of my books. This is of course perfectly fine, because I'm like that too—there are many writers out there for whom I am not the perfect audience, including some for whom it would seem I should be the perfect reader. People are quirky and don't always work the way they're supposed to. Likewise, I have no beef with the (mostly vaguely) negative review; as I've said before, a good (i.e., well thought-out) negative review can be better and more interesting than a positive review, and anyway I'm generally of the opinion that the books I write are good enough to release. So there's that.

What the review made me feel, paradoxically enough, was a bit of sympathy for the reviewer, who (I imagine), once confronted with yet another of my books, sighed heavily and then set themself down to the mostly unpleasant task of reading an author they have regularly found unsatisfactory. And along with that sympathy, a bit of befuddlement, because, well. They're reading that author (namely: me) *why*, exactly? This particular reviewer was not assigned the book for a gig; they were reading it on their own recognizance. So I suppose that my own thought on the matter is, why would you do that to yourself? Life is often unpleasant enough without choosing to fill your recreational hours pursuing a book from an author with whom ample previous readings have shown you have little rapport.

Here's my thing about my own writing, which I've noted before: I write my books to be generally accessible, and generally enjoyable, for just about anyone. I cast a wide net, as it were. But within that general intention for a general audience, there will always be *particular* people who will discover I am not their ideal writer. For whatever reason: Perhaps they don't like how I write dialogue, or plot the stories, or feel like I should be writing the book differently from how I am actually writing, or so on. Yes, it's sad, for both of us; I like to sell books, and I assume these particular readers like to read books. When a writer and a reader find their respective books and tastes don't match, there's always a sad little *moue* of the mind, a wistful wish for what could have been. But then you both go on with your lives. For the writer, there are other readers. For the reader, there are other writers. That's how it works.

As a writer, I'd like readers to give me my work a fair shake—to try what I write to see if we're a good fit. But if they try it and after a couple of fair-minded attempts they decide I'm just not the writer for them, then from my point of view the obvious solution is to acknowledge the fact and thereby avoid the task of grimly tromping through my future books. Because clearly I am not making them happy, and I have to admit that as a writer I don't enjoy the idea of someone joylessly hauling themselves through my prose for whatever reason they determine that they absolutely *must*. I really don't write books to be joyless slogs. Unless it's your job (or, in the highly specialized case of awards like the Hugos and Nebulas, you're reading a slate to determine your voting), there's probably not a good enough reason to do that to yourself.

I mean, if you've determined I'm not the writer for you, it's okay to check in every three or four books and see if I'm still not working for you. Who knows? Maybe I'll have changed my writing and/or something about you will have changed, and then suddenly what I write will work for you. Groovy. But otherwise I really would suggest taking the time you're using to unenthusiastically trudge through one of my books and devote it instead either to writers you know you love or (even better!) in the pursuit of newer authors who are looking for their audiences. You could be that audience! It's worth giving *them* a fair shake, rather than looking at one of my books and thinking to yourself, *oh, crap, another Scalzi book. Here we go.*

Don't go. You don't *have* to go. If you don't really enjoy what I write, stop reading it. Read something else, from someone else. If for some reason you need my permission and blessing to do so, here it is. I sincerely hope you find another writer whose work you like better.

Joe Barton Just Wants to Have His Life Back

Jun
18
2010

There are many ways to distinguish between the two major political parties in the United States, but one of the more obvious ways is in how they choose to implode. Democrats, for example, tend to implode in slow motion, when their own aimless, plodding inertia turns them into lugubrious and easy targets for the right wing media, which scurries around them, draping yet another thin, disingenuous stratum of "they're socialist grandmother killers!" over them until the whole sludgy edifice collapses from the accumulated weight, and the Democrats are crushed underneath. Republicans, on the other hand, implode like old, fat, gassy stars, when the depleted fuel of their empty ideology can't sustain further inward pressure from their personal idiocy, and the whole mess sucks down and then spectacularly erupts into a blazing display of abject stupidity.

And then you have something like what happened yesterday, when Texas representative and ranking Republican member of the House's energy and commerce committee Joe Barton apologized to BP for having to endure the "shakedown" of agreeing to put $20 billion in an escrow account to help pay for the damages the company inflicted on the Gulf of Mexico. Shortly thereafter Barton was forced by the Republican leadership both to apologize for his apology and to retract it, which he did, in exactly the same manner a 10-year-old boy whose mother is standing behind him with a well-used wooden spoon apologizes to his sister for putting a dog turd in her bed. Barton didn't apologize because he felt he did or said anything wrong; he did it because the alternative—losing his standing on the energy and commerce committee—would be more painful.

It's this fact which is the real problem for the Republicans. The Republican leadership is righteously pissed off at Barton at the moment, but the question not answered is: Is it pissed off because he said something that does not reflect the Republican point of view on the escrow account, or is it pissed off because Barton, the House GOP point man on energy, was stupid enough to *say it out loud* at a congressional hearing? The phrases "shakedown" and "slush fund" as regards the escrow account didn't come out of nowhere—other Republicans and right wing media were already using the terms before Barton made an ass of himself with them. The major difference is that when Michele Bachmann and Sean Hannity punt the terms about, they're part of the GOP "socialist grandmother killer" strategy of dinging the Democrats over the long term, and the Republican leadership doesn't have to engage with it directly and can distance itself from it if need be while still benefiting from getting the meme out there.

But when Barton, poster boy for the House GOP energy policy, used them, there was nowhere for the GOP leadership to hide. It had to either disavow the statements and step on Barton's head, or hand the Democrats a really thick board to smack Republicans with from here to November. So the leadership disavowed the statements and in doing so killed off any benefit they get from Bachmann or Hannity burbling on about shakedowns and slush funds because now they are explicitly contrary to the GOP position, and any further leakage of the phrases from backbenchers and right wing media is going to be used by the Democrats as further proof of the GOP's utter insincerity on the matter. But some folks won't get the memo, which is to say the Democrats probably still have a nice thick board to use between now and the elections, which Barton didn't just hand to them but personally engraved and then dropped trou and bent over to receive his beating.

I don't want to suggest the GOP isn't going to pick up seats in the House and Senate in November—I suspect it will—but I don't think it will pick up enough seats to take the majority from the Democrats in either chamber and I suspect that a large part of that will be because of the complete mess the party is currently making of its oil spill messaging, and in particular its association with and affinity for BP. One, I'm not at all sure why any Republican would want to be seen taking the side of a massive foreign corporation over the American citizens and small business owners whose livelihoods are now threatened by that massive foreign corporation's neglect and ineptitude. Two, in particular, I'm not at all sure why the Republicans would want to be seen doing that in the American South, where the majority of its political base lies. Three, nobody who isn't stupid and/or reflexively partisan would pretend that if a Republican president had negotiated the exact same escrow account with BP that Bachmann, Hannity, Barton et al, wouldn't be falling all over themselves to point out how it's an example of how Republicans work with private business to solve problems rather than trying to have government be the solution in itself and forcing taxpayers to foot the bill.

Basically there's little in the GOP oil spill positioning that isn't a) initially following the mantra of "Whatever Obama does is Socialist," b) a confused and hasty backtrack from that position when the GOP realize that most people are not interested in blaming Obama, they're interested in blaming BP, which to be *fair* is responsible for having its oil rig blow up, killing 11 workers, and gushing millions of barrels of crude oil into the Gulf of Mexico. Part of the reason for this is that I don't think the GOP as it is currently intellectually constituted is able to handle getting off the script regarding point a), or doing anything but responding petulantly and defensively regarding point b). It and its members (and media) are so used to their "socialist grandma killer" talking points, and in trying to help the Democrats do their slow motion implosion that they just don't notice that when it comes to BP and the gulf, they're setting themselves up for their own implosions of supernova magnitude.

Joe Barton had to go up like an oily Roman candle for this to impinge in the GOP consciousness. I wonder how many more GOPers will have to go up for it to really sink in.

Just Plain Stupid

Jun
6
2011

Dear Andrew Weiner:

Seriously, dude? You're not some frat boy, you're a congressional representative. You shouldn't have to be *told* "no sextweets for you," you should know it on your own. And if you didn't know it, that other congressional representative—from your own state!—who made an ass of himself on Craigslist earlier this year should have been a warning. But, I don't know. Maybe you thought this was the sort of thing that only happened to Republicans. Surprise! Married Democrats probably shouldn't do certain things *either*, and mailing around pictures of your swaddled member is one of them.

Ugh. I've been waiting for this particular announcement since Weiner admitted that he couldn't be sure the picture wasn't of him. I'm going to say it again: One probably does know one's own package, and at the very least one also knows if one makes a habit of sending ill-advised pictures of one's self on the Tubes. As soon as Weiner employed that particular hedge, the clock was on the play and it was just a matter of time until he either he admitted it, or the evidence piled up at his door. Weiner picked the more honorable route in terms of dealing with it (that is, after having lied about it to begin with), but once more: Dude. What were you thinking. And the answer, quite obviously: He wasn't thinking at all, or more aptly wasn't thinking with his brain.

For the record, I have no real issue with people sexting or sex-tweeting or sex-whatever-ing their little brains out; if it gives you joy, go ahead. Everyone has their hobbies. That said, this particular hobby does come with repercussions and responsibilities. Toward the former, as suggested earlier, this is one of those hobbies contraindicated by high-profile public service, especially if one has no stomach toward owning up to it when caught (and one would be caught sooner than later). Toward the latter, the relatively newlywed Mr. Weiner should have disclosed to his wife his little hobby, which he apparently did not until this morning, which was no doubt the least comfortable conversation in the history of the Weiner-Abedin breakfast nook.

If she had been fine with it—and who knows? There have been stranger things—then, well. *Still* not smart for a congressman, but then it would fall under the "hey, their life" category. But, look: When you're married or otherwise in a deeply serious relationship, all the cards are out on the table. No one likes surprises, and more to the point, your spouse (or the equivalent) deserves better than to get a surprise like this.

In sum: Stupid. Just plain stupid.

Kodi, 1997–2010

Jul
17
2010

In 1998, Krissy decided that we should have a dog. This precipitated a philosophical discussion between the two of us as to what constituted a "dog." Krissy, whose family had had a number of smaller dogs over the years, was inclined toward something in the Shih Tzu or Maltese direction of things. I, however, steadfastly maintained that if one is going to own a dog, then one should get *a dog*—a large animal, identifiably related to the wolves whose DNA they shared, who could, if required, drag one's unconscious ass out of a fire. More practically, there was the fact that at the time I owned a 30-pound cat named Rex, whose default disposition was such that a dog smaller than he would be in very serious danger of being either eaten or being sat on and smothered in the night. It wouldn't be fair to bring a small dog into our home.

And thus, it was decided that, indeed, we would probably get a big dog. And as it happens, when this decision was made, our good friend Stephen Bennett mentioned to us that, as we were looking for a dog, he knew of a puppy that was available. A friend of his had put down a deposit on an Akita puppy from a local breeder, but then moved somewhere pets weren't allowed. So an Akita pup was up for sale, at a substantially discounted price. Normally the phrase "discount puppy" is one fraught with danger, but Stephen had heard good things about the breeder, so we gave her a call.

It turned out that actually two puppies were still available, one a boy and one a girl, so we went over to the look at them. Krissy had originally wanted the boy puppy, but he seemed distant and diffident and didn't seem to want to have much to do with us. The girl puppy, on the other hand, went right up to Krissy and seemed to be just plain delighted to see her. Five minutes later, it was decided that the girl puppy was our puppy. As it happened, it was indeed the pup Stephen's friend had planned to buy, and in anticipation of that, the breeders had already started calling her the name that not-actually-former owner had planned to call her: Kodi.

Having bought the dog, I then went home and researched Akitas, and just about had a heart attack, because it turns out that Akitas are a dog that can go one of two ways: They can be an utterly delightful dog, clean and intelligent and devoted to family, or they can be twitchy neurotic creatures who were originally bred to hunt bears and will be happy to challenge you for alpha-hood in the family if you give them the chance. What made the difference between the one and the other? Basically, how much time you spent socializing them. Spend enough time and attention to socialize them well, you get the good Akita. You don't, and you don't.

Fortunately, if you want to call it that, something happened that allowed me to spend all sorts of time with my new puppy: I got laid off from AOL. Thus, during Kodi's entire puppyhood, I had nothing better to do with my time than to spend it with our new pet. Partially as a result of this, and partially out of her own good nature, Kodi became the best of all possible dogs, or at the very least the best of all possible dogs for for me and for Krissy. Athena came along, almost exactly a year younger than Kodi, and our dog took to her immediately, sensing a younger sister rather than competition for affection.

Kodi was a good dog for all of us, but it's fair to say that while she loved me and Athena, she adored Krissy. I like to tell the story of how I went away on my book tour in 2007, and I was gone for three weeks, and the day I came back, Krissy went to the airport to pick me up. When we got out of the car and opened the door to the house, Kodi came out and greeted me in a way that translated into *oh, hey, you're back. Nice to see you.* Then she went over to Krissy and greeted her in a way that translated into *OH MY GOD I THOUGHT I WOULD NEVER SEE YOU EVER AGAIN AND NOW YOU'RE BACK AND I LOVE YOU SO VERY MUCH.*

And she had been gone for maybe two hours. I once told Krissy that the very best day for Kodi would be one in which Krissy came back home every ten minutes. Krissy was Kodi's world, her sun and her moon, her waking thought and her dream.

Krissy never took that for granted, as one being given unconditional love might. She returned that love. She delighted in the fact that Kodi was *her* dog, even in its most exasperating moments, such as when the dog couldn't stand to be more than five feet from her and was simultaneously having deep and abiding intestinal issues. You take the bad with the good, the cat litter breath with the soft, happy puppy sighs, the dog farts with the unalloyed happiness that a dog who really loves you provides. Krissy loved her dog, and loved everything that went with the dog, from start to finish.

Kodi's love for my wife amused me and I would occasionally feign jealousy, but I never doubted that Kodi loved me too, and cared for me as well. To explain how I know this I have to tell you about two separate events. The first happened the night of the day my daughter was born. The second was a few days after my wife miscarried what would have been our second child. In each case I was home while Krissy was somewhere else—in the hospital recuperating from giving birth for the first, and at her work for the second—and in both cases I was suddenly and extraordinarily overcome by my emotions. For the first, the indescribable joy that comes in meeting your child for the first time. For the second, the grief that comes from knowing you will not meet the child who could have been yours. And each time, I was frozen, unable to process what was happening to me, or what I was feeling.

Both times, Kodi did the same thing. She came into the room, saw me, walked over to the chair in which I was sitting and put her head in my lap. And both times I did the same thing. I petted her head, slid out of the chair and on to the floor, and held my dog while I cried, letting her be the one to share both my joy and pain, so I could go on to what I had to do next. Both times she was patient with me and sat there for as long as I needed. Both times my dog knew I needed her. Both times she was right.

I haven't written or spoken of either of these before, even to my wife. They were something I kept for myself. But I want you to know about them now, so that you know that when I say my dog loved me and I loved her, you have some idea of what that actually means.

Akitas are large dogs and live, on average, for nine or ten years. Kodi lived for almost thirteen, and twelve of those were very good years. In the last year, however, age caught up with her. She slowed, and she panted, and finally it had become clear that she had begun to hurt. While Krissy and I were in Boston this last week, we got a call from the kennel where we boarded our dog when we traveled. Kodi had had to be taken to the vet because she was listless and she wasn't eating. X-rays at the vet showed she had a tumor in her abdomen, which was likely causing internal bleeding. There was some question whether Kodi would make it until we got home. We asked the vet to do what she could. She did, and yesterday afternoon we drove straight from the airport to see our dog.

In the end it was simple. We walked Kodi into the sunlight and then Krissy laid down in the grass with her and held her dog close and let her dog go, both at the same time, bringing to an end a journey that began with Kodi walking up to Krissy and into her life, and our lives, twelve years before. I'm thankful our dog waited for us so we could be with her. But I'm even more thankful my wife could hold her dog one last time, feel the happiness Kodi felt in her presence and she in hers, and to have her arms be the last thing her dog felt in this life as she passed into the next.

Now she is gone and we miss her. We are glad of the time she was with us. She was loved, by my wife, by our child and by me. I wanted to share a little of her with you, so you might remember her too. She was a good dog.

Lie to Me

Sep
15
2008

One of the more depressing articles of this political cycle popped up on Slate today, asking not why McCain's campaign is outright lying about so many things in its political ads and messaging, but why Obama *isn't*. Sure, it says, Obama's stretching the truth here and there, but when someone notes facts, the Obama campaign amends the message. When the McCain people get caught in a lie, on the other hand, they more or less shrug and continue the lie, on the grounds that it's working. And well, it *is*, as anyone who can read a poll can see. Therefore, since outright lying and distortion seems to be what people want, one has to wonder why Obama isn't doing more of it.

As fantastically depressing as the thesis of the piece is, it points to a fact that is alas well in evidence, which is that the McCain campaign is the *reductio ad absurdum* of the GOP strategy that "facts are stupid things"—and that from the simple *realpolitik* point of view that winning isn't just the important thing, it's the only thing, it might be onto something. It's a campaign that will lie and continue to lie when called on its lies because as far as it can tell it's being rewarded for doing so. As the article notes, the GOP has spent the last several presidential cycles inculcating the idea to its partisans and to the public that truth is a relative thing and that an actual, verifiable fact can and should be discounted if it is presented by someone whose politics are not your own—and indeed the very act of pointing out facts is a suspicious activity in itself.

It's entirely possible that the McCain campaign will benefit from a critical mass of people—and not just dyed-in-the-wool, will-vote-

Satan-into-office-if-he-wears-a-flag-pin Republicans—who have been primed by years of intentional and structural undermining of the legitimacy of fact, to accept bald-faced lying as just another tactic; people, in other words, who know that they are being lied to, know the lies are being repeated in the face of factual evidence, and know the campaign knows it is lying and plans to continue to do so all the way to the White House…and see that sort of stance as *admirable*. Can you blame McCain for taking advantage of this dynamic? Well, quite obviously, you can, and should. It's one thing to imagine one's self a "maverick" for speaking truth to power; it's quite another thing to be a "maverick" by deciding to lie one's way into power. However, it's also amply clear that many who *should* blame him, or would be outraged by Obama lying in such a transparent and recurrent fashion, *won't*.

And *this* is the interesting thing about this particular election cycle. I'm not suggesting that distortion and lying are new to this presidential election cycle (it goes back to at least the 1800 election, when Adams and Jefferson teed off on each other), and I'm not suggesting the Obama campaign is comprised of innocent does who would (gasp!) never stretch a truth for political gain. I am suggesting the McCain campaign is the first campaign, certainly in modern political history, that has decided that truth is entirely optional, and isn't afraid to come right out and say it. And it's working—and might well work all the way to the steps of the White House.

If it does, that will be an interesting political lesson for the GOP. It will be confirmation of the actual "Bush Doctrine" of "do and say whatever the hell you want, because no one has the will to stop you." When there is no real-world penalty for lying, distorting and demonizing, then the only thing to stop you is your own moral compunctions. However, if McCain actually had any moral compunctions on this point, he wouldn't be running the campaign he's running now. And I would suggest that a man who shows no moral compunction in pursuit of power is not a man who will suddenly find those compunctions once he *has* power. An election is a job interview, people. If someone lies to you during a job interview, and says to you "yes, I'm lying, what of it?"

when you catch them in the lie, and you hire them anyway, well. You shouldn't be surprised at what comes next.

To go back to Obama and whether he should embrace the philosophy of flat-out lying, perhaps it makes sense for him to do so, but I certainly hope he *doesn't*. Not because I think it's better to have honor than power (although I don't think it's a *bad* thing to have honor rather than power) but because I believe that someone should be making the argument that one can win an election by something other than a willful determination to lie in people's faces, and to encourage them to cheer those lies.

The fact of the matter is that at this point in the election, it's not just about what positions the candidates hold on various political subjects. It's also about how the candidates, and the parties behind, choose to see the people they intend to lead. The GOP and the McCain campaign, irrespective of its political positions, sees the American voter as deserving lies, lots of lies, repeated as often as necessary to win. And maybe they're right about it. We'll know soon enough.

Living Like Fitzgerald

Oct
22
2009

With a hat tip to the estimable writer Walter Jon Williams, I came upon an article which examines the tax returns of one F. Scott Fitzgerald, of whom you may have heard, over the length of his writing career from 1919 through 1940. It turns out that during those years, Fitzgerald more or less consistently clocked $24,000 in writing income, which the author of the article, employing a 20:1 ratio of money values then to money values now, offers as the equivalent of making $500,000 a year in today's dollars. This is a nice income if you can get it, and Fitzgerald got it in an era in which his tax rate was something on the order of 8%.

What's interesting for modern writers, however, are the little tidbits that let you know how much things have changed—and how much, alas, things have stayed the same.

For example, here's one fun fact: The engine of Fitzgerald's income (at least until he went to Hollywood) was not his novels but his short stories. He considered them his "day job," a thing to be endured because writing them would allow him the financial wherewithal to write the novels he preferred to do. And how much did he make for these short stories? Well, in 1920, he sold eleven of them to various magazines for $3,975. This averages to about $360 per story, and (assuming an average length of about 6,000 words) roughly six cents a word.

To flag my own genre here, "Six cents a word," should sound vaguely familiar to science fiction and fantasy writers, as that's the *current* going rate at the "Big Three" science fiction magazines here in the

US: *Analog* (which pays six to eight cents a word), *Asimov's* (six cents a word "for beginners") and *Fantasy & Science Fiction* (six to nine cents a word). So, sf/f writers, in one sense you can truly say you're getting paid just as well as F. Scott Fitzgerald did; but in another, more relevant, "adjusted for inflation" sense, you're making five cents to every one of Fitzy's dollars. Which basically sucks. This is just one reason why making a living writing short fiction is not something you should be counting on these days.

(Mind you, science fiction writers of the 1920s weren't making what Fitzgerald did, either—indeed, if they were writing for *Amazing Stories* (the first SF magazine, which debuted in 1926), it was an open question as to whether they'd get paid at all; publisher Hugo Gernsback loved his "scientifiction" but he had liquidity problems, which is why he lost control of the magazine in 1929.)

In 1920, Fitzgerald also had his first novel published: *This Side of Paradise*. He made $6,200 on it for the year, from a royalty rate of 10% (later bumped up to 15%), on a cover price of $1.75. Using the 20:1 multiplier, we can say hardcovers in the US, at least, have gotten a lot cheaper, but that royalty rates for authors are essentially unchanged 90 years later; I myself make a 10%–15% royalty on my books.

It's also interesting to note that *Paradise* was Fitzgerald's bestselling book while he was still alive, and that it sold less than 50,000 copies at the time. This would be similar to someone selling 150,000 copies of their book today: A solid seller, to be sure (I wouldn't turn down sales like that) but no *Twilight*, or even *The Secret History*. It's also a reminder that the main portion of Fitzgerald's literary fame had to wait until he was dead and unable to appreciate it—*The Great Gatsby* regularly sells in excess of 200,000 copies a year these days (hello, high school reading lists!), but sold only 25,000 copies while Fitzgerald was alive. I'm sure Fitzgerald would be happy being considered a writer for the ages—he was somewhat embittered at the end of his life that his literary star had fallen so dramatically—but I also suspect he wouldn't have minded all those yearly sales happening today occurring while he was still alive and having use of the money. He certainly could have used it.

Which is of course the other thing; in this era or the 1920s, a half million dollars (or its real money equivalent) is not an inconsiderable sum—and yet Fitzgerald had a hard time keeping it. Much of that was due the cost of tending to Zelda, his increasingly mentally erratic wife, who was frequently in psychiatric hospitals—yes! Health care was expensive then, too!—but some of it was just money just leaking out all over the place, as money seems to do around those creative types. And then there was Fitzgerald's desire to live well, with servants and nice houses and such, and his wee problem with alcohol. Eventually Fitzgerald's financial issues became significant enough that he felt obliged to work in Hollywood—*Hollywood!* of all places—which he found remunerative but degrading.

The lessons here: Do keep track of your money, try to live within your means, avoid debilitating addictions if at all possible and, for the nonce at least, try to have decent health insurance. That'll help you keep your cash as a writer, whether you're making $24,000 a year from your writing, or $500,000.

On my end of things, while I wouldn't mind getting paid like Fitzgerald (in the "half a million" sense, not the "$24,000" sense), I don't think I'd want to *live* like him. Aside from the fact that I'd have less than four years left on my life, he doesn't seem to have been very happy in his life while he lived it, and that wasn't something that having a significant income was going to fix. I might have wished for him a little less money (and the need to acquire it), and a little more peace of mind.

The Lost Art of the Pretentious Video

Jun
14
2009

As much as I am a child of the 1980s, I will not say that the music of the time is better than the music of today or any other era, for reasons I have noted before. However, I will maintain that there was one thing the 80s did better than any other era before or since, and that is make truly spectacularly pretentious music videos.

Take, as a representative sample, the video for "Alive and Kicking," by Simple Minds, which I should note is a song I like, and available for your viewing on YouTube.

Our pretentious ingredients:

1. Initial God-eye view of band with lead singer Jim Kerr in messianic/crucified position;
2. Rock band performing in the Rousseauian splendor of nature with full kit, far from maddening crowds or electrical outlets;
3. Band dramatically posed, staring into the far distance, photographed from below for extra iconographical goodness;
4. Lots of shots of Jim Kerr emoting like a latter day Byron;
5. Gospel singer inserted for musical credibility.

Just a simple glance at this video tells us: "This is a video made in a time when no one thought anything about the cost involved in hauling a Scottish band out to the Catskills and putting them in the middle of a bunch of arty crane shots." Why do it? Why not? We're going for mythology here, son. This isn't just a band, these are *masters of emotional grandeur.* And if it takes posing them precariously on a cliff next to a waterfall without regard to the safety and well-being of the bassist to get that through your MTV-addled head, that's just what we'll do. Bassists are cheap and plentiful anyway (except for Sting, that posh bastard). This is a gorgeously pretentious video.

Now, sadly, it's also a gorgeously pretentious video that fails miserably, for the following reasons:

1. The "crucified messiah" pose worked only for Bono, and even then only in 1987, and it certainly doesn't work for a dude who looks like a leprechaun wearing his dad's sport jacket;
2. If you put a rock band in nature, it should look like it might survive a night or two without access to hair gels;
3. Any mythological iconography inherent in dramatic posing is undercut by 80s clothing and hairstyles;
4. In every closeup Jim Kerr appears dazed, as if he was clubbed in the temple just before cameras rolled, and his dancing style looks like what would happen if someone attached electrodes to his spine and zapped him at random;
5. The gospel singer in fact highlights the staggering inauthenticity (or at least, total goofiness) of the rest of the band.

But hey, pretty countryside.

They don't make videos like this any more, not because musicians have run out of pretension—that's really not *ever* going to happen—but because who can afford to anymore? The music industry has cratered and MTV doesn't run videos anymore, and the idea that a band might spend a quarter of a million dollars on film crew transportation and crane shots for a video that's going to be seen in a three-inch YouTube window is, shall we say, an idea whose time is past. It's easier and cheaper to record something ironic using a $200 Flip video recorder. This video is as unlikely now as OK Go's treadmill video would have been in 1987. This is not a bad thing—I prefer the OK Go video, personally—but it is a reminder that times change.

So reflect a moment on the great pretentious videos of the 1980s. There were some before, there were some after. But never as many, and rarely as pretentious in sum. Of course we didn't know it at the time. You never know what you've got—and how ridiculously pretentious it is—until it's gone.

Lord of the Tweets

Nov
27
2011

Last night both my wife and child were out for the evening and I was alone with a Lord of the Rings movie marathon on Encore, and access to Twitter. What happened next will now be revealed.

Oh, hey, a Lord of the Rings movie marathon. Suddenly all my plans for industry fall to the wayside. #TheBloodOfMenIsSpent

"The Mimes of Moria" is the name of my next band.

Wife is at a rock concert tonight. I'm watching cable TV at home. Thus are illustrated the differences between us.

OSHA clearly has no jurisdiction in Moria.

Thanks to the Lord of the Rings, I always think of Kazakhstan as having Balrogs.

"You shall not pass!"—The Balrog's algebra teacher.

I just realized that if you wanted to be a rebel in Lothlorien, you would wear bangs.

I'm imagining a Ken Burns' documentary of the events in The Lord of the Rings.

Cue the long pan of the Alan Lee artwork.

It is odd to think it's actually been ten years since "Fellowship of the Ring" came out.

The Two Towers is now on. I hold the minority view that it is the best film of the trilogy.

That said, I'd've trimmed back the ent scenes pretty severely.

I SWEAR I did not realize I was making a tree pun in that last tweet.

I am suddenly aware of just how little difference there is between Orlando Bloom's Legolas and certain sparkly vampires one could name.

Orcs vs. Stormtroopers. GO. On second thought, never mind. Neither side aims well enough for it to be interesting.

And now for no good reason the image of Legolas with a Justin Bieber haircut just popped into my head. I'm sorry.

A name like Grima Wormtongue should have been a tipoff.

Little known fact: Theoden's previous advisor was named Pervert McTraitorpants.

On the other hand, the name "Rasputin" meant "Debauched one," and that didn't stop Nicholas II. Conclusion: Kings are dumb.

Fun fact: Shadowfax, the horse Gandalf rides, had a younger, hipper sibling named "Darktweet."

I wonder what dentists think when they look at Orcs. I suspect "that's a sailboat right there."

They could have just distracted the Wargs by throwing a bunch of red bouncy balls and yelling "fetch."

The orcs would be awesome in a Road Warrior movie. The orcs probably WERE in a Road Warrior movie.

If the co-star of The Hangover made a porn film, they could call it "Helms Deep." #ImSorryAgain

Specifically one thing that bothered me about the Ent scenes is the the green screen is qualitatively less good than elsewhere.

Now we're at the "We paid Cate Banchett to be in this film so we might as well use her for exposition" scene.

Everyone in Middle Earth writes in the same font. THAT'S JUST NOT REALISTIC.

Dear world: I am deeply disappointed there is not a dubstep version of the Smeagol Fish Battering Song.

Frodo just admitted to being in a same sex relationship with Gollum. Sam will kill him!!

"Tricksy Master" is the name of my BDSM bar band.

Dear Aragorn: go right ahead and pose heroically on a mountain top. No rush to get to Helm's Deep. It's not like an Uruk army is coming.

Every time an ent is on the screen I think Robert Plant gets a tingle.

Related: the dude outfitting Theoden looks like David Gilmour. I want him to break out the solo to Comfortably Numb.

Now Aragorn is trying to cheer up the boy who has been chosen for the Hunger Games.

The men of Helm's Deep are saved! The League of Bowie Impersonators has arrived!

All the elves look like they really could use a low-tar cigarette right about now.

For those of you who don't know, there's a very Helm's Deep-like battle sequence in "Kingdom of Heaven," also starring Orlando Bloom.

Dear sound effects people: The Wilhelm Scream is the Rickroll of your industry. Time to retire it.

Helm's Deep explosion: One of the top five explosions in film history. Discuss.

The Legolas Arrow Eye Stab never gets old. The shield surfing, however.

Now at the scene where elf is stunned that someone as pretty as he can die.

The Two Towers may have the most neck wounds of any film ever made.

I wonder what ents do when they come across a book. I imagine there's a lot of screaming.

The ents are marching, first to Isengard and then to a Phish concert.

I strongly believe Theoden could benefit from mood levelers.

Gimli is taking to that horn like it's the world's biggest hookah.

The horses of the Rohirrim: "You want us to gallop down WHAT?"

At the "Ents go Orc bowling" scene.

Burning ent putting himself out in the flood: Still cool.

Sam doing his Saint Crispin's day speech. Undercut by his 70s roadie haircut.

Gandalf now foreshadowing. Movie nearing the end.

Mordor's going about it all wrong, incidentally. Harness all that geothermal energy, sell it to the humans, LIVE LIKE KINGS.

Movie done. I wasn't intending to livetweet it incidentally. It's just that I'm ALL ALONE. With a computer. And cable TV.

And yes, Encore is showing Return of the King next. So if you're sick of the tweets, probably best to unsub for the night.

The very first time you ever see Smeagol he's impaling a living creature, so it's not as if what happens to him afterward is surprising.

The One Ring is bad for your teeth. Pass it on.

Sitcom proposal: Frodo and Sam are roommates, Gollum is their cranky landlord. Gandalf as the wacky neighbor with a cat.

First time I've noticed the ents in the background, still throwing rocks at Saruman's tower.

Merry and Pippin doing product placement for Green Dragon ale. I remember Middle Earth before it went corporate, man.

Gollum is the 1%.

You'd think they could password protect a palantir.

Merry and Pippin having a spat. They're adorable.

It must be tiring to be an elf and always have to walk in slow motion.

They are reforging the sword of the king. Which will be given to Connor McLeod. IN MY CROSSOVER FANFIC #AragronConnorSlashFTW

Let's be honest and admit that Gandalf's people skills leave much to be desired.

I knew Osgilliath was doomed when the Starbucks closed up. All 16 of them #OrcsHateCoffee

Minas Morgul glows like an XBox.

And yes, that would make the Eye of Sauron the Red Ring of Death.

Also, I don't care if they're evil, I want a Nazgul.

Say what you will about the Orcs, you don't get be one of their leaders just by having a nice head of hair #MeritocracyIsUgly

Of all the Hobbits, it's not entirely surprising that Pippin is the one that starts fires.

I wonder what horrible thing you have to have done to be assigned to Beacon Patrol.

This may be a bit of futconning, but I think Eomer would be even more awesome if he spoke like Leonard McCoy.

Gandalf, walking around with that Nazgul repellent in his staff, only thinks to use it once. #NotATacticalGenius

We are now at the scene that suggests that Thanksgiving at the Steward's House is never not awkward.

If I were Sam, I would not be sleeping that close to a cliff edge with Gollum around.

We're at the emo-est parade ever. "You're all doomed. Here's some flowers."

It's nice that in Middle Earth you can become Steward of Gondor without ever learning to chew with your mouth closed.

Does anyone other than me notice the similarity of the falling necklace to the falling necklace in The Exorcist?

Aragorn will not be wanting to swing that sword around in a thunderstorm.

We're at the "Eowyn discovers that proximity does not trump a hot elf" scene.

Also, for those who asked: I am totally sober right now. Believe it.

The whole city of ghosts part here is a little too "Haunted Mansion" for me.

Given the sooty barrenness of Mordor, the support logistics of the orc army are being seriously glossed over here.

Once again: Gandalf—not a people person. #WhatDenathorNeededWasAHug

That Orc general is badass. Good looking, too, in a John Merrick sort of way.

If Gandalf would only use his Magneto powers, this whole battle would be over in, like, a minute and a half.

Frodo should have turned back at "The walls are sticky!" We should ALL turn back when the walls are sticky.

It's out of character for Sam not to have collected up the Lembas bread before he ran back up the mountain in a rage.

You know what would kill Shelob, don't you. A good hard whack with "A Dance With Dragons." #ALargeBookIsComing

Frodo, Gollum and the rest are easier to understand if you think of this movie as Peter Jackson's remake of "Requiem for a Dream."

Here comes my favorite, most Peter Jackson-esque line: BRING WOOD AND OIL

It says something about me that I have no problem with a 10 foot spider but I get annoyed that it has a stinger.

Elijah Wood spends a lot of time in these films expelling foamy spittle to signify pain. #ThatsActing

Theoden's speech to the troops is pretty damn fatalistic. "Everyone! We're going to die! Whoooo!"

These Orcs act like they've never seem stampeding horses before! Weren't they at Helm's Deep? Oh…right.

Denethor falling from a great height ON FIRE is why Peter Jackson was destined to make these films.

Here come the Oliphants. In the super-extended version, the riders of Rohirrim counter the Oliphants with T-Rexes. It's a true fact.

Wow, things are going terribly for the defenders of Minas Tirith. If only some sort of Deus Ex Machina would show up to save their bacon!

Oh look! A Deus Ex Machina in the form of an unbeatable ghost army! That's convenient.

Seriously, that flail? It's like a chandelier on a chain.

Eowyn is No Man! And somewhere Odysseus is considering a copyright infringement suit.

We'll not speak of Legolas' Oliphant Adventure.

We're at the "Eowyn and Theoden recite Luke and Vader's lines from Jedi" scene.

Hope the people of Minas Tirith like Oliphant barbeque.

Aaaaand now we're at the point where one goes "wow, this movie is still going?" no matter how much one is enjoying it.

Sam is dedicating his murders to friends and quipping as he stabs people in the back. How far he's come.

Also, Sam as ringbearer is like the tribute band singer who replaces a front man in the real band. He knows it won't last.

Mount Doom: The name's a little on the nose. You'd think someone would have suggested rebranding to "Mount Pleasant" by now.

Every time the Orcs march I start hearing the Flying Monkey March from Wizard of Oz in my head.

I *did* warn people I would be tweeting a lot tonight. Don't worry. It's just until this movie ends, seven hours from now.

Next, I'll livetweet Berlin Alexanderplatz!

It never actually ends, you know. One eventually just leaves to go pee.

You have to give Gollum credit for persistence. His can-do spirit is what America needs in these hard times. #Gollum2012

We're at the "Frodo's paid the florist and the caterer and everyone's at the chapel but he still can't commit" scene.

And then Gollum comes along to steal the bride. #ItsAllInTheSubtext

I'll say it: Gollum and Frodo's slap fight? Embarrassing for them both.

But of course there's Sam to swoop in for the rebound.

We're at the "Sauron's Tower clearly not built to code" scene.

Sam and Frodo have a bubble of conveniently non-superheated air around them. Which is a lucky thing!

We're at the "Sam's deathbed conversion to heterosexuality" scene.

Aragorn is crowned king; spends the rest of his life settling taxation and usage rights issues. #KingBetterAsAConcept

Elrond clearly still believes Arwen is marrying down #Elf-ElitismIsSickening

At the "We've told Bilbo he's going with the elves, and at his age that's what the nurse's aides at the home will look like" scene.

Frodo smiles as he leaves because he knows he's stuck Sam with an open tab at the Green Dragon #ItWasAThingBetweenThem

Aaaaaaand now I'm done tweeting the movies. Tell the people who unfollowed they can come back now.

Luck

Nov
3
2011

I'm a lucky bastard, and sometimes it annoys me when people don't acknowledge that fact.

In most cases they mean well, because most discussions of luck around me come up in the context of my fiction career, when I note that I got lucky when *Old Man's War*, my first published novel, was not only plucked from online obscurity by Tor Books but then became one of the big science fiction books of its year. This precipitates comments suggesting it wasn't about luck at all, and that I shouldn't underestimate my own efforts/skills/timing or whatever. My response, aside from thanking these folks for their upvote, is point out that of all the writers currently practicing the craft, in the science fiction genre or out of it, I really am the last one who needs to be reassured of his skills and talent. I'm good at what I do, both in writing and in marketing myself. Trust me when I say I'm not running down my skills or abilities. Indeed it's because I am *not* notably neurotic about those things that I can say, with a full, clear and reasonably objective point of view, that aside from anything else in my life, I have been lucky. Extraordinarily so. It does nothing to minimize what I have done purposefully in my life to acknowledge that fact and to be grateful for it.

What is luck? At the end of the day, it's the good things that happen to you that you simply don't or can't control. Stepping away from a curb the second before a car you didn't see barrels right over where you just were. Finding a $20 bill on the sidewalk. Stepping into a restaurant for a bite to eat and seeing an old friend you lost contact with years ago just before she steps out the door. These are all some obvious examples of luck. It works the other way too; you can step toward a curb just as a car you didn't see plows into it and into you; then you are *un*lucky.

In either case the event is not something you consciously or purposefully controlled. You can argue left and right about how much "luck" has to do with any particular event: In the case of me getting lucky with *Old Man's War*, I still wrote the book, and I still had, for the time, a robust presence online which meant it had a better chance to be seen than perhaps another similar novel presented online would have. Both of these had a significant impact on my luck. Be that as it may, ultimately I had no control over Patrick Nielsen Hayden going to my site, reading the entire novel on his own time, and deciding to make an offer on the book outside of the usual submission channels. Had he not decided to do just one of those things (and particularly the last one), it's pretty obvious that my life would be a different one than I have now.

However, this is not even the best example of what an incredibly lucky bastard I am. The best example is me meeting my wife. Many of you know that I met my wife in 1993 when I was doing a feature story for the newspaper I was working for at the time. The story was on a local DJ; I followed her around all day, including to a gig at bar, at which Krissy and her friends chose to show up, and at which she saw me dancing with someone else and decided to approach me later that evening. We then danced several times that night and then made arrangements to see each other again, and everything went from there. It's a nice story.

Here are some things to consider:

1. I was originally supposed to follow the DJ in question on an entirely different day, when she was supposed to do an evening gig at an entirely different bar in an entirely different city. If the story had gone as originally scheduled, I would not have met Krissy.

2. The bar we did meet in was in a city that neither Krissy nor I lived in; she and her friends went to that bar specifically because they liked the DJ. I don't think I had actually ever been in that city before that night. If it hadn't been for the specific DJ, doing that specific gig on that specific night, I wouldn't have been there, and I wouldn't have met Krissy.

3. Even if Krissy had decided to go to a bar in my town one night, I don't drink, and as a result, outside of science fiction conventions (which I did not go to at the time, nor did Krissy), I never go to bars. If I had not been doing this particular story, which occasioned me being in a bar for work, I wouldn't have met Krissy.

4. If I had decided that being on job meant I couldn't do any dancing, Krissy wouldn't have seen me on the dance floor and become interested in meeting me. And then I wouldn't have met her. Note, incidentally, that asking random women to dance is not what I usually did at the time; in fact, I'm pretty sure that night was the only time I'd ever done it.

5. Krissy tells me that she saw me because she was getting a drink at the bar and I happened to be dancing at that time. If I had decided to skip that particular song—or if the random woman I had asked to dance had decided not to dance with me—Krissy wouldn't have seen me, and given how crowded the bar was that night and the fact she was with friends and probably would have spent most of her time with them had she not seen me on the dance floor, it's entirely possible we would not have met.

6. If Krissy had made the assumption that the person I was dancing with was my girlfriend, she might not have approached me. And then we might not have met.

7. And so on.

If you add all this up, the odds of me having met my wife, given who I was, where I lived and what I usually did with my time, are so *infinitesimally small* as to be almost completely non-existent. Pretty much the only chance I would have ever had to meet her was that one time, that one night. You know, there's a word for meeting one's lifelong love on the single night in either of your lives that you would have ever had the chance to meet. It's called "luck."

When I want to drive myself hair-pullingly crazy, I think about all the ways it would have been so *easy* not to have met my wife. And then I call up my wife and tell her just how happy I am that she's in my life, and that I love her and that when she comes home I'm totally gonna *rub her feet.*

So when I tell you that in my life I have been blessed with an extraordinary amount of luck—more luck than one person should probably have, in fact—don't rush to assure me that luck has nothing to do with where I am in life today. I do appreciate the thought, to be sure. And I know you mean well. But I know the truth. I'm a lucky bastard. I'm thankful for it.

McKean's Inversion

Aug
11
2011

For no particular reason, I thought of an observation that lexicographer (and old college pal) Erin McKean had about the word "classy," the gist of which was that if someone used the word to describe themselves, it was often quite obvious that they were in fact the opposite. Someone else calls you "classy"? Maybe you are. Call someone else "classy"? Maybe they are, too. Call yourself "classy"? It's what you're trying to sell yourself as, not necessarily what you are.

It occurs to me that this idea has application outside of the word "classy," since I've often found that the adjectives people use to describe themselves exist on a spectrum with "aspirational" on one end and "delusional" on the other, with otherwise very little correlation to who they actually are:

"I am a humble man."

"I'm punctual."

"I'm a funny guy."

And so on.

As there already exists a "McKean's Law" with respect to words ("Any correction of the speech or writing of others will contain at least one grammatical, spelling, or typographical error"), allow me instead to suggest what I will henceforth label "**McKean's Inversion**," to wit:

The adjective a person says they are is frequently the thing they are not.

To put it in writing terms, it's a fine example of "show, don't tell." Classy people don't need to assert they're classy, they do classy things. Funny people don't have to assure you they're funny, they simply make you laugh. Kind people don't need to verbally advertise their kindness, because it's evident in their lives. All of which is to say the way to be *seen* as funny, or kind, or humble, or classy, is to *be* that thing. And if you are, chances are pretty good other people will note it.

In any event, keep McKean's Inversion in mind the next time you have the urge to tell rather than show what you see as your own best qualities. People may not have a term in their head for McKean's Inversion, but, believe me, they know it exists.

Meanwhile, On the Home Front, I Have Growing Suspicions My Male Cats Are Totally Gay

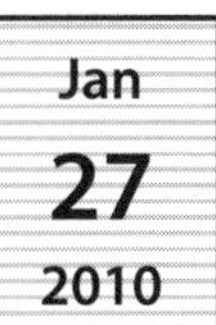

It's because in the last several days I have come across Zeus and Lopsided Cat openly and enthusiastically grooming and gently headbutting each other in open, conspicuous places, followed by a casual glance over to me as if to say "What? You have a problem with two male cats showing their affection for each other *in their own home?*"

For the record, I do not. Indeed, I celebrate their feline gayness, inasmuch as two cats who have had their gonads removed can be said to be gay, which I think is a fair amount, since "gay" encompasses more than physical sexuality and gonads (or lack thereof). And anyway, what sort of hypocrite would I be if I supported same-sex marriage but viewed my two male cats tongue-bathing each other and thought, *dude, that's just wrong*. It's not. Go, Lopsided Cat and Zeus! I wish you joy.

That said, it *is* kind of sudden. Lopsided Cat has generally viewed Zeus as something of a nuisance, to be smacked about whenever the younger cat got too uppity but otherwise to be ignored. For Lopsided Cat to go from benign neglect of his fellow cat to open affection seemingly in the space of a few days is a little weird. But then, I don't speak cat. Maybe this has all been simmering under the surface, like how in all those romantic comedies the leads can't stand each other and then suddenly they're mad for each other. This is like that. With cats. Who may be gay.

I know some of you are thinking, "yes, yes, but what does *Ghlaghghee* think about this turn of events?" She is perhaps unsurprisingly perfectly okay with it. Ghlaghghee has always struck me as an unusually tolerant cat (although she, like Lopsided Cat, has been known to smack around Zeus when he gets out of line), and so her apprehension of these current events seems to be along the "Oh. Huh. Well, okay, then" line. Which of course is just fine with me. It'd be sad to have to have a talk to her about embracing diversity, not the least because I don't speak cat. So that's one awkward discussion avoided. For which I think we are all grateful.

Middle Ages Me

Mar
15
2011

Charles asks:

If you were born in the dark ages, and couldn't be a writer, how would you earn a living? Technology related jobs are out, because remember it's the DARK AGES. I don't see you as the farmer type, so what would you do?

Well, first, I'm not 100% behind the phrase "dark ages," which implies, basically, that from the collapse of Rome until roughly the time of the Renaissance, there wasn't a whole lot going on in Europe, intellectually and culturally speaking. This is not entirely true, as any student of European history will tell you. Likewise, as French historian Jacques Le Goff reminds us, "Those who suggest that the 'dark ages' were a time of violence and superstition would do well to remember the appalling cruelties of our own time, truly without parallel in past ages." Look at the last century and see if you can disagree with this point.

As for technological advances, there was a lot of them about, actually, but in a manner we don't much think about. The development of the heavy plow, for example, was literally cutting-edge technology in the 7th Century; sure, it doesn't look like much next to your shiny new iPhone, but on the other hand your shiny new iPhone can't break up the heavy soils of Northern Europe and lead to massive advances in the ability of the people there to feed themselves. If you've got any ancestors from above the Danube, you might be glad one of them thought up the heavy plow. Add in the horse collar, which arrived in Europe in the 11th century or so, and suddenly those same farmers could plow the same fields in half the time. No, they couldn't play Angry Birds. But back in the day, they had *real* angry birds. Stealing grain. So *there.*

Be that as it may, the question remains: What would the John Scalzi of, oh, let's say, 1011, be doing with his time?

To begin, if he was my current age of 41, there's an excellent chance he would already be dead. Infant and child mortality killed off a large number of folks who would never see the other side of a fifth birthday; add to that the general less-than-advanced state of medicine of the eleventh century AD, and there's a good chance that either disease or injury would have claimed me by now. And even if it had, I would still be *old* at 41; it seems unlikely I'd have many of my teeth still, my various injuries and years of almost certain hard physical labor would have taken its toll on my body, and so basically I'd probably be hunched, creaky and gumming my food.

And what would my job be? Easy: Peasant farmer.

Which, I know, Charles suggests he doesn't see me as. Thing is, in 1011, pretty much everyone was a farmer. Yes, there were other jobs, and other social strata, but if we're looking at actual statistics, guess what? Odds are, you're probably a peasant farmer. And certainly in my case it seems to be likely. Look at my last name: Scalzi. In Italian, it means "barefoot." Tell me that doesn't just *scream* "hardy peasant stock." So, yes, if I'm in the eleventh century, and still alive at my advanced age, then I'm almost certainly a farmer. And I probably think it *sucks*, but then, it's not like I have all sorts of options.

That said, there's a small possibility that at an early age someone saw some small spark of intelligence in me, in which case there's a chance that might eventually find my way into a religious order, which given who I am today might seem somewhat ironic and amusing, but in the eleventh century might strike me as a pretty good deal, all things considered. If I joined an order that followed the Benedictine Rule, I would have some access to reading and the intelligence of the time, and would be in a community of like-minded individuals, and in any event knowing me I would prefer that life to looking at the ass end of an ox for most of my days.

In either case I probably wouldn't have become me—that is, the witty, snarky writerly type you all know and appear to tolerate. But we're talking the eleventh century here. It was not a quality era for snark. I do imagine that in my village or order I would be known for my quirky sense of humor, but I also suspect that's about as far as it would go. I suppose there's some very small chance that I could be something along the lines of a wandering entertainer, going from court to court with my tales, perhaps with musical accompaniment. But I don't exactly see that as a *good* life, in 1011.

But let's suppose that in my 11th century character creation mode I rolled all natural 20s and ended up having the option of being anything I wanted to be. What then? Well, my first option would be not to be born for another 958 years (or so), because I like me some air conditioning and Internet and human rights and modern medicine. Barring that I would go for, oh, I don't know, a royal court historian somewhere; a gig that keeps me out of having to take an arrow in the thigh (or alternately, running someone through with a pike) in a war, or watching an ox's ass while it pulls a plow, or in fact very many of the really stinky and inconvenient aspects of life in the 11th century. What about being a prince or a knight? Yeah, no. Lots of wars. Lots of death. Lots of being away from family for years while you fight for a boggy chunk of land. Pass, thank you. Court historian will suit me just fine.

But in point of fact, what I'm rather more likely to be is a peasant farmer, and also, at age 41, stone cold dead. I'll stick with the 21st century.

My Life Is Good But I'm Worried Yours is Better

Sep
21
2009

Cartoonist Tim Kreider writes over at the *New York Times* about something he calls "the Referendum," in which people in their early middle age (think 40 to 45) look at the lives of all their friends and try to figure out how their own lives match up to theirs. This is basically indistinguishable from what everybody does all the time—20somethings look at their lives relative to their other friends too, I assure you, or at least did when I was that age—but Kreider's thesis (or at least what I got out of it) was that at about 40 years of age, this comparison is more pertinent and poignant, because by that time you've already made all sorts of life choices that will define the rest of your life, and in some ways it's just too late to go back and start over.

Essentially, at 40 or so, you've become who you are going to be for the rest of your life. Which means that, when you look at your friends' choices, you do so with some measure of romanticism and envy, because those choices will no longer ever be yours. The only positive note about any of this (or so says Kreider) is that your friends likely look at *your* life through rose-colored glasses as well. Basicially, at 40, everyone's over-romanticizing the life of their contemporaries.

It's an interesting thesis, and in some ways dovetails into something I've thought for a while, which is that one's 20th high school and college reunions are really the only ones that one needs to attend, because they're the ones that let you see who all your classmates became when they grew up. At the reunions before the 20th, people are still figuring out what they're doing with their lives; the ones afterward you show up just to find out who's still breathing. But basically while one always has to leave room for epiphanies, freak-outs and karma, I do think when you see someone at 40, they are who they who they have become and will likely be for the remainder of their time on the planet. I could be wrong on this; ask me again when I'm 50. But it seems that way to me now.

I don't know how much I agree about the rest of "The Referendum," however. Or more accurately I think that I agree that "The Referendum" functions, but only to the extent one is unhappy with one's own choices in life, or sees the choices one's made in terms of what one's lost in other opportunities. I suspect people who are satisfied with the choices they've made with their lives (rather than being resigned to them) look at things differently—they look at the lives their friends have and see the value of them and the cool things those lives offer, but wouldn't trade because their own lives have enough value for them.

For example, this paragraph, in which Kreider, single and without children, discusses his friends with children (and, also, homes):

But I can only imagine the paralytic terror that must seize my friends with families as they lie awake calculating mortgage payments and college funds and realize that they are locked into their present lives for farther into the future than the mind's eye can see. Judging from the unanimity with which parents preface any gripe about children with the disclaimer, "Although I would never wish I hadn't had them and I can't imagine life without them," I can't help but wonder whether they don't have to repress precisely these thoughts on a daily basis.

This is a fairly depressing way of looking at life with children and mortgages, and so quite naturally if this is how you're doing it, you'll be romanticizing the lives of your friends without either. But it's not impossible to look at college funds and mortgage payments as part of a long-term process that results in a) responsible, productive adults you've had a hand in creating and b) a place you own and stake a claim to, both of which are in their way laudable and worth the time and commitment. Now, maybe neither of these things are *monumental,* in terms of asking "what have I done with my life," but it doesn't mean that either is not desirable or worth doing. Not every desirable or good thing in one's life is or should be monumental.

I think the real thing that bothers me about Kreider's "Referendum" is that it seems to deny both agency and optimism, the latter not in the "hey! It's a sunshiny day!" sense but in the "work as if these were the early days of a better nation" sense. Our lives are a combination of the choices we make, for better or for worse, and events that are largely out of our control, which we then have to deal with. It's also a continuing process, to which we have to commit every morning when we wake up. I think Kreider's "Referendum" is a tapping into the desire to escape one's life rather than to commit to it. And, I don't know. I think that's not a way to go through life, if you can avoid it.

Now, you may say, it's easy for me to have this perspective because in many ways I have an enviable life. Which is true, and I don't want to pretend otherwise. But, you know, Tim Kreider and most of his pals undoubtedly have enviable lives, too; as one interviewer put it to Kreider, "You draw at home and you hang out with friends and drink and stuff, and then, at the end of the week, you produce a cartoon? And that's your job…Please allow me to congratulate you on having the best life of all time." To be very clear about it, anodyne musing about one's position in life relative to one's chums is the sport of the privileged, like polo or key parties. The issue in this case isn't privilege, it's perspective. It's one of those enviable problems to have.

Or to put it another way, if you're really spending time fantasizing about your friends' lives, and they are equally spending time fantasizing about yours, there's a good chance both of your lives are, you know, *pretty good*, and maybe you should focus on that instead. It's just a thought.

Neil Armstrong and Futures Past

Aug
27
2012

I was two months old when Neil Armstrong landed on the moon and 43 when he died, and in between those two events the future changed. When Armstrong landed, a human future in space seemed inevitable—we'd landed on the moon, after all. How long could it possibly be until we had moon colonies, space stations where thousands lived, stuck by centrifugal force to walls which were their floors, and a second space race to Mars? Why, not long as all, it seemed, and so I lived the first decade of my life breathlessly waiting for the moon colony and all the rest of it. And also drinking Tang because, hey, I wasn't quite ten, and Tang was pretty awesome when you're that age.

Four decades on, we never did get the mechanistic, physical future required for those moon colonies and space stations. In point of fact that future was expensive, and once the "landing on the moon" bragging rights were taken by the US, we apparently lost interest. Gene Cernan was the last man on the moon, and he left that orb in December of 1972; we're coming up fast on the 40th anniversary of his departure, and more people seem to know about the Mayan Apocalypse than that particular anniversary. Yes, it makes me sad.

I don't mind too much the future we've gotten so far. I like the Internet, and my cell phone, and my television bouncing to me from space, and all the other things that have come from what has essentially been the less expensive path of least resistance. I think the things that NASA has done with its robotic craft, which are now on Mars and over Mercury and pushing through the heliopause at the very edge of interstellar space, are nothing short of miraculous. This future has been pretty good for me. But I don't think this future had to be exclusive of the future that Neil Armstrong seemed to herald, and for which he was our icon; maybe we could have had both, had our will to go to the moon been matched by a will to stay and build there.

We can still go back to the moon, of course. We can still go and build and stay and use the moon as our first stepping stone to other worlds. Anything is possible. But for me Armstrong's death forever closes the door on a certain possible path the we could have taken, the one where that first small step and giant leap was not essentially taken in isolation, but was followed by another step and another leap, followed by another, and so on, one right after another, without pause and without interruption. Even when or if we return to the moon, we will never live in Neil Armstrong's future.

I wonder how Armstrong himself felt about that. He lived down the road a piece from me; people I know had the honor of meeting him and described him, in so many words, as one of the best of men. Back here on Earth he did not seem to go out of his way to call attention to himself, and while he encouraged people to keep alive the spirit of exploration and service that he exemplified, it doesn't seem that he spent a lot of time beating a drum in public. For all that, I read that when he was 80, he volunteered to be the commander of a mission to Mars, should anyone want him for the job. I would guess he wanted to live in Neil Armstrong's future, too. I'm sorry for him he didn't get to.

The New York Times: We May Slide Into Irrelevancy But At Least We Update Daily

Jun
7
2009

***The New York Times* is engaging in another one of those delightfully passive aggressive stories it does about blogs, this time focusing—about a decade too late—on the bloggers who quit blogging when they realize that just because they write something online doesn't mean anyone is going to know it is there. I say this is a decade too late because I certainly remember the grousing in 1999 or thenabouts by folks discouraged that no one was beating a path to their virtual doors, and I remember the newspaper stories about just that fact. What's old becomes new again, apparently.**

The *Times* also notes that of the millions of blogs that exist, only a tiny margin get a readership beyond the blogger and the blogger's mom ("OMG I can't believe my mom read what I wrote about her on my blog"), and thus as a consequence most are eventually abandoned. But again, this is no real surprise; the numbers are larger now but the percentages of abandoned blogs has been fairly consistent for years. The vast majority of blogs, in fact, have nothing but the following three posts:

Post One: "Here's my blog! This is where I'm going to share all my thoughts about life, the universe and everything! It's going to be great and I can't wait to tell you all what I'm thinking about everything!"

Post Two: "Hey, sorry I haven't updated in a while—life's been crazy. But I'll be back soon."

Post Three: "Here's a picture of my cat."

And then it's done.

Nothing wrong with this—writing on a regular basis is work, even when you're ostensibly doing it for fun, and it shouldn't be a surprise not a lot of people really want to work that hard. Also and perhaps more to the point, I suspect many people who start blogging realize fairly quickly that they either don't like sharing all their thoughts to the world, or that their thoughts, while interesting to them, appear fairly banal once they're typed out, and it's better just not to post them for the sake of posting them. And there's nothing wrong with this either, and indeed the blogger is to be congratulated for that bit of personal insight. Most blogs are abandoned because they should be.

The thing about this *Times* piece is that it feels almost endearingly anachronistic; not to run down blogs, but they're not exactly the hot new kid on the block these days, are they. These days it seems like the only people starting new blogs are laid-off journalists, which says something both about blogs and these journalists. Everyone else has moved on to Facebook and Twitter. Which is something I personally applaud; I like my blog, but I'm a wordy bastard, by profession and by inclination, and online social networks actually do a far better job of what people wanted blogs to do, which is be a way to act and feel connected online with friends and family. No one gives a crap if your tweet or status update is short and utterly inconsequential ("Hey! I just ate a hot dog!")—indeed, that's kind of the point.

So it's worth noting that even on Twitter, with its absolute ease of connecting with people and its inherent design promoting short, deep-thought-free posting, the vast majority of Twitter accounts rarely update, and have fewer than 10 followers. Which is to say the same communication dynamic applies everywhere online, regardless of whether it's a blog, or Facebook page or Twitter account or whatever. It's *hard* to make interesting content, whether it's a 670 word blog post or a 140 character tweet. People might initially think they're up to it, but they find out quickly enough that they're not. Which, again, is perfectly fine. There's no inherent virtue in being a wordy bastard. Some people are; most people aren't.

I expect the *Times* will catch up on this news about Twitter in another eight years or so, assuming (he said, snarkily) it's still around then. Set your timers now.

Next Morning Presidential Election Thoughts

Nov
7
2012

Last year in October, I did a book tour of Germany. Every night I was there, after my reading, I would have dinner with some of the Germans who were kind enough to have hosted me on the trip. And almost without fail, after enough time had passed that they felt comfortable with me, the more-or-less same question would come up. Paraphrased, it is thus: "Okay, seriously, what is going on with your politics over there? You're scaring the hell out of us." And specifically, they wanted to know what was going to happen to President Obama, which the Germans, to a person, saw as a reasonable and moderate leader. They were terrified that he would not be re-elected.

Here's more or less what I said to the Germans then: "Look, all the political noise is going to get much worse in 2012 because it's a presidential election year and that's how we get. It's going to get loud and weird and you're going to be much more scared before it's all over. But in the end Obama's going to win, because he's doing as well as he can under the circumstances, and because things are slowly turning around, and because the GOP is running its B-team running for President. It's going to be close, but Obama's going to do it."

So to all of my German friends: See? Just like I told you.

Four years ago, there were a lot of people who believed that Obama's election heralded a material change in American politics. I would argue that it's this one that's the actual signifier of that change. Look: It's one thing for a black man with a name like "Barack Hussein Obama" to win an election after eight years of a GOP presidency that culminated with two wars and the greatest economic crisis in eighty years. It's another thing entirely for that same black man with a funny name to win a second term in the face of an unimpressive economic recovery and the full, uncontained and often unreasoned fury from his opposing side. For better or worse, Americans view one-term presidents as losers or historical flukes: See Gerald Ford, Jimmy Carter and George HW Bush as examples of this. Barack Obama, whatever else you will say about him—and many will—can no longer be categorized as a loser or a fluke. He won both the electoral and over 50% of the popular vote twice, which is the first time since Reagan that any president managed that.

More to the point, two years after a mid-term election that swept into office some of the most recalcitrant opposition that any modern president has seen, and after four years of dealing with a GOP whose major legislative goal (as Mitch McConnell so memorably put it) was to make Obama a single-term president, Obama's electoral map was strikingly similar to his first; he lost only two states from 2008. This was a close election, on the popular election front. But after all the noise and thunder and intonation, and assuming Florida falls into the Democratic tally, as it appears likely to do at this point, Obama walks out of the election with 50% more electoral votes than Romney.

This wasn't a squeaker, and Obama didn't just get lucky. To be clear, he *did* get lucky, most obviously in drawing Mitt Romney as an opponent, who gave Obama far too many opportunities to punch at him, and in a GOP which persists in fielding candidates far to the right of the US population as a whole, giving the Democrats a field of bogeymen with which to scare its voter base. But Obama also won because he was canny: how Obama won Ohio this year will be required reading for political wonks for decades. And he also won because of demographics—a word which is currently being used as code by the right for "people who are not straight white men." Well, as it happens, there *are* lots of people who are not straight white men in these here United States, and whatever code word you want to use for them, it turns out that their votes count just the same as anyone else's. Unless the GOP is irretrievably stupid, this is the last presidential election they'll assume they can win entirely white.

And saliently, Obama successfully made the argument that he was doing his job, despite (and sometimes in spite of) a solid, unified wall of opposition from the GOP. At the end of the day, luck, campaign smarts and "demographics" aren't going to make the case for a re-election by themselves. People have to believe he's getting things done. It appears they do.

Obama is not a fluke or a historical blip. You can argue he won his first presidential election on credit, and I'll let you have that argument. It's four years later, and the voters have seen him in action. This election he had to win with what was on his ledger. He won it, and he won it big enough to forestall all doubt. If you are one of those who will persist in thinking he's there by accident or by trivial circumstances, you're delusional. And you're likely doomed to see your preferred presidential candidates lose. This isn't Reagan's America anymore, or Bush's. It's Obama's. You should get used to that.

For all that, four years ago when Obama won, I offered readers here a reality check regarding their expectations for the man. Here is the reality check this year:

* **The House is still in GOP hands.** In the Senate the Democrats do not have a filibuster-proof majority. We have a divided government, and the GOP standard operating procedure is to oppose every single thing Obama is for. Don't expect *that* to change.

* **You've had four years to see how Obama works and how he does his job.** If you're expecting that to change, you haven't been paying attention.

* **Obama is not a liberal.** He's definitely not a socialist. He's a moderately left-leaning centrist. Anyone who believes (or at least says) otherwise on either side of the aisle is speaking rhetorical

nonsense. Obama will lead from the center. That's what he does. That's who he *is.*

* **Those who dislike Obama for whatever reasons they do are still there.** And they dislike him even more today. They also dislike what he represents: The end to a comfortable (for them), right-leaning United States. You will not stop hearing from them.

* **The presidential election settled one thing: Who is president for the next four years.** All the rest of it is up in the air. And a lot of it will be up to you, and us.

How do I feel about Obama's re-election? As I said last night: Relieved. Pleased. And ready to move forward.

Congratulations to our president.

Congratulations to the United States.

Let's get to work.

A Note to the Anonymous Man Sitting in the Bathroom Stall Next to Me Earlier Today

Aug
16
2008

It's not necessary to narrate.

Really.

That is all.

And Now, For No Particular Reason, a Rant About Facebook

Jan
19
2011

A friend of mine noted recently that I seemed a little antagonistic about Facebook recently—mostly on my Facebook account, which is some irony for you—and wanted to know what I had against it. The answer is simple enough: Facebook is what happens to the Web when you hit it with the stupid stick. It's a dumbed-down version of the functionality the Web already had, just not all in one place at one time.

Facebook has made substandard versions of everything on the Web, bundled it together and somehow found itself being lauded for it, as if AOL, Friendster and MySpace had never managed the same slightly embarrassing trick. Facebook had the advantage of not being saddled with AOL's last-gen baggage, Friendster's too-early-for-its-moment-ness, or MySpace's aggressive ugliness, and it had the largely accidental advantage of being upmarket first—it was originally limited to college students and gaining some cachet therein—before it let in the rabble. But the idea that it's doing something better, new or innovative is largely PR and faffery. Zuckerberg is in fact not a genius; he's an ambitious nerd who was in the right place at the right time, and was apparently willing to be a ruthless dick when he had to be. Now he has billions because of it. Good for him. It doesn't make me like his monstrosity any better.

Which is of course fine. The fact is Facebook isn't made for someone like me, who once handrolled his own html code and then uploaded it using UNIX commands because he was excited to have his own Web site, and back in 1993 that's how you did it. I've been maintaining and actively updating my own site in one form or another for the better part of two decades now, and (quite obviously) like to write at length on whatever thought is passing through my brain at the moment. Committed loggorheic nerds like me don't need something like Facebook. It's made for *normal* people, the ones who just want to stay in contact with friends and post pictures for them to see and maybe play a game or two, and have a single convenient place to do all that sort of stuff online. Facebook is the Web hit with a stupid stick, but that doesn't mean people are stupid for using it. They see Facebook as letting them do the things they want to do, and not making them jump through a bunch of hoops to do it. Again: Fine.

But again, also: Not really for me. I look at Facebook and what I mostly see are a bunch of seemingly arbitrary and annoying functionality choices. A mail system that doesn't have a Bcc function doesn't belong in the 21st Century. Facebook shouldn't be telling me how many "friends" I should have, especially when there's clearly no technological impetus for it. Its grasping attempts to get its hooks into every single thing I do feels like being groped by an overly obnoxious salesman. Its general ethos that I need to get over the concept of privacy makes me want to shove a camera lens up Zuckerberg's left nostril 24 hours a day and ask him if he'd like for his company to rethink that position. Basically there's very little Facebook does, either as a technological platform or as a company, that doesn't remind me that "banal mediocrity" is apparently the highest accolade one can aspire to at that particular organization.

So, you ask, why do I use Facebook? The answer is obvious: Because other folks do, and they're happy with it and I don't mind making it easy for them to get in touch with me. But my Facebook immersion is relatively shallow; I save the majority of my deep thoughts for this Web site and the majority of my short thoughts for Twitter, so Facebook tends to get whatever's left. I don't use much there that would allow some obnoxious third-party program to either clutter up my wall or inform all my friends that I've bought a pig in a video game; they don't give a crap and I wouldn't want to inflict that information on them. I work on the assumption that Facebook is working by default to make me look like an asshole to everyone who's connected to me, because I've seen it do it to others. As a result I think I've managed to avoid being such to others there. Or at the very least, if I'm an ass on Facebook, it's my own doing and not because of Facebook. Which is all I can ask for.

I really do wish Facebook were smarter and less obnoxious to use. I wish I could sign on to the damn thing and not have the first thing I feel be exasperation at the aggressive dimness of its UI and its functionality. I wish I could *like* Facebook. But I don't, and I'm having a hard time seeing how I ever will. I understand there's a value for Facebook making itself the stupid version of the Web. I really really really wish there wasn't.

So what's left to me is to take comfort in the fact that eventually Facebook is likely to go the way of all companies that are stupid versions of the Web. This is not to say that Facebook will ever go away completely—its obtuse process for deleting one's account at the very least assures it will always be able to brag of its membership rolls. But you know what, I still have accounts for AOL, Friendster and MySpace. Ask me how often I use them.

Obama's First 100 Days: A Complete and Utter Failure

Apr
29
2009

Why? Well, I'll tell you.

1. I'm continuing to go bald.
2. I haven't lost any weight since January 20.
3. I AM STILL AGING.
4. In March, one of my cats (or more—conspiracy!) peed in the corner of my closet.
5. My hot chocolate this morning was *distinctly* unsatisfactory.
6. Last week, after four years of service, my beloved Vans sneakers—the ones with bats on them—ripped, making them unusable, and Vans *doesn't make them any more.*
7. Rosario Dawson has *not* phoned my wife to get clearance from her for a sanctioned night of Grainy-Sex-Tape-Posted-to-BitTorrent-Worthy Debauchery™ with me.
8. I was not transformed overnight into a ninja spy with mega awesome secret LASER POWERS.
9. I still have to brush my own teeth; no one else will do it for me.
10. I have not been provided a 2010 Mustang. I mean, really. It's not like I'd hold out for a GT. The V6 Premium package would be just fine. I'm not *greedy.*

President Obama has had 100 days to address each of these issues of *vast national importance.* How many of them has he tackled? *Not a one.* This is the change we can believe in? *I don't think so.* I did *not* vote for

Obama just to have ripped sneakers, unsatisfactory beverages and *no spousally-approved hot sex with Rosario Dawson in my bitchin' new muscle car.* There's a word for the emotion I'm feeling right now, Mr. President. And that word is: *Betrayal.*

Yes, I understand that President Obama has said that sacrifices need to be made by each of us. Fine. In the spirit of this national sacrifice, *I will still brush my own teeth.* But Mr. President, you have to meet me half way. Where are my ninja powers? And my Mustang? And why are my telomeres still degrading, meaning that every day I look more and more like Ernest Borgnine? This is not the America I want to live in, Mr. President. You have to do *your* part, too.

And the fact is, he hasn't. Not a single one of the items above, which Mr. Obama agreed to solve when he and I met *in my mind* on that hot sunny day last August when I was trapped in a car with the windows uncracked, has been resolved. You can't tell me I haven't been patient. The dude has had 100 days with the entire apparatus of the United States government at his disposal. It's not like he has *other* things to do. These things should have been dealt with, quickly, forcefully, fully. But they have not. And now look at me. I'm a middle-aged balding man smelling of cat pee. And it's *all Obama's fault.*

For shame, Mr. President. For *shame.*

And thus, for your first 100 days, Mr. President, you earn a richly-deserved **F**. But I still have hope that in the next 100 days, you will stop doing whatever distracting things you are doing and *finally* focus your attention on the things that really matter; specifically, that thing about Rosario Dawson. America *needs* that one. Yes it does. *Desperately.* Oh, and the Mustang, too. Thank you.

Observations on a Toothache

Sep 3 2009

Well, I'm scheduled at the dentist at 3pm to deal with the cracked molar, and until then I have a toothache which occasionally throbs up, but is mostly under control at the moment thanks to the dynamic duo of ibuprofen and Orajel. Be that as it may it's too distracting to allow me to be terribly creative at the moment, so instead allow me to offer some thoughts on me and my toothache.

First, I feel lucky to be alive in the relatively small slice of human history during which dentistry is a licensed medical profession, said doctors have an understanding and appreciation for basic hygiene, and we have access to lovely, lovely mouth-numbing painkillers. Considering the vast majority of humanity typically had their teeth pulled by people who also doubled as hairdressers, and had to feel every single yank and twist until it was over, the advantages to being alive now should not be understated.

Second, this is a reminder that sometimes things just happen. Four years ago today, as it happens, I wrote my "Being Poor" essay, in which one of the things I noted was "Being Poor is hoping the toothache goes away." To which some arch twit who thought he was very clever responded in the comments that being poor doesn't excuse people from brushing their teeth, and did not appear to want to be convinced that the simple act of brushing one's teeth does not mean one then has blanket immunity from all subsequent dental issues.

And, well: Hello, I brush and floss my teeth daily. I go to regular checkups as recommended by my dentist. I do not chew rocks or coat my teeth with a solution of sugar and acid directly before I go to sleep. I do everything I'm supposed to do for my teeth and mostly none of the stuff I'm not, and yet one morning—today—I woke up and one of my teeth was cracked. Why? Oh, possibly because I'm a 40-year-old man and this particular molar has been in constant use in my mouth since I was twelve or so, and also possibly because *shit just happens*, and also possibly because a tooth brush is not, in fact, the magical talisman against life that this smug jackass appeared to think it was.

Now, fortunately for me, I don't have to just hope that this toothache goes away. As soon as I realized this wasn't just some random transient pain I hopped on the phone, called my dentist's office, and was delighted that he was able to drop me into his schedule for the day. I can do this because I have dental insurance and can afford the co-pay without problem. That said, it's not hard to imagine a situation where I wasn't so fortunate, without having to resort to being poor. I could be unmarried, for example, since my insurance comes through my wife. Alternately I could stay married and have my wife unemployed, laid off because of cuts her company made due to the recession, and then the full cost of the insurance we have would fall on us, at least until the COBRA runs out, and it would be an open question as to whether we could afford it.

If my wife couldn't find another job with health/dental benefits—and where we live there are lots of jobs that skip that part—it'd fall on me to cover it. I'm a successful writer, but I also know that much of my success comes from luck; there are other writers who work as hard and are as good at writing as I, who are not as financially successful. I could be in a situation where I (like most writers) don't make a whole lot of money and would have trouble purchasing a health and dental plan for myself, much less my wife and our child. If I didn't have dental insurance, I might have to decide whether I want to fix my tooth or pay some other bills first; I might decide it makes more financial sense to chew on aspirin for a while.

And so on. Again, these are some of the situations one might find one's self in without having to go all the way to being *genuinely* in poverty here in the US. Not all of these situations are entirely under one's control, and not all of them are one's *fault*. There are lots of people who have cause to hope the toothache goes away, and to dread if it doesn't, and not just because some guy is fiddling around in their mouth with a high speed drill.

This is what it is (which is not to say it is what it *has* to be, which is another thing entirely), and what it *does* is remind me that I really am a fortunate bastard in lots of little ways that don't bear thinking about until thinking about them is required. I don't stay up nights thinking "gee, it's nice that if I crack a tooth I can take care of it with a minimum of fuss," but when I *do* crack a tooth, I think it's worth noting that there are many ways in which it would be a serious problem, were my life just a degree or two off the direction it's going.

It's particularly useful when I'm feeling smug and thinking my life is as it is solely because I made it that way on my own. In the real world, what we do with our lives matters, but our lives are lived in a world that is more than just what we make of it. And sometimes you get toothaches.

Omelas State University

Nov
10
2011

These things should be simple:

1. When, as an adult, you come across another adult raping a small child, you should a) do everything in your power to rescue that child from the rapist, b) call the police the moment it is practicable.
2. If your adult son calls you to tell you that he just saw another adult raping a small child, but then left that small child with the rapist, and then asks you what he should do, you should a) tell him to get off the phone with you and call the police immediately, b) call the police yourself and make a report, c) at the appropriate time in the future ask your adult son why the *fuck* he did not try to save that kid.
3. If your underling comes to you to report that he saw another man, also your underling, raping a small child, but then left that small child with the rapist, you should a) call the police immediately, b) alert your own superiors, c) immediately suspend the alleged rapist underling from his job responsibilities pending a full investigation, d) at the appropriate time in the future ask that first underling why the *fuck* he did not try to save that kid.
4. When, as the officials of an organization, you are approached by an underling who tells you that one of his people saw

> another of his people raping a small child *at the organization, in organization property,* you should a) call the police immediately, b) immediately suspend the alleged rapist from his job responsibilities if the immediate supervisor has not already done so, c) when called to a grand jury to testify on the matter, avoid perjuring yourself. *At no time* should you decide that the best way to handle the situation is to simply tell the alleged rapist not to bring small children onto organization property anymore.

You know, there's a part of me who looks at the actions of each of the non-raping grown men in the "Pennsylvania State University small-child-allegedly-being-raped-by-a-grown-man-who-is-part-of-the-football-hierarchy" scandal and can understand why those men could rationalize a) not immediately acting in the interests of a small child being raped, b) not immediately going to the police, c) doing only the minimum legal requirements in the situation, d) acting to keep from exposing their organization to a scandal. But here's the thing: that part of me? The part that understands these actions? That part of me is a *fucking coward.* And so by their actions—and by their inactions—were these men.

At least one sports columnist has made the point that Joe Paterno, the 40+ year coach of Penn State, who was fired last night (along with the university's president) by the university's board of trustees, should be remembered for all the good things he has stood for, and for his generosity and principles, even as this scandal, which brought his downfall, is now inevitably part of his legacy as well. And, well. I suspect that in time, even this horrible event will fade, and Paterno's legacy, to football and to Penn State, will rise above the tarnishment, especially because it can and will be argued that Paterno did all that was legally required of him, expressed regret and horror, and was not the man who was, after all, performing the acts.

Here's what I think about that, right now. I'm a science fiction writer, and one of the great stories of science fiction is "The Ones Who Walk Away From Omelas," which was written by Ursula K. Le Guin. The story posits a fantastic utopian city, where everything is beautiful, with one catch: In order for all this comfort and beauty to exist, one child must be kept in filth and misery. Every citizen of Omelas, when they come of age, is told about that one blameless child being put through hell. And they have a choice: Accept that is the price for their perfect lives in Omelas, or walk away from that paradise, into uncertainty and possibly chaos.

At Pennsylvania State University, a grown man found a blameless child being put through hell. Other grown men learned of it. Each of them had to make their choice, and decide, fundamentally, whether the continuation of their utopia—or at very least the illusion of their utopia—was worth the pain and suffering of that one child. Through their actions, and their inactions, we know the choice they made.

On How Many Times I Should Get Paid For a Book (By Readers)

Apr
7
2010

Randy Cohen, who writes the "Ethicist" column at the *New York Times*, caused a minor fracas this week when he told someone who had purchased a hardcover copy of Stephen King's *Under the Dome* and then also downloaded a pirated electronic copy for travel purposes, that they were ethically in the clear for the illegal download. Cohen's reasoning is, hey, the guy *paid* for the thing, and because he paid for it once, he should have the right to enjoy it in whatever format he likes. Therefore the download, while illegal, was not unethical.

Personally I think Cohen is pretty much correct. Speaking for myself (and *only* for myself), when I put out a book and you buy it for yourself in whatever format you choose to buy it in, the transactional aspect of our relationship is, to my mind, fulfilled. You bought the book once and I got paid once; after that if you get the book in some other format for your own personal use, and I don't get paid a second time, *eh*, that's life.

So, as examples: If you bought the paperback copy of one of my books and then liked it so much that you pick up a cheap remaindered hardcover edition for archival purposes, great. If you buy a hardcover copy, lose track of it, and then pick up a used paperback copy for re-reading, groovy. If you buy a trade paperback edition of one of my books and then happen to find a free electronic version of the same book, which you then download onto your cell phone for travel purposes, that seems reasonable to me.

Now, in each case, if you *decided* to pay me or any author a second time, I wouldn't complain—indeed, please do! Athena's college fund thanks you. And it's what I do; for example I recently paid for and downloaded an authorized electronic copy of China Mieville's *Perdido Street Station* because I wanted to read it again and my trade paper copy is currently in a box in my basement. I didn't want to bother to dig it out, I didn't want to have to troll the underside of Teh Internets for a pirate copy, I can afford the $6.39 an authorized copy cost, and I like paying authors. Likewise I usually buy new editions of books I've lost or displaced, again because I can afford it and because philosophically I am inclined to do so.

I pay the authors more than once, because I can and I think I should. However, I also put such actions in the ethical category of "morally praiseworthy but not morally obligatory"—that is, I believe my transactional responsibility to the author was fulfilled the first time I paid her. Additional payments to the author are optional, and indeed are sometimes transactionally difficult. If a book is out of print I may have no choice but to buy a used physical copy, for which an author gets nothing, or acquire an unauthorized electronic edition, which again gives nothing to the author.

The moral issue with unauthorized/pirated electronic copies of works has to do with the fact that a) they were put out online by people who didn't have permission to do so, and b) that it makes it easy for people who haven't paid for the work and have no intention of paying for it to acquire it and share it with other people who also have no intention of paying for it. These are *separate moral issues* than the issue of whether someone who has paid full freight for an author's work should feel bad about acquiring a second copy of the work for personal use without additional financial benefit to the author.

To be *very* clear, I think the person who puts an unauthorized edition of a work of mine online is ethically and legally wrong to do so; that guy is ripping me off. I don't take kindly to it and neither do my publishers, who have lots of lawyers. Please don't post my work online without permission, and please don't share unauthorized copies with others. I thank you in advance for your sterling morals in this area.

But if that work *is* out there online, and the guy who just bought an authorized version—thus paying me and the people who worked on the book—downloads it for his personal use, am I going to be pissed at him? No, I don't really have the time or inclination. Maybe it would have been marginally more ethical for the fellow to have, say, scanned in each individual page and OCR'd it himself, thus making the personal copy he's allowed to make under law, rather than looking for it online. And maybe I'd ask him how it was he got so knowledgeable in the ways of the dirty, dirty undernet, where pure and innocent books are exposed to bad people, and suggest to him that he get his computer checked for viruses. But at the end of the day, he *did* pay me, and paid my publisher.

(That said, I do think there are limits to this. For example, I think an audio book and a text book are two separate things, because a significant part of the audio book is the performance of the reader, an aspect that is not there in the original book. Likewise buying a book doesn't give you a free pass to torrent the movie version of the book; alternately, having bought a Halo video game doesn't give you a moral green light to snarf down a Halo novel. Etc.)

If I had my way about these things, I'd be doing with books what movie companies are now doing with DVDs and blu-rays, which is to bundle a legal electronic copy of the work in with the hardcover release. There are distribution issues with doing something like this (unlike physical movie media, books are typically sold unsealed) but these aren't unsolvable; I think in a later post I'll talk about this in more detail.

But the point to make here is that these days, people are deciding that when they buy a book or a movie or a piece of music, they're buying the content, not the format. As a writer I don't have a philosophical problem with this, since I write content, not format, even if publishers want that content to fit a particular format. And as a consumer, I think there's a certain point at which you get to say "you know what, I've *paid* for this already, and I'm done paying any more for it." Both of these are why I say that if you've paid me once for a book I've written and what you've enjoyed, we're good. Pay me again if you like; I won't complain. But once is enough.

On the Asking of Favors From Established Writers

Sep 15 2009

It looks like it's time to do a little more head-knocking regarding the life of a writer, so let's just start knocking heads, shall we.

Dear currently unpublished/newbie writers who spend their time bitching about how published/established writers are *mean* because they won't read your work/introduce you to their agent/give your manuscript to their editor/get you a job on their television show/whatever other thing it is you want them to do for you:

A few things you should know.

1. The job of a writer is to write. So, I'm looking at one of my book contracts. It says that I need to write a certain type of book (science fiction) of a certain length (100,000 words) by a certain time (er…Hmmm). In return, I get paid a certain amount of money. So that's the gig.

Here's what's *not* in the contract:

1. That I critique the novels of other people;
2. That I offer any advice to people on how to get published;
3. That I arrange introductions to my agent, editor or publisher;
4. That I do any damn thing, in fact, other than write the book I've agreed to write.

The job of a writer is to write.

To which you may say, "Yes, but—" To which I say, you've gone one word too far in that sentence. There is no 'but' involved. Once again: *The job of a writer is to write.* Anything else a writer does is entirely on his or her free time and subject to his or her own whim.

Commensurate to this:

2. A writer's obligations are not to you. Here is the list of the people and things to which I am obliged, in roughly descending order:

1. My wife and child.
2. My work.
3. My friends and the rest of my family.
4. My editors and producers.

Now, you might notice that you are probably not in that list. You know why? Because you and I don't share a life bond/genetic consanguinity/mutually beneficial business relationship.

Now, as it happens, I also feel an obligation to my various "communities"—the spread-out groups of people who share common interests with me—and one community I think about quite a bit is the community of writers. However, two things here. First, my sense of obligation to the community of writers is both voluntary and rather significantly less compelling to me than the obligations I feel to those enumerated above, and also does not mean I feel obliged to any particular member of that community (i.e., you). Second, there are lots of other writers who may not feel a similar communal obligation.

You may or may not feel this is proper on their part or mine, but so what? It's not up to you. Which brings us to:

3. The person who determines what a writer should do for others is the writer, not you. Why? Well, quite obviously, because it's not your life, and you don't get a say. And if you're somehow under the impression that well, yeah, actually you *do* have a say in that writer's life, take the following quiz:

Think of your favorite writer. Now, are you:

1. That writer?
2. That writer's spouse (or spousal equivalent)?
3. Rather below that, a member of that writer's immediate family?
4. Rather below *that*, the writer's editor or boss?

If the answer is "no" to the above, then guess what? *You don't get a vote.* And if you still assume you do, that writer is perfectly justified in being dreadfully rude to you. I certainly would be. I certainly *have* been, when someone has made such assertions or assumptions. And if necessary, I will be happy to be so again.

Beyond this, you don't know the circumstances of the writer's life, so you don't know what his capacity is for doing extra-curricular good deeds for random strangers, or his interest, or his ability. The writer may simply not have the time. He may not have the connections. He may not feel competent to evaluate your work. Or he may just not want to, because after everything else he does, he's *tired* and just wants to kill zombies on his computer.

Again, you may object to this, or feel your favorite writer should make a special exception for you and your work. But again: So what? It's not *your* life.

4. Writers are not dicks for not helping you. Let's say you ask me to read your work and I tell you "no." What happens then?

a) **You perish in a burning house.**
b) **You starve to death.**
c) **You die due to sepsis of the blood because both your kidneys have failed.**
d) **You are smothered by adorable kittens and fluffy bunnies.**
e) **Nothing.**

The correct answer is "e". Because you know what, my refusal to read your work has not damaged you or your work in any way. This is not a life or death situation, and all the normal ways of intake into the world of professional writing—the various query and submission processes, the workshops and writers circles—remain as open to you as they ever were.

Let's review. When you ask me (or any writer) to read your work, you are asking for a *favor.* A favor is generally understood to be something that someone is not obliged to do and is indeed an imposition, to a greater or lesser degree, on the person being asked by the person asking. People are not dicks for refusing to grant a favor, and someone who believes them so either doesn't understand the nature of a favor, or is a bit of a dick themselves for thinking that favors *must* or even *should* be granted.

Along this line:

5. People asking for favors from writers often don't understand the consequences of that favor. You know, right after I announced that I was hired as the Creative Consultant for *Stargate: Universe*, people I didn't know came out of the woodwork asking me if I could hook them up with gigs or send along their scripts or if I could give them the e-mail of the producers so they could talk to them about this great idea they had. You know what would have happened if I had done any of that? If you say "oh, you'd probably have gotten *fired*," you'd be *absolutely correct*. It would have been frankly *insane* for me to jeopardize my gig that way. I ended up putting up a note telling people to stop asking, but I still to this day get people who think that it's somehow *logical* to ask a complete stranger who knows nothing about them (and who they know nothing about) to carry water for them.

When you ask a favor of a writer, you're asking her to take time from her own work and/or her own life. You are asking her to assume you're not crazy or won't turn spiteful or angry when she can't give you 100% of what you want. You are asking her to assume that 10 years from now you won't sue her because something she's written is somewhat tangentially related to something you asked her to read. You're asking her to assume that continually pestering her own contacts on behalf of people she doesn't know at all won't jeopardize her own relationships with those contacts. And so on.

6. People asking favors from writers are often crazy in some undiagnosed way. Yes, I know. *You're* not crazy, and you won't become an asshole to the author, and you won't sue them even though that story is *exactly like yours was*, sorta. But there are two things here.

First, the people who ask a writer to do things for them underestimate the number of times authors get asked for these sorts of favors. People: you're not *special* when you ask us for our time/effort/connections. Personally, I started getting asked for hook-ups by strangers when

I was still in college (I was freelancing for the *Sun-Times* then), so that's two decades of being solicited, and no, not even posting a "why I won't read your unpublished work" post here stops it, because lots of people believe, oh, *that* doesn't apply to *them*.

Second, ask a writer and they will tell you a horror story of trying to help out someone by critiquing their novel or some other nice thing they tried to do in their capacity as a writer, only to have that person go *completely nuts* on them, for whatever reason. The specifics will vary, because crazy is a multi-headed hydra of abject terror, but just about every writer I know has a story. Some, who still believed in the fundamental sanity of people after such an experience, have two. Almost none have three.

The point is, *you* may be a nice, sane, rational person who will be grateful for any help you get from a writer. The problem is, other people out there are *flat-out bugshit nutbags*, and they are asking for the same things you are. It only takes one of them to ruin it for the rest of you, and the problem is that from the *outside*, you all look pretty much the same. Sorry.

7. Writers are not mystical door openers. At least not in a professional sense. If I read your novel and critiqued it, the critique will tell you how to make the novel more like something I want to read. But you know what? I'm not an acquiring editor at a publisher, and what I consider readable and what that editor were to consider saleable are likely not in parallel. Likewise, I could introduce you to my agent or editor, but I guarantee you that neither of them are going to suspend their judgment to rely on mine; they will happily reject your work if it doesn't suit their needs, even if I love it insensibly.

The most I or almost any other writer can get you, professionally speaking, is a small jump ahead in a line. But if your writing doesn't work, you're still going to get rejected. And if I spend all my time touting people who my agent and editor end up rejecting, in a very short period of time I'm going to become someone you definitely *don't* want on your side.

What it comes down to is that the belief that selling work really comes down to who you know is magical thinking, or at the very least it's *wildly overrated* in terms of what actually sells work. Yes, there are authors for whom their assurance of a blurb on your cover *might* convince a publisher to buy your novel, sight (and quality) unseen. Currently, they are called "Stephenie Meyer" and "Dan Brown."

As for every other writer in the land, well, it's nice you imagine us with such mighty powers. But you really are better off simply submitting your work the regular way.

Finally, there's this:

8. Writers remember: If you ask for a favor and I say no and your response is to throw a fit about how elitist writing assholes such as myself are pulling up the ladder after us and we all *suck,* I will remember that. If you ask for a favor and I say yes and you don't end up getting what you want and you throw a fit about it, I will remember that too. If you ask for a favor and I say no and your response is gracious, I will also remember that. And if you ask for a favor and I say yes, and you *do* end up getting what you want, I will remember how you respond to that as well. As will any writer in my position.

What will it mean that we remember these things about you? On one hand, it might not matter much. On the other hand, writers, like all professionals, talk shop. We talk shop with other writers, with editors, with publishers and with everyone else in our little industry. Occasionally we *are* in a position to help people. Occasionally we're in a position to influence the selection of a writer for an assignment. Occasionally there'll be work we've been offered and can't take, but will be in a position to suggest someone who can. Occasionally we'll switch hats and become editors or producers and be in a position to buy work. And then, of course, remembering *will,* in fact, matter.

It doesn't mean I or anyone else will take the opportunity to be a *dick,* mind you. We will simply remember who we think is worth helping or considering, and who is not.

And that's something for *you* to remember.

And now we're done.

On the Passing of Ray Bradbury: "Meeting the Wizard"

Jun
6
2012

As many of my readers know by now, Ray Bradbury, science fiction grandmaster, has passed away. To note the day, and what he meant to me, Subterranean Press has graciously allowed me to reprint here my introduction to its edition of Bradbury's *The Martian Chronicles*. It's called "Meeting the Wizard".

W

When I was twelve a wizard came to town.

And immediately I have to explain that comment.

First: Quite obviously, the wizard under discussion is Ray Bradbury.

Second: Understand that when you are the age you are now, and the age I am now, an author coming to town to talk about his work is no magical thing. The author may be your favorite author, and you may be genuinely excited to hear him or her speak—you may even be nervous and hoping you don't act like a complete fool when you get your forty seconds of conversation with them as they sign your book. But you know them as what they are: an author, a person, an ordinary human who happens to write the words you love to read.

But when you were twelve—or perhaps more accurately, when *I* was twelve—things were different. To begin, authors were not just common schmoes who happened to string words together. They were, in a word, mystics. When I was twelve I had been a reader for a decade and a writer for about a year, and in both cases at a stage where I was old enough to finally understand that writing didn't just *happen*; it was an expression of both will and imagination.

What I didn't know—and honestly at age twelve couldn't have known—was how to put the two together. I would walk through the stacks of my local library, where I spent a genuinely huge amount of my time, running my hands along the spines of the books, wondering that each book represented a single person. How did they make it happen? I could barely manage four pages in a lined composition book before I began to sweat. Here were whole books of dense, close-set, unlined words, spanning hundreds of pages.

I simply couldn't grasp how it could be done, and I think now that I believed something at age twelve that I would describe as a literary consonant to Clarke's Law: that any sustained effort of fiction writing was indistinguishable from magic. Magic was the only way people could possibly write as long, and as well, as they had to in order to make a book at the end.

Therefore: Authors were wizards.

And Ray Bradbury, to my mind at least, had to be the top wizard of all. Because of all the wizards practicing their craft—or of the ones I was reading at the time, which is possibly an important qualification—he was clearly the one most in control of his magic, the one who again even at the age of twelve I could see was doing something with his words that no one else I was reading was doing.

I should pause here to note that my introduction to Ray Bradbury had come the year before, in Mr. Johnson's sixth grade class at Ben Lomond Elementary, when I was assigned by my teacher to read *The Martian Chronicles*. Now, understand that being assigned a book is no positive thing. It's a well-known fact that if you wish to inspire in a child a vast hatred of any single book, all you have to do is assign it to him in school. This generally works like a charm, and is why, for example, I to this day loathe George Eliot's *The Mill on the Floss* with the sort of passion normally reserved for ex-spouses or whatever presidential candidate it is you're damn well not voting for.

Fortunately for me and for the book, there were two significant mitigating factors. The first was that I had already been inducted into the cult of the science fiction geek; the door had opened in the fourth grade, with a copy of Robert Heinlein's *Farmer in the Sky*. I had wasted little time getting myself over the threshold, burning through the school library's rather meager collection of science fiction—mostly Heinlein juvies and a few poor imitations of Heinlein juvies, their titles and authors now lost due to pre-adolescent critical expunging from memory. I was primed, basically, to receive the book.

The second factor was that the book came, not from an approved curriculum list, but from Mr. Johnson himself. Every student has the teacher who looms in memory, and Keith Johnson is mine—a fine, handsome and fearfully smart man who didn't take any crap (which is an excellent trait in handling sixth graders) but who also saw each of his students as an individual (which is an *exceptional* trait in handling sixth graders). Mr. Johnson gave me *The Martian Chronicles* to read and said this to me as he handed it over: "You *should* be reading this." He also said it was one of his favorite books.

To get the book, vouched for in that way, felt like an intimacy between the two of us. I realize using the word "intimacy" there opens things up to an unseemly interpretation, which would be, mind you, ridiculous. What it means is that while in no way stepping out of the teacher-student relationship, Mr. Johnson was treating me as a confidant, and even in a small way as an equal: *This book means something to me*, he was saying. *It might mean something to you, too.* It was, in other words, a powerful recommendation.

And Mr. Johnson was right. It meant something to me. *The Martian Chronicles* is not a child's book, but it is an excellent book to give to a child—or to give to the right child, which I flatter myself that I was—because it is a book that is full of *awakening*. Which means, simply, that when you read it, you can feel parts of your brain clicking on, becoming sensitized to the fact that *something is happening here*, in this book, with these words, even if you can't actually communicate to anyone outside of your own head just what that something is. I certainly couldn't have, in the sixth grade—I simply didn't have the words. As I recall, I didn't much try: I just sat there staring down at the final line of the book, with the Martians staring back at me, simply trying to process what I had just read.

I could tell you now about all of it—I'm a good enough wizard on my own now—but that would take more space than you would have tolerance for in an introduction. I know you are eager to get through this and start re-reading the book you love.

But I will give you one example: *The Martian Chronicles* was the first book to make me understand that words themselves, and in themselves, had power. The genre of science fiction vaunts itself as the literature of ideas, which seems a bit much. It's more to the point that it's the literature of *engineering*, originally springing forth from the minds of proto-geeks fascinated with the technical potential of the future. These men (and occasional women) used words as fine-tooled machines to work those ideas into print, practically rather than poetically.

There's nothing wrong with this. I largely stand in this tradition myself. What it does mean, however, is that much of science fiction prose reads flat. Great colorful playful ideas, packaged in a big cardboard box.

Ray Bradbury's words are not a cardboard container for his ideas. His words have weight and rhythm and pace and form; they are a scaffold of filigree for his ideas to weave themselves in and around, taking form through them. Bradbury's people did not exist for the sake of exposition or simply to have things happen to them: He sketched them in what they said (or didn't say), and how they said them or not. Words gave rise to character, economically but fully revealing a spaceman disgusted with his people, two strangers from different times meeting on a road, a man who learns he's okay being alone, a father teaching his children about who the Martians truly are.

The Martian Chronicles was the first science fiction book to make me feel a character's righteous rage (not to mention the concept of ironically literal death, both in the same chapter) and the first science fiction book to make me feel loss and loneliness in my gut, doing it without featuring a single human, save as a shadow on a wall. And more than the first science fiction that did all these things: the first fiction, too.

The Martian Chronicles, in short, showed me what words can truly do. It showed me magic.

And now you might understand how, at age twelve, I was amazed beyond words that this wizard was coming to town, and would be somewhere I could meet him and see him, in the flesh, for myself. Because I was geek enough to be well-known to all the librarians, who were hosting this wizard's appearance, I managed to wheedle my way into being in the group that would welcome him to the library and would get him ready to meet his public in our library's common room, which we grandly but not wholly inaccurately labeled a "forum." I would meet this wizard of all wizards, I would spend time with him, and perhaps I might even get him to show me some of his secrets. It was an excellent plan.

Which didn't work. Ray Bradbury's magic is strong, but the black magic of the 210 Freeway at rush hour is stronger—Bradbury arrived only minutes before he was set to speak. Nevertheless, the librarians, knowing how excited I was to meet him, pushed me forward and introduced me to him, and gave me a prime opportunity to talk magic with the wizard.

At which point my tongue, previously full of questions, fell out of my head, and all I could do was squeak about how much I liked his books. As I recall, the wizard tousled my hair, said something I don't remember except that it was kind, signed the copy of *The Martian Chronicles* I had in my hand, and then went up to our forum to do another kind of magic, which was to entertain a room full of admirers for an hour.

I would say that I never got another chance to have the wizard show me his magic, but that's not quite true. I never have met Ray Bradbury again in person. His magic, however, is there in his work. When you read it, if you pay attention, the wizard shows you all his magic and power. If you're smart, you see how it works. If you have some talent, you might be able to pull off a trick or two. Will you become a wizard? Well, that depends on many things, some of which will not be under your control. But you won't be able to say that this particular wizard has not been generous with his magic.

What I have never gotten another chance to do, however, is to thank the wizard, for what he's showed me and taught me and how he's inspired me to use my own magic. This seems as good a time and place as any. So thank you, Mr. Bradbury, for all of it.

And now, like the rest of you, I'm off to read *The Martian Chronicles* another time. I suspect this wizard has more magic to show me here. I want to see it.

The Only Time the Conservative Politicians Ignore Warren Buffett

Aug
15
2011

It's when he tells them it's okay to tax the rich more, as he does in a recent *New York Times* opinion piece. Indeed, Buffett is not only saying that it's okay to tax the rich, but that the rich *ought* to be taxed more, because they are disproportionately shielded from the "shared sacrifice" that the rest of America's citizens are being asked to shoulder:

> *While the poor and middle class fight for us in Afghanistan, and while most Americans struggle to make ends meet, we mega-rich continue to get our extraordinary tax breaks. Some of us are investment managers who earn billions from our daily labors but are allowed to classify our income as "carried interest," thereby getting a bargain 15 percent tax rate. Others own stock index futures for 10 minutes and have 60 percent of their gain taxed at 15 percent, as if they'd been long-term investors...*
>
> *Last year my federal tax bill—the income tax I paid, as well as payroll taxes paid by me and on my behalf—was $6,938,744. That sounds like a lot of money. But what I paid was only 17.4 percent of my taxable income—and that's actually a lower percentage than was paid by any of the other 20 people in our office. Their tax burdens ranged from 33 percent to 41 percent and averaged 36 percent...*
>
> *[T]hose making more than $1 million—there were 236,883 such households in 2009—I would raise rates immediately on taxable income in excess of $1 million, including, of course, dividends and capital gains. And for those who make $10 million or more—there were 8,274 in 2009—I would suggest an additional increase in rate.*

Buffett's opinion piece does not only suggest raising taxes on the rich; he also and reasonably points out that there is a need to trim back spending, obliquely referring to "promises that even a rich America can't fulfill." Fair enough; there's not a lot of specificity there, but then, the piece isn't about those things, it's about taxes. Buffett's point there is simple: The rich, in fact, will do just fine if you raise their taxes a bit. They will do just fine because, among other things, they are doing just fine already.

The worries for the tender sensibilities of the rich has been a hallmark of conservative American politics since time immemorial, but the current gag-inducingly lickspittle levels of it are a bit much. Among other culpable parties, I lay some blame for this at the altar of Ayn Rand, who imagined a world in which the titan of industries "go Galt" in the face of creeping socialism. Over time the rather silly book this scenario plays out in has been confused by the greedy and clueless (and cynically touted by the greedy but somewhat more crafty) as a reasonable simulacrum of the real world, to the extent that I think there's a genuine fear by the credulous—which unfortunately correlates to the most vocal elements of both Republican primary voters and politicians today—that if the state moves to raise taxes on the wealthy, the lot of them will flounce in a huff, taking their money with them and retiring to a crevasse where they will await the end of the world. This sort of madness is gussied up and made slightly more respectable by rhetorical feints, like calling the very rich "job creators," as if the investment bankers profiting by passing off crappy mortgages as AAA investments ever created a job, or the folks who increase shareholder value by laying off ten of thousands of workers are job creators.

Leaving aside the fact that raising taxes on the capital gains that people accrue by pushing around electrons in a financial system that ultimately is not tied into any tangible measure of value is not the same thing as nationalizing real-world industries, in the same way that being tickled by a feather duster is not the same thing as being attacked by a large flock of angry geese, this misapprehends the psychology of those who desire to become very very rich, or who are already very rich and wish to be more so. The sort of person who is very rich does not become so by flouncing when the rules of the game change, to sulk in a gully. The sort of person who is very rich becomes so by understanding the rules of the game and *leveraging them to their maximum benefit*. This is why there have *always* been the ridiculously rich, even in times when the top marginal tax rate in the United States was 92%. The very rich don't flounce, they fiddle. They always have. They always will. The fantasy of the enraged rich packing up and going is just that, a fantasy.

It's not a particular surprise that recent polls say the majority of Americans would like to see the wealthiest Americans taxed more, because most Americans seem to realize that bringing in more revenue is an essential part of dealing with debt. The problem here as I see it is that the majority of people who agree that taxes need to be raised are somewhat squishy on the subject, while the minority of people who are opposed to *any* taxes being raised *ever* are very very very very opposed. They are so opposed that there's little chance of reasoning with them; even Warren Buffett, by many measures the most successful investor of the last half century, is unlikely to get them to entertain the possibility that the very rich will survive a few ticks up on their marginal income rates. They'll happily take his advice on any other aspect of the business world except for this.

This does raise the question: In matters of governmental fiscal policy, if one is to follow the advice of someone who is not an economist by profession, is it smarter to follow the economic advice of a man who has played the financial world to the tune of $50 billion in personal wealth, or that of a writer who bent her own moral and philosophical rules to take government assistance when it was fiscally convenient for her to do so (although she of course had a fine rationalization for that, which is generally consistent with how many conservatives square away their use of government services and programs they oppose)? The answer to this question for many conservative folks is not about what is smart, but rather what is politically and philosophically orthodox, so I wouldn't expect much by way of an answer here.

As someone who in the short term benefits from the current conservative overweening solicitousness for my financial well-being, but who in the long-term would like a solvent, financially-stable country with a healthy middle class and solid if basic social net, I find myself generally aligned with Buffett here. Yes, please, raise taxes on the wealthiest Americans, and I include myself in that (although I'm definitely waaaaay down the list from Mr. Buffett, and indeed below his suggested cutoff; even so). It's not the *only* answer to the financial mess the United States finds itself in these days. But it is *part* of the answer. You don't have to be worth $50 billion to see that.

An Open Letter to MFA Writing Programs (and Their Students)

Nov
15
2010

Dear MFA writing programs (and their students):

Recently *New York* magazine published a story, in which Columbia University's graduate writing program invited James Frey to come chat with its students on the subject of "Can Truth Be Told?" during which Frey mentioned a book packaging scheme that he had cooked up. The contractual terms of that book packaging scheme are now famously known to be egregious—it's the sort of contract, in fact, that you would sign only if you were as ignorant as a chicken, and with about as much common sense—and yet it seems that Frey did not have any problem getting people to sign on, most, it appears, students of MFA programs. Frey is clearly selecting for his scheme writers who should know better, but don't—and there's apparently a high correlation between being ignorant that his contract is horrible and being an MFA writing student.

I don't blame Columbia University's graduate writing program for inviting James Frey over to talk to its students about "truth." If there's anyone who knows about the word *truth* contained between ironic quotation marks, it'd be James Frey, and it's probably not a bad idea for the kids to see a prevaricating hustler up close to observe how one of his kind can rationalize bad actions and even poorer ethics as transgressive attempts at literature. It's always a joy to see how a master of bullshit spins himself up; publishing and literature being what they are, the students should probably learn to recognize this species sooner than later, all the better to move their wallets to their front pockets when such a creature stands before them.

What does bother me, however, is that Frey apparently quite intentionally was working his way through MFA programs recruiting writers for his book packaging scheme. You could say there's an obvious reason for this, which is that MFA writing students are likely more competent at writing than your average schmoe writer on the street (this is a highly arguable contention, but never mind that now), and they're all in one place, which makes for easier recruiting. But I suspect there's another reason as well, which is that in general it appears MFA writing programs don't go out of their way educate their students on the publishing industry, or contracts, or much about the actual business of writing.

And so when someone like James Frey breezes in and starts blowing smoke about collaborations, the response is this—

> *We were desperate to be published, any way we could. We were spending $45,000 on tuition, some of us without financial aid, and many taking out loans that were lining us up to graduate six figures in debt. A deal like the one Frey was offering could potentially pay off our loans and provide an income for the next decade. Do a little commercial work under a pseudonym, sell the movie rights, and never have to suffer as a writer in New York. We wouldn't even need day jobs.*

—followed by a number of students receiving and then signing a contract that pays them next to nothing, and offers a deal so constrictive that by the terms of the contract Frey could publish works under their names and keep them from publishing again (via a gloriously vague "non-compete" clause). Frey was no doubt counting on the students being starry-eyed at the presence of a real-live bestselling author (even a disgraced one) who was waving a movie deal in their faces, but one reason he *could* count on it was because he was speaking to an audience whose formal educations did not include learning how to spot a crappy deal.

So, MFA writing programs, allow me to make a suggestion. Sometime before you hand over that sheepskin with the words "Master of Fine Arts" on it, for which your students may have just paid tens of thousands of dollars (or more), offer them a class on the business of the publishing industry, including an intensive look at contracts. Why? Because, Holy God, *they will need it*.

Now, perhaps you are saying, "We focus on the art of writing, not the business." My answer to that is, please, pull your head out. Your students are not paying as much money as they do for your program strictly for the *theoretical* joys of writing. They are paying so they can publish, and it's a pretty good bet, considering how many of those Columbia folks scrambled to pitch to Frey, that they actually want to be published *commercially*, not just in university presses, in which (sorry) low advances and small print runs don't matter since it's just another line on the CV. Yes, you are teaching an art, but whether you like it or not you're also teaching a trade—or at the very least many of your students are coming to learn a trade, and put up with the art portion of it as part of the deal. Teaching them something about the trade will not hurt your program.

And then you might say, "there's no point in teaching them about the business because if they go the commercial publishing route they'll have agents." To which I would say, wow, really? "Other people will handle the dirty money part" is a response that a) shows a certain amount of snobbery, b) sets up a writer to be dependent on others because she is ignorant of the particulars of her own business. You know how every year you hear about an actor or musician who has been screwed by his accountant or business manager? That's what happens when you don't pay attention—or more relevantly don't have the *knowledge* to pay attention.

To be clear, I don't want to paint literary agents, *et al* as suspicious and shady characters; I have two literary agents (one for fiction and one for non-fiction) and they are super-smart and do a great job for me, and I'm glad they do their job and leave me to do mine, which is writing. But you know what? Part of the reason I know they're doing a good job is because I know my own business, which makes it easier for me to know what they are doing. It also means they know that they can discuss business with me on a realistic and sensible level. Beyond that, not everyone has an agent, or (alas) a good one if they have one.

Finally, you may say "We don't have anyone on our faculty who can/wants to teach that course." Well, presuming that your university doesn't have a business or law school on campus, from whom you might borrow an appropriate professor every now and again, I can't help but notice that adjunct professors are very popular in academia these days, and I'm guessing that maybe you could find someone. Try a working agent, maybe. Point is, if you wanted to offer this class, you could.

There is no reason not to offer a class on this stuff. And maybe students will choose not to take that class. But if that's the case, at least *then it's all on them.* Your students are all presumably adults and are responsible for their own actions, to be sure. But if you're not giving them the tools to know when a huckster is hucking in their direction, if they get hulled, some of that's on you.

Speaking of which, let me now turn my attention away from the MFA writing programs and to the writing grad students themselves:

Dudes. *Learn about the industry,* already, *before* you sign a contract. Otherwise you're going to get shaved by the first jackass who waves a publishing deal in your face. Yes, I know, you're smart and clever and you write really well. You know what, your belief in your intelligence and your cleverness and your writing ability as a proxy for knowing everything you need to know about the world is *exactly* what's going to get you screwed. Because being smart and clever and writing well has *nothing* to do with the backend business of the publishing industry or reading a contract knowledgeably and dispassionately. Think about those MFA students who are now slaving away for Frey on the worst contract just about anyone in publishing has ever seen. I'm pretty sure they all think they are smart and clever and write well, too.

If your MFA program doesn't have a class on contracts and the publishing industry, ask for one. Because, Jesus, you're spending enough for your education. You might want to get some practical knowledge out of it as well. If it can't or won't offer that class to you, a) complain and b) seek out that information. The writers' organization to which I belong, SFWA, sponsors Writer Beware, which offers some of the basics about avoiding scams and bad practices, and has an informational area which includes sample contracts. Other writers' organizations also have information for you, and most bookstores will have sections on writing and the business of writing. Find that information, learn it, and use it before you have anything to do with anyone trying to make a deal with you.

But why you should have to pay extra for this essential bit of education, or search for it outside your writing program, mind you, positively baffles me.

Osama, Obama, and Us

May

2

2011

And now, some further thoughts on the death of Osama bin Laden.

* In a very practical sense, bin Laden's death doesn't change anything, particularly in the short run. He's been on the run for years, al Qaeda is designed to be decentralized, the scope of our military operations in the Middle East far exceed the boundaries of bin Laden's group. Today we still have troops in Afghanistan, and their job there will not be any easier today than it was yesterday. The Middle East itself is not the same region it was a decade ago; it seems to have developed a home-grown taste for democracy. So on and so forth.

But in an existential and psychological sense bin Laden's death makes a huge difference. Dude's been out there for years, and the fact The Most Powerful Country in the World™ couldn't get to him was an overarching narrative frame for much of what else the US did in the last decade. But in the end we did get to him, and the frame has changed. No longer was the US engaged in a futile pursuit of a man who killed thousands of our citizens and would die of renal failure far out of its reach; now the US engaged in a ceaseless pursuit, and in the end bin Laden received a form of justice from his actions, i.e., an American bullet in (or as seems likely more accurate, through) the brain that conceived of 9/11.

Changing the frame from "hapless" to "implacable" means something to us as Americans and also, I expect, means something to others as well, particularly for the folks for whom "bin Laden is laughing at the US" was part of their worldview. What effect the existential impact of bin Laden's death will have on the practical life of the US and the rest of the world over the long term is something we'll get to find out in the coming months and years. No matter what, however, bin Laden will still be dead, and that has a cathartic, and I optimistically suspect in the long run *useful*, finality all its own.

* In the immediate aftermath of Obama's announcement of bin Laden's death last night I saw some folks on my Twitter feed note that it was too bad we killed him rather than captured him and put him on trial. I would have been happy with that as an outcome, but I can't say that I would have been *happier* with that outcome than what actually happened. Bin Laden killed in a firefight with US operatives, none of whom were killed? All right then. No complaints on this end and good shooting.

There would have been some pleasure in seeing him in the dock, being confronted with his crimes, ably represented by the best defense his money could buy, getting buried by the evidence, and then kept in a tiny cell for as long as we could keep him alive. But inasmuch as I expect that bin Laden was akin to the types who maintain that a fringe on a court flag means it's a court of the admiralty and therefore can't try them for tax evasion—and was perfectly happy to have murdered lots of innocents in any event—this works too. I don't imagine bin Laden was hoping to spend many days in a courtroom, either. In this one thing I don't feel it to have been much of an imposition to oblige him.

* The fact that a closet Muslim socialist WHO ISN'T EVEN AN AMERICAN is the one who gave the order to kill the bogeyman who has haunted the US for a decade will be a terribly inconvenient fact for a lot of folks. Well, let it be. If only for a moment, it serves to remind us that the job of a president is a serious one, while the job of tearing down a president can be done by morons, and often is. This definitely puts Obama's birther jabs at Donald Trump over the weekend at the White House correspondent's dinner in a whole new context; as someone else has noted, Obama's not a guy you want to play poker with, because he's got the straightest face in the business.

People are already speculating what this means for Obama in 2012. I think it means that any rumblings about a Democratic primary challenge are now done. It also makes it more difficult for the GOP to paint him as Carter II: The Quickening, although of course they certainly will try to do so; they can't help themselves, and I think at this point the Democrats would invite them to keep trying. In a larger sense, if the economy falters Obama will still be vulnerable in his quest for a second term. But if it's coming along, then 2012 won't be a happy presidential election cycle for the GOP. Dude had bin Laden killed. Kind of hard to top.

Oscar and Me

Mar
3
2010

Because the Oscars are coming up, I dug out of the archives this story I wrote for the *Washington Post* about ten years ago, about when I borrowed my friend's Oscar statuette. Enjoy.

Oscar and Me

Some time ago, I needed an Oscar—(Why? Does it matter? If you thought you could legally get hold of an Academy Award, wouldn't you? Now, then)—and as it happened, I knew where to find one. My friend Pam Wallace had picked one up for writing a little film called "Witness." I asked if I might borrow it. Sure, she said; she trusts me, and besides, she knows where I live.

Hours later, the Oscar was mine, wrapped in a beach towel and stuffed into the trunk of my car. I'd hit the brakes, there'd be a soft thunk as the Oscar hit its head on the tire jack. It would be the first of many indignities that Oscar would suffer in his three days with me. As you might imagine, having an Oscar, even for just three days, is an educational experience. Here's what I learned.

1. Oscars Are Heavy. An Oscar weighs about 8 1/2 pounds, about as much as a newborn baby, and people react to both much the same way—they hold them gently with both hands, stare at them lovingly and pray they don't accidentally drop them. The side effect of this weight is that one gets physically tired of handling an Oscar; hold one too long and your arm cramps. A friend of mine once said to me, "Man, if I had an Oscar, I'd wear it around my neck." This is inadvisable. In addition to Oscar being the ugliest neckwear since disco medallions, your neck would develop such a crick.

You'd think the heft of the Oscar would underscore the solid Midwestern craftsmanship that goes into making the things (they're made in Chicago by R.S. Owens & Co.), but the fact of the matter is…

2. Oscars Are Kind of Flimsy. Flick the base with your finger, and it resonates with a static-like buzz reminiscent of an AM transistor radio. This is truly disappointing; you'd think the most coveted trophy in the world would have a sturdier base. In fact, up until 1945, it was made out of Belgian marble. I suppose they thought that after the ravages of war, taking marble from the Belgians would seem kind of mean. De-marbleized, today's Oscars are notably top-heavy, which I expect leads to a lot of unintentional drops and falls. Pam's Oscar, in fact, has a chip gouged out of its forehead from such a calamity. You can peer right in and see what passes for Oscar's brains. Which leads to the next Oscar discovery…

3. Oscars Aren't Golden All the Way Through. It's something of a shock to examine Oscar's insides and find they are made of the same britannia metal (90 percent tin, 10 percent antimony) that goes into making flatware. Your fork is Oscar's cousin. In a way it's entirely appropriate to have the symbol of Hollywood be base metal innards covered with a thin golden coating. But, you know, whatever. An Oscar is still an Oscar. In a world where the vast majority of humanity couldn't tell the difference between a Pulitzer Prize and the Best of Show ribbon given to hogs at a county fair (the difference: Best of Show winners get stud fees), the Oscar is immediately recognized, admired and coveted. How recognized? How coveted? Consider the following…

4. Everyone Has an Oscar Acceptance Speech. Every single person I handed the Oscar to did the same thing: Placed the Oscar at a tilt—one hand mid-statue, the other cradling the bottom of the base—looked to the middle distance (where the television cameras would be) and said, "I'd like to thank the academy for this award…" It's positively Pavlovian.

This makes sense. The only time most of us actually see an Oscar is when someone's just won it. There's no other context. You don't see them in people's yards, like lawn gnomes. They aren't photographed visiting the Grand Canyon or Yosemite. They're not in a book titled "Where's Oscar?"

Oscars exist solely to be followed by a speech. Not to make one would be to violate the fundamental laws of the universe. The Academy Award that people see themselves winning is a personality test in itself. The vain "win" Best Actor or Best Actress; the control freaks, Best Director; the frustrated intellectuals, Best Screenplay. Passive-aggressives choose supporting actor categories. No one ever pretends to be the producer; no one knows what producers do. No one ever pretends to win the minor categories either, like sound effects editing or art direction. Everyone knows that after 30 seconds, these people are cut off by the orchestra conductor.

Everyone wants an Oscar, but what do you do when you get one? For everything it represents (fame, fortune, a real chance that you will get to date someone like Gwyneth Paltrow), ultimately the Oscar itself is nothing more than an art deco tchotchke. Perhaps this is the cause of the final Oscar discovery…

5. People Who Have Oscars Are Far Less Impressed With Them Than People Who Don't. Hollywood is rife with stories of Oscar winners using their statuettes as doorstops, to prop up tables or to smash bugs (or budding screenwriters) crawling around their desks. Jodie Foster was told by her local video store staff that if she won the Oscar for "The Silence of the Lambs" and brought it in for them to look at, she'd get a free rental. She did, and did, and did. Even my friend Pam treats her Oscar with something less than total reverence. When it's not being borrowed by goofball pals, it's covered by a gorilla puppet her son made in elementary school.

You could argue this is a sort of protective false humility, since the only thing Hollywood likes less than someone without an Oscar is someone who wins one and gloats (henceforth to be known as "James

Cameron Syndrome"). There's something to this, but there's also just the fact that even the extraordinary becomes boring after a while. I stand testament to this—the first day I had the Oscar in the house, I stared at it like a graven image. The second day I got used to it. The third day I was using it as a paperweight. Which precipitated the following exchange between me and my wife:

Wife: Where'd you put the phone bill?

Me: I dunno. Did you check under the Oscar?

God, I loved saying that.

A Passing Thought

Jul
28
2010

I now have in my possession a pocket-sized computer which, when I speak a question to it ("Who is the author of *Kraken*?" "Who was the fourteenth president of the United States?" "What is the name of John Scalzi's cat?") provides me an answer in just a few seconds. If I take a picture of something, the same pocket computer will analyze the photo and tell me what I'm looking at. Oh, and it makes phone calls, too. Among other things.

None of that is the cool part. The cool part is, when I speak a question to my pocket computer and it gives me a bad answer, *I get annoyed*. Because here in the future, when I talk to my pocket computer, I expect it to get the answer right the first time.

I think I've said before that one of the neat things about getting older is that you really do become aware just how much things change. To be more specific about it, as you get older, at some point you cross an arbitrary line and are aware that you are now living *in the future*. I'm not precisely sure when it was I crossed my own arbitrary Future Line, but I'll tell you what, I'm well past it now.

That is all. Carry on.

The Paul Ryan Pick

Aug 11 2012

Two things:

1. It's really the best Romney could do. If it sounds like faint praise, well, it is, but the fault is neither Romney's nor Ryan's. It's the GOP's, because its current bench of viable national players is pretty thin at this point. I mean, I looked at the list of VP prospectives and, with the exception of the possible positive optics of Marco Rubio, didn't see a whole lot of *there* there. Pawlenty? Portman? I'm just going to go over here and take a nap. Governors Christie, McDonnell and Jindal are probably happy to sit out 2012 and prep for 2016 instead (or 2020, if it actually rolls that way), and other than that, who really is there for the GOP?

Some folks hinted toward Condi Rice, who, to be honest, I think would probably be an excellent VP. But she's got the stink of the Bush Administration still on her, and anyway, the fact that she's not safely married off *to a man* would probably freak out a lot of the GOP base. Given the field of whackjobs and dimwits that contested against Romney in the primaries, he couldn't reasonably expect to tap one of them and not scare away every independent voter in the land (the one exception to this, Jon Huntsman, is a fellow LDS Church member, and I'm pretty sure an all-LDS ticket would sorely test those across the political spectrum for whom all they know of the LDS Church is what they saw on *Big Love* and that Broadway musical). So no love there.

With Ryan, Romney does himself no damage with GOP voters, and indeed quite the opposite: Ryan is well-liked in the party in general and also in Washington (where as I understand it even people who don't share his politics find him to be a pleasant fellow to work with and be around). He has no major personal skeletons in the closet, and has solid conservative credentials. As the House Budget Committee chairman, and the author of a number of proposed budget plans, he is what passes for a serious thinker in the Republican Party these days. Ryan can help deliver Wisconsin to Romney, which is 10 electoral votes he's going to need, and I suspect the thinking is that he might be able to put other parts of the Midwest into play as well, including Ohio, which right now is leaning Obama. And it signals to GOP voters that Romney—former Governor of the gayest commonwealth in the Union, who socialized medicine while he was in office there—is solidly behind the current conservative blueprints for the future of America. After all, Ryan is the architect of those blueprints, and those blueprints really do offer a solid contrast against what Obama has to offer (Romney maintains he is going to put together his own budget plan rather than run on Ryan's, and I wish him the best of luck convincing anyone of that).

So, yes, Ryan really is the best Romney could have done. Now a substantial number of GOP voters will be voting *for* him (or at least for the ticket), rather than simply against Obama.

2. Ryan is the fellow that Obama's used as a rope-a-dope punching bag at least a couple of times now because of his economic plans, and if you're under the impression Obama's not going to do it again, bigger and better than ever before, just you *wait*. There's also the question of whether Ryan does anything to bring in independent and undecided voters in any way. I don't think he does directly because generally speaking VP candidates don't really do that except possibly in their own state, and he'll only do it indirectly if voters twig to his economic plans, which will now be pressed to the forefront. That's going to be a matter of selling, and of selling a vision that someone else (read: Obama and all the

SuperPACs on his side of the divide) will be spending the next three months punching at, hard.

It's going to be a challenge, in part because I suspect there's a growing belief that the rich aren't in fact holy job creators, nor would it invoke the end times if they were taxed a bit more, and partly because at the end of the day Obama is like Clinton and Reagan before him: A charismatic leader blessed with a leaden opponent. Nor is Ryan much help in that department. He may be likable but he's not exactly charismatic; he comes across as the overly earnest sort who really believes what he believes and is sad and hurt when you don't believe it with him. I suspect Biden is going to eat him alive in their debate. And in any event, even if Ryan had the charisma of Brad Pitt, he's still not the fellow in the big chair; that's Romney. Romney's biggest problem is still Romney.

On a personal level, while I believe that Ryan is the best Romney could do under the circumstances, I think this suggests something not very good about the circumstances. I don't think Ryan rises to Newt Gingrich levels of "a dumb person's idea of a smart person," but I have to admit being flummoxed by the amount of regard the GOP and conservatives have for his economic blueprints. Ryan has publicly distanced himself from Ayn Rand, whom he reportedly admired, which I think speaks well of him (if you consider Ayn Rand a serious political thinker rather than a philosophical and economic dilettante with a flair for potboilery prose, you get put into the "hasn't quite grown up" category in my brain). His economic thinking, however, still bears the smudgy marks of the pseudo-objectivist doctrine that modern conservatives have, with its belief in the inherent malignancy of government and the inerrancy of private enterprise. His economic plans strike me as naïve at best and disingenuously meretricious at worst. That they are now the guiding star for the GOP's plans for the US makes me want to get the lot of them into a doctor's office to see if they are, as a class, suffering from hypoxia. Ryan would be the first into the examination room. I don't doubt his sincerity, but I do doubt his good sense.

That said, I don't see Ryan's brand of economic thinking going anywhere anytime soon. More to the point, there's nothing about Paul Ryan being elevated to Vice Presidential candidate that is anything but good for Ryan. If Romney wins, then quite obviously Ryan is going to have a nearly clear path to put his economic vision into effect. If Romney loses, no one in the GOP is going to blame Ryan or his economic plans for it; everyone will blame Romney for being a weak candidate and his team for not selling Ryan's economic plan to the nation the way it should be been sold. Ryan goes back to the House (he doesn't have to give up his seat unless Romney wins) a tragic conservative hero and positions himself, and his economic plan, for 2016. There's not a whole lot of downside to this for Ryan.

At least on paper. It'll be interesting to see how it works out for him, and for us, in the real world.

PEAK GINGRICH

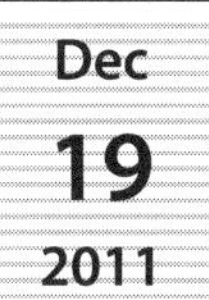

Talking Points Memo notes that Newt Gingrich's poll numbers peaked a few days ago and now seem on a decline of the sort one sees on rollercoasters or cliffs. I'd personally like to think it was because Gingrich blathered stupidly about how he'd arrest federal judges whose rulings he didn't like; there is a word for the sort of leader who responds to the Constitutionally-approved concept of the independent judicial branch by threatening its members with arrest, and it's not "president."

But that's only a specific case of a more general issue with Gingrich, which I imagine the GOP electorate is now remembering about him: Gingrich, bless his heart, can only give a stab at being a statesman in brief, isolated bursts. Then his Gingrichosity shines through, he decouples prudence from his pie hole, and he starts doing the 68-year-old poltiwonk version of a college freshman midnight bull session, only in public and in front of cameras, and without someone there to say "whoa, duuuude, you're getting *pretty out there*" before passing over the bong to mellow him out. He just can't shut up.

It's not *just* that he can't shut up. It's that Gingrich is also apparently incapable of distinguishing which of his ideas are reasonable, and which ones have been beamed in straight from a transmitter located on a high mountain deep in the heart of FrothyLand. It's not that Gingrich doesn't have some good ideas in his head. He does. The problem is they share space with some *absolutely terrifying* ideas. When Gingrich prepares to hork an idea out of his mouth, he doesn't roll it around first to see if it tastes bad. He just spits it out, and there it is, on the carpet, Gingrich looking at you in that way he has, the way that says *yet another brilliant thought from the mind of Newt. You're welcome.* And then the idea rears up, hisses at you, and tries to mate, horribly, with your shoe.

This is why, should Gingrich buck the current trend and gain the GOP nomination, the *absolute worst thing* he could do is have a Lincoln-Douglas-style debate with President Obama. Seriously: an hour to ninety minutes of raw, unscripted, *uninterrupted* Gingrich? There is no limit to the size of the hole that man will dig for himself, all the while thinking how dazzling he's being. And there's Obama, grinning his ass off, letting Gingrich dig, waiting for his turn. If we know anything about Obama, it's that he knows how to stay focused and on message. He'd do just fine in a long form debate; you might not like the policies he espouses but you can bet he'd promulgate them in a safe and sane-sounding way, which, to anyone not already in the Gingrich camp, and with the fortitude to withstand an entire three-hour debate, would be all he would need. Obama might bore you, but he wouldn't scare you.

Dear Newt: Obama would *love* to do a Lincoln-Douglas debate with you. He would love it more than *candy*. But it looks like he won't get that chance.

Mind you, Gingrich's essential Gingrichosity is not the only reason he's trending down at the moment. The scads of negative ads his opponents are targeting at him are doing their fair share as well, and as I understand it Gingrich's campaign is cash-poor enough that responding to those ads has not been something he's been about to afford much of (he did just make an ad buy in Iowa, but it's small compared to the ad buys of Romney and Perry). Even so, I don't think Gingrich being Gingrich helps him any.

He can draw this out a while (and make no mistake that the Democrats would *love* for him to do that, as long as humanly possible) but at the end of the day the reason I suspect we've hit and passed the Peak Gingrich moment is because ultimately Gingrich reminds people of someone who is an unpleasant showoff. The person he's reminding them of is possibly him.

Procreation

Mar
31
2009

M asks:

If we procreate, we doom civilization through overpopulation and depletion of resources. If we don't procreate, we doom civilization through exacerbating an aging population. What's a potentially procreative person to do?

I don't think it's as bad as that, personally.

For one thing, personally speaking I don't think an aging population is a civilization killer, if for no other reason than that in a relatively short period of time the problem of an aging population solves itself (think about it for a minute and you'll figure out how). Nor do I think that in theory an intelligently-handled reduction in population (via natural attrition through old age, to be very clear about that) would be a horrible thing; the problem is I wouldn't expect it to be particularly well-managed, and indeed in the places where the populations are aging and the birthrates are declining there seems to be bit of confusion on how to handle the issue.

On the other side of the coin, while personally I think seven billion people is more people than the planet actually needs to have on it, there's no reason why we couldn't manage ten billion or fourteen billion or even 25 billion—if again the population was managed in a way that we don't abuse or overtax our planetary resources. This would mean drastically changing how people lived, driving down their overal energy and resource use, vastly improving their reuse and recycling processes, changing how they eat and generally getting them to keep from killing the shit out of each other. But again, the issue isn't whether it's theoretically possible but whether people would do what's required to make it happen.

Or to put it another way: the issue isn't how many people the planet has; the issue is how the people who are on it (however many there are at any given point) handle their resource management and way of living. And in point of fact we do a really crappy job of it overall. For one thing, resources are highly unevenly distributed (said the guy living in the country that consumes 25% of the world's energy while having only 5% of the world's population); for another thing, the lifestyles, desires and goals of the people of the whole world are too heterogeneous to make coordinated and evenly distributed resource management possible—which is a nice way of saying that your average American likes his big house and all his toys and doesn't want to ditch them all to live a lifestyle resembling that of, oh, your average Kyrgyzstani (additionally, one suspects the average Kyrgyzstani would like to live like the average American, given the choice, which complicates matters).

This is actually something I think about a fair amount. Truth to be told, I personally have far more crap than I need and most of the time even want (thanks to being a packrat), and I live in a house with more space than I or my family use, on land we don't really do anything with. I suspect strongly we could downsize—in terms of what we have and use—by a rather substantial amount before we felt a real change in our overall quality of life, and we could downsize rather substantially more than that before it became actually uncomfortable. This is relevant to the question at hand because in either case of a declining or rising population, a downsizing in *things* is likely to be a long-term result. In any event: I think the population issue really is a stalking horse for resource issues; those are what I worry about in the long run.

Nevertheless. As regards procreating, my thought on the matter is that if you are procreatively inclined but are worried about a growing population, have one kid; if you're worried about a declining population, have two. Here in the US, the "replacement rate"—that is, the number of births required to counteract the number of people the nation loses from death, is 2.1 kids per fertile woman, so having two is doing your part, and you can assume other people having more, combined with the US immigration rate, will keep our overall population from decline. In other countries your replacement mileage may vary, but one or two is a reasonable rule of thumb here.

I wouldn't worry personally about whether having even the one will send the overall world population spiralling into some sort of Malthusian nightmare, as US/Western world births are an overall drop in the bucket in terms of worldwide population growth, i.e., when the worldwide famine hits, it won't be your fault for having a kid (it might be your fault for driving an SUV, however, to go back to the resource issue). But if you are worried about that but still want to have kids, well, you know: It's called adoption, and in general I think it's a very cool thing, and encourage you to go that route. And if you don't want any kids at all, then don't have 'em, of course. Kids are a good way to have a complete life, but you know what, there are other ways to a complete life that don't include them, too.

But overall, unless you're having a dozen or so children, and they're having a dozen (and so on), however many children you're having is not really going to make a difference in whether civilization collapses. What will make a difference is how you (and the rest of us) manage the resources we have. The irony is, if civilization collapses, chances are very good the birthrate will go up as well. It's what would happen after that which would likely constitute the tragedy. So, you know. Let's work on that resource thing.

Portrait of a Closet Introvert

May
31
2009

I was very recently asked if there was something that I knew about myself that no one else believes when I tell them. I suspect that the question was meant to elicit a confession that I was born with twelve toes, or that I get sexually aroused in the presence of yogurt (neither of which, incidentally, is true, I *swear*), or something along that line, so I sort of blew off the question at the time. That said, the question's been lingering with me for a few days, primarily because there is something about me that I know is true, which (almost) no one else believes about me, and that is that I am an introvert.

The reason almost no one believes it is because I quite admittedly exhibit the signs of being a shameless extrovert: I'm very social, I don't get lost or withdrawn in large groups, I handle public appearances and performances adeptly and in general I give the impression of enjoying being around people, including people I don't know particularly well. That's pretty textbook extroversion right there.

Naturally I admit to all the above. I *do* like people, I do enjoy myself in social situations, I like meeting new folks and (if I may say so) I'm pretty well socialized for someone who is both a writer and a geek. I'm not faking my generally sociable nature. But I think there's a difference between playing well with others, and *genuine* extroversion, in which being with other people is energizing to that person. As much as I like people and being with them, I'm not energized by them; sooner or later I turn into a pumpkin and go off to have time by myself, in order to recenter and hit the "reset" button, and to be presentable to other human beings once more. Which is to say the way I energize is to spend time by myself, which is a classic introvert thing.

I've always known this about myself, but the event that really brought it home to me was the book tour I did for *The Last Colony*. I had a great time doing the readings and signings and meeting people, but the moment I was done with the last bit, I was done. I had friends who saw me on the tour and a number of them remarked on the fact of how dazed I was after an event. It was true, and it wasn't just because I was tired; it was because I was peopled out. For me, doing an event like that is the human interaction equivalent of mainlining three king-sized Snickers bars: Yes, I'm *on*, but then, *wow*. Sugar crash.

There's a similar thing that goes on with me at science fiction conventions, particularly when I'm a Guest of Honor; during the day if I'm not on a panel or have some other commitment I'm often in my hotel room in order to conserve my sociability for scheduled events and for evening partying and hanging out. It's not to say I have to force myself into being a social person—as noted before I do actually like being sociable and partying, it's one reason I do so much of it. It's more of being aware of what my own limits and needs are. If I don't get a certain amount of alone time, I get cranky. And that's not good for anyone.

This is why, incidentally, living out in the middle of nowhere in rural Ohio is not actually a hardship for me. My geographically closest close friend is about an hour away; on a day-to-day basis I just don't get out much to see anyone. How do I feel about that? Just fine, thanks. Being alone works for me; I get writing done, I get thinking done, and generally speaking I keep myself suitably amused. I really like seeing my friends when I see them, and I wish I saw them more (including the one just an hour from me). But I'm not going stir-crazy out here in the sticks. It suits my temperament well.

Also, you know: hi, people coming to my blog. Thanks for providing me daily low-impact fraternization. The Internet was made for introverts, I suspect. In all, I'm covered on a day-to-day basis.

So, yes: Introvert. You might not see it when you meet me. But it's there.

Post-Election Notes For the GOP (Not That They've Asked For Them)

Nov
7
2012

Having just voted against both its presidential and Ohio senatorial candidate, I am reasonably sure the GOP doesn't want any notes from me about its failures last night. On the other hand, I am a white, male, well-off, heterosexually-married, college educated fellow, which means according to the exit polls at least, I am the GOP "demographic" down to the last jot and tittle. Maybe it'll listen for just that reason.

So, fellows! Some notes for you. Please note this is addressed to the party leaders, not the party members.

1. Recognize your brand is damaged. You can't seriously be considered to be the party of fiscal probity at this point; your record for the last thirty years makes this laughable. Bush shot your international relations standing in the foot. All you have left is social issues, and—surprise!—on social issues, most people who are *not* you think you're intolerant at best and racist, sexist, homophobic and bigoted at worst.

Seriously, guys: What does the GOP actually want to be the party *of*? At this point, and for the last few years, it's been "The Party of Not Obama." This is not a good way to run a railroad.

2. Deal with your base. Your base is killing you. Did you *see* your presidential nominee slate this year? I know your base was excited about them, but from the outside we were all, like, "seriously, WTF?" The fact that an unrepentant bigot like Rick Santorum managed to pace Mitt Romney for the nomination as far into the process as he did should have sent up enough red flags to rival Beijing on May Day. Then it makes the (relative) moderates who eventually win the nominations spend too much time tending to its issues and selecting awful vice presidential candidates. Sarah Palin terrified the non-base voters she was supposed to attract. That Paul Ryan counts as an "intellectual" in GOP circles speaks to the almost unfathomable poverty of your brain trust at the moment. That these two were brought on to bolster their respective presidential candidates with the party's base should throw up all sorts of warning signs.

Your base is fine for now with mid-terms, when you're dealing with House races, and districts that have been gerrymandered to allow for genuinely horrible politicians to be elected (yes, on both sides, but we're talking about you for now). For presidential elections, when you have to deal with a national electorate? They're a bad foundation. They're going to keep making you fail. If you don't want to believe it, two words for you: Akin, Mourdock. If you think they only lost *their* races, think again.

3. Accept the fact that the US is browner and more tolerant than you are, and that you need to become more of both of these things. By "tolerant" I mean that we're okay with gays marrying and women deciding what to do with their own wombs and that we think science *doesn't* want to shiv Jesus in the night when no one is looking. By "browner," we mean, well, *browner.* Lots of Latinos and blacks and other ethnic minorities out there. More every day. And very few of them want to have anything to do with you. Both of these mean that lots of younger white people don't want to have anything to do with you either, because—again, surprise!—many of the people who they love and grew up with in this browner and more tolerant nation are the folks you spend a lot of time railing against, in code or just straight up. And that's bullshit.

I am a white, well-off, college-educated man married to a woman. And in my family and close circle of friends I have Hispanics, African-Americans, Asians, gay, bisexual and trans people, religious, agnostic and atheist, able-bodied and disabled. You lose me when you classify any of them as *the other.* They're not the other; they're us.

4. Stop letting your media run you. Look, guys: Fox News and Rush Limbaugh don't actually care about the GOP. They really don't. They are in the business of terrifying aging white people for money. To the extent that your political agenda conforms to this goal, they're on your side. But when you step outside of their "terrify aging white people for money" agenda, they're going to stomp on you. How many GOP politicians have had to grovel at Limbaugh's feet because they said something he didn't approve of? Stop it. Tell him to fuck off every once in a while. It'll be good for you.

And while you're at it, tell Grover Norquist to fuck off, too. The fact this dude keeps the lot of you from facing economic reality with that damned pledge of his is an embarrassment.

These are the things I would start with.

Do I expect you to consider them? Not really, no. What I expect you to do is the same thing you've been doing for the last twenty years, which is to decide that the problem with the GOP is that it's not socially conservative or fiscally irresponsible *enough,* cull anyone who doesn't subscribe to the new tighter and angrier level of orthodoxy and go from there. If that's the direction you go, I wish you joy in it, and look forward to years and years of Democratic presidents.

Reality Check

Nov
5
2008

For those who need it:

1. It was Obama who won, not necessarily the Democrats. Which is why, while the Democrats gained in both the House and the Senate, they don't appear to be having the blow-out additions to their numbers some folks seemed to think would happen (note that at least a couple of Senate races are still in play). Which suggests, to me at least, that rather than the Democrats putting wind into Obama's sails, they rode on his coattails. I think people who are under the impression the *Democrats* now have a mandate are misreading what happened yesterday. It's *Obama* who has the mandate. The Democrats are along for the ride. Don't think Obama, at least, isn't aware of this. Which brings us to:

2. The United States did not become a deep blue paradise overnight. Fox News will not implode. Matt Drudge will not spontaneously combust. Rush Limbaugh will not choke on his own tongue. And aside from all those pleasant images, America is the same essentially purple-y place it was yesterday. If you need proof of that, please to see the results of Proposition 8 in California, which, alas, seems headed for a win, along with amendments and resolutions in other states intended to make sure same-sex marriage is illegal in those places. It would be tempting to imagine that this is a departing knife twist by religious and social conservatives before they start to tear at each other's intestines ("I can't have Sarah Palin but at least I can screw the gays"), but that's delusional thinking. There are more pro-Obama, pro-Prop 8 (and etc) types out there than some folks are ready to admit. Which brings us to:

3. Obama will not give you everything you want, when you want it. Since Obama seems to have this crazy idea that he might want to be president of the whole damn country, I think he's going to be small-c conservative in his battles, at least the early ones, and will likely stick to the economic issues that got him elected. Anyone who's observed the man in the campaign who is also not totally high on crazy wing juice (either the right or left vintages) will note that Obama is a man of exceptionally practical strategies; one of those strategies is to lead people to where *he* wants to go by using the paths *they* like to go by. Per point 2, this means frustrating people who want to go off the beaten paths. Which brings us to:

4. Your next president is going to disappoint you. Barack Obama does not fart cinnamon-scented rainbows. He is not trailed by angels and unicorns. Reality does not reshape itself to his wishes. Dude's a human being, and a politician, and he's going to have to work with other human beings who are also politicians. Per point 2, some things you want him to do he won't be able to do, and some of the things you want him to do he won't want to do, so they won't get done. He will make mistakes. He will make errors. He will be caught flat-footed from time to time. He will be challenged by antagonists, foreign and domestic, who will have an interest in seeing him faceplant. He will piss most people off. His approval rating will drop below 50%. *He is going to disappoint you.* Get used to the idea.

5. Last night's election didn't change the country; it offered a chance for the country to change. Which is something Obama himself pointed out last night, because he's a smart man like that. He will effect some of that change through the power of the presidency, and through his relationship with Congress, but ultimately what will change things is whether people want change and are willing to work for it. Elections are the easy part, basically. Now comes the work. As the saying goes, you have been offered a country, if you can keep it. It's up to you more than it's up to your next president.

Regarding Snobbery

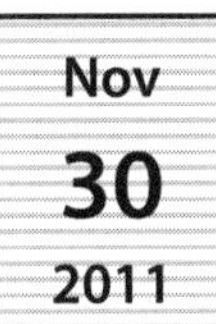

propos of nothing in particular, a few thoughts on the subject of snobbery.

1. One is perfectly within one's own prerogatives to feel snobby about things, if one feels invested in them in one way or another.
2. However, being a snob often makes one look like an asshole.
3. It especially makes one look like an asshole if the basis for one's snobbery lacks an adequate foundation. For example, if despite rhetorical flourishes and handwaving, one's critical thesis devolves to "This stuff is awesome because I like it; this stuff sucks because I don't; those who like the things I do not are stupid," then one will look like an asshole.
4. If one's critical thesis exhibits this level of foundational poverty, no amount of rhetorical flourish or handwaving will hide it. One's pleasure at the presumed rhetorical cleverness will likely be noted, however, and added to the tally of things that make one look like an asshole.
5. Likewise, gathering friends of like-minded snobbery and exegetic facility will not make your common critical thesis better. It merely means that as a group you enjoy the smell of your own farts. This is nice for you, and likely obvious to anyone outside your circle.
6. If one's feeling of snobbery leads one to believe that one is in fact some way superior to those who do not hold the same snobbery,

then one is at severe risk of crossing over from merely looking like an asshole to actually being an asshole.

7. A reason for this is that one is exhibiting a childishly binary way of looking at the world, and while that is fine for a child, who may not know better, one is an adult and should have the ability to exhibit complexity whilst thinking. Because it is polite to assume that an adult is, in fact, not stupid or incapable of complex thought, the maintenance of such a binary classification system relating to people suggests one might be an asshole. There may be other reasons for this choice besides being an asshole, but if Occam's Razor teaches us anything, it is that the simplest explanation is often the correct one.
8. If one uses such simple, non-complex binary sorting to classify others as inferior in some manner, it does not make one any more of an asshole, but it may mean that one's sense of irony is not as finely tuned as one would hope.
9. If one declares oneself publicly to be a snob, then one actively invites scrutiny of the sort detailed above, often by those with the means to determine whether the snobbery proclaimed is warranted by anything other than one's own estimation of self-worth. There are more of such people than you may expect.
10. It is worth considering what benefits one ultimately receives in declaring one's snobbery. There may be fewer than one thinks.

Thank you for your attention.

Reminder: There's No Actual Office for "President of the Left"

Jul 2 2008

Apparently some Obama supporters are shocked and appalled to discover that now that he's out of the primaries, their man is running to be the President of *all* the people in the United States, not just the people in the United States who have the "Yes We Can" YouTube video bookmarked on their Web browser. Well, you know: *Surprise*, people. For example, Obama's supporting an extension, with significant caveats, of some of the faith-oriented policies started by Bush, has gotten a lot of folks spun up. But from where I stand it makes perfect sense.

1. Many evangelicals are disenchanted with the GOP, and young evangelicals in particular seem to be coloring outside the lines, politically speaking, more and more these days. Splintering off young evangelicals, perhaps on a permanent basis, would be like cutting off the GOP's fuel supply for future elections, given that the evangelicals have been in the tank for the GOP for at least three decades. Even just putting them into play on a regular basis means the GOP has to fight (and use money to fight) for a demographic it took for granted just a single presidential election cycle ago.

2. It's an act of political ball-cutting. There's nowhere on Obama's political agenda that McCain wants to go, because the GOP base is already horrified that the man is not conservative enough for them. But Obama has some room to snack on elements of McCain's potential agenda, and in doing so make an appeal to voters (and not just those noted in the first point) that McCain's people probably thought they wouldn't have to fight for. Whether Obama gets those voters is immaterial to the fact that for the relatively low cost of giving a speech on the subject of faith-based programs, he's just committed McCain to spending a lot of time and money to keep them in his camp.

3. There are still places in the United States—some which I can see right out my *window*, thank you very much—where there lives a significant number of people who are under the impression Barack Obama is an *Islamicist* mole whose first act as president will be to suicide bomb himself in the Oval Office. Obama is many things, but "dumb" isn't one of them. If he simply denies or tries to ignore the "Obama will fly a plane into a building" meme, it'll fester. If he offers a substantive example of an actual policy that counteracts that meme, he's got a tool he can use to beat it, or at least beat it down.

4. The is the part where I'm confused that people haven't figured this out yet: Obama clearly doesn't just want to win, folks. He wants to win *big*. We're talking about Super Bowl blowout big. Spanish-American War big. *Friends* vs. whatever the hell was on TV against *Friends* big. 400+ electoral votes big. He wants a *generational* vote, like Reagan had in 1980—and given the abysmal standing of the GOP and the sitting president at the moment, it's entirely possible he can *get* it with a little outreach and some strategic tacking to the center.

The folks who are currently braying about how Obama is where is he is right now because he *didn't* swing toward the center are somewhat disingenuously forgetting how well Clinton did in the last few Democratic primaries, appealing to more conservative Democratic voters. Remember how the primaries went *all the way to the end?* Yes, good times, good times. Anyway, those folks can conveniently forget the lessons of the last few Democratic primaries; Obama really can't, and apparently hasn't.

5. Obama's probably also aware that he's got the left in the tank. Some folks on the left were goofy enough in 2000 to think that voting for, say, Nader, wouldn't make a huge difference in the end, so why not make a cute little protest vote. Here in 2008, anyone on the left who *isn't* planning to pull a lever for Obama probably has congenital brain damage. Seriously, there is unlikely to be another chance for the left to so definitively remake the political map as it has this year, if the folks on the left simply don't *lose their shit* at the idea of Obama trying to widen his margin of victory, the better to make the case that his election represents a major shift in US politics.

Now, I'm a firm believer in never discounting the Democratic party's ability to snatch defeat from the jaws of victory; I'm still appalled at the incompetence of the Kerry campaign in 2004 and for that matter, the bad strategy of the Gore campaign in 2000, which involved separating their man from the most popular president in recent history. In this case I think the people involved in the presidential campaign are doing pretty smart things, and it might be the *other* folks who blow it.

To them I would suggest that they consider that the Obama campaign is paying them a compliment, in that they are making the (not necessarily self-evident) assumption that they're all smart enough to realize that tacking toward the center in the campaign is going to pay huge dividends for the left when at the end of the 2008 election it finds itself in charge of the executive and legislative branches, and finds itself in a position to fill two or possibly even three seats on the Supreme Court in the next four years, *and* possibly in the bargain create a sturdy new left-leaning political base that lasts as long as the GOP base that Reagan used as a foundation three decades ago. I guess we'll see if that compliment pays off.

Personally speaking I'm not hugely thrilled with every move Obama has made recently; I don't like the continuation of the faith-based office that much (which should not be a huge surprise), although my real ire is for his position on the FISA "compromise" bill which will hopefully die in the Senate sometime next week. On the other hand, I have strong suspicions that President Obama would nominate to the high court the sort of judges that would see the FISA "compromise" bill as fundamentally unconstitutional, and in the meantime his positioning deprives the right-wing shouty chorus of some oxygen during his presidential campaign.

Which is to say that I'm fundamentally unsurprised to discover that Barack Obama, who has been in politics for a number of years, is a *politician*. And a politician who wants to win as big as he can.

Reminder: Tis the Season Not to Be an Ass

Dec
21
2011

Question from e-mail:

Any thoughts on the current state of the War on Christmas™?

I think it's about as silly as it ever was, considering that Christmas has conquered December, occupied November and metastasized into late October. To suggest that the holiday is under serious threat from politically correct non-Christians is like suggesting an earthworm is a serious threat to a Humvee. This is obvious enough to anyone with sense that I use The War on Christmas as an emergency diagnostic, which is to say, if you genuinely believe there's a War on Christmas, you may want to see a doctor, since you might have a tumor pressing on your frontal lobes.

But—but—what about all those horrible atheists taking over holiday displays with crucified Santa skeletons? Surely that's evidence of a war! Well, no, it's evidence of some non-believers taking a page out of the PETA playbook, i.e., being dicks to get attention and to make a point. I do strongly suspect that if we didn't have some certain excitable conservatives playing The War on Christmas card when a business says "Happy Holidays" rather than "Merry Christmas," and such, there would be less incentive for certain excitable non-believers to make a public show of desecrating Christmas symbols, but that's just an opinion and I don't have anything to back that up. What I do know is that the War on Christmas crusaders and the Santa crucifiers deserve each other; the rest of us, unfortunately, have to watch them both make public asses of themselves.

This is not to say that non-believers have to passively suck it up during the Christmas season; they have as much right to public display space as anyone and in a theoretical sense I'm glad they're out there to remind people that not everyone defaults to Christian or even "religious." I like it better when they do it in a manner that doesn't explicitly say "take the symbols you cherish and shove them right up your ass." But then I'm also the sort of non-believer who doesn't take every public religious display as an intentional slap in the face. When people put up Christmas displays, or (to the point) when municipalities allow public space to be used for them, I don't see them as a Christian majority saying "bow down to our hegemony, heretics and infidels," I see them as people saying "Yay! Christmas!" Which is a different motivation entirely.

Here's the thing: If you're using the holiday season to go out of your way to be an asshole to someone, believer or non-believer, you're doing it wrong, and I wish you would stop. That's not a war, it's a slap fight and it's embarrassing. As a non-believer, when someone says "Merry Christmas" to me, I say "Merry Christmas" back, because generally speaking I understand that what "Merry Christmas" means in this context is "I am offering you good will in a way I know how," and I appreciate that sentiment. Left to my own devices, I use "Happy holidays" because I know a lot of people who aren't Christians (or at least Christmas-centered) and that seems the best way to express my own good will; the vast majority of people get what I'm doing and appreciate that sentiment too.

I think most people get the idea that regardless of religion or lack thereof, we've designated this time of year as the one where we make an effort to be decent to each other. Accept it. Welcome it. Live it, in the best way you know how. Be tolerant and gracious when others share this sentiment in a way different than you would. Look for what they're saying *means*, not just the words they use to say it. It would be a fine way to have everyone enjoy the season.

The Ripper Owens Syndrome

Mar
2
2009

Here's my problem: Unlike a fair number of people of my general political description, I don't buy into the trendy sound bite that Rush Limbaugh is the true leader of the Republican Party. The bad news, though, is that for the life of me I can't think of who *is*—and I suspect neither can anyone else, which means a professional attention-seeking loudmouth like Limbaugh seems to have the gig for no other reason than no one else has stepped up. He's not a leader, he's just wearing bells and spangles, and everyone's looking at him and cheering as he capers. If you're looking in from the outside, the one everyone's paying attention to looks like the leader.

What really worries me is that if this vacuum at the top of the GOP goes on for long enough, then Limbaugh eventually *will* be considered the GOP's true leader, because he does a fairly impressive act of looking and sounding just like a GOP leader should look and act, even if at the end of the day all he's doing is mouthing the GOP Greatest Hits to a bunch of people who are doing the political equivalent of holding up lighters when their favorite-but-now-unfashionable power ballad gets cranked up at a concert.

Indeed, Limbaugh is the GOP manifestation of what I call The Ripper Owens Syndrome, in which a tribute band version of the lead singer performs the function of mimicking the actual lead singer so well that the real band hires him when the actual lead singer takes a hike—thus dooming the band to a shadowy half-life in which it releases albums no one buys and it becomes its own cover band and plays the state fairs and is generally miserable. Not that the new lead singer minds; he's having a ball—until he gets unceremoniously dumped by the band a couple of years later. Because the fact is, there's more to being the lead singer than just standing up there and singing the same dozen songs someone else wrote and that everyone already knows.

Where the analogy breaks down is that poor Ripper Owens was (sorry, Mr. Owens) some schmoe from Ohio who got a break from a band cynical enough to use him for life support; Limbaugh, on the other hand, has his own immense popularity and is canny enough to sense the vacuum at the top of the GOP as an opportunity for him to wield some genuine political power without that annoying intermediary step of having to get elected, either by the public or by the party. But what's good for Limbaugh is not necessarily good for the GOP—nor is it good for the country as a whole.

The real problem with Limbaugh is not his political positions, which are the bog-standard GOP sour mash of once-upon-a-time genuine conservatism denatured through three decades of 100 proof Will to Power, which makes sense because it's not like Limbaugh is interested in or capable of generating original political thoughts on his own. The real problem with Limbaugh is at the end of the day he's an entertainer, and his shtick relies on political division and dissension.

When Limbaugh bloviates that he wants the President of the United States to fail, his motivation is not a genuine passion for conservatism, or alternately a genuine nilhilistic embrace thereof, in which he believes it's better for civilization to collapse than liberalism to succeed. Limbaugh wants to the President of the United States to fail because saying so is the sort of attention-getting jackassery that gives him a goose in the ratings. Expecting him to retract such a comment is just going to get him to double down on it. Limbaugh wants Obama to fail because it's good for his livelihood; whether it's bad for the GOP or the US as a whole is really not Limbaugh's problem.

You can't blame an attention-seeking blowhard who makes a living saying outrageous things for doing what he does; it's not like Limbaugh has anything else going for him. The GOP, on the other hand, ought to know better than to allow itself to be played by someone whose goals are short-term and selfish and at the end of the day only marginally aligned with the long-term goals of the GOP. But that's the GOP these days, isn't it: so rudderless that even its executive class seems to have confused its top salesman with the CEO.

Or maybe it's they actually prefer it that way. Maybe the GOP is happy to be its own cover band. In the short term, I can't say this bothers me, because unlike Limbaugh, I have no desire for the president to fail, if for no other reason than if he fails, he's likely to take the country with him. It's not as if the GOP has a plan to get us out of this jam, other than to shout "tax cuts!" while running in tight little circles. In the long term, of course, it's depressing and worrying. The GOP needs to figure out what it stands for and how it's going to effectively embody genuine conservative thoughts and positions moving forward. It's certainly not going to do it with Limbaugh at the mike. There are only so many GOP Greatest Hits he knows, and there aren't that many state fairs left to play.

Romney and the LDS Church

Feb
4
2012

Question from the gallery:

How much do you think it will matter that Mitt Romney is a Mormon? And does it matter in your own thinking about him?

Since I think at this point it's all but certain Romney will be the GOP nominee, I'm not sure it's mattered greatly in a negative sense. I'm pretty sure in a couple of cases it will work to his advantage; for example, tonight, in the Nevada caucuses, as Nevada is the state with the 7th largest population of LDS folk (4th biggest per capita), LDS folk tend to skew Republican/conservative, and in the 2008 Nevada caucuses, LDS folks who voted GOP went 90% for Romney and were 25% of the caucus voters. So, yes, in Nevada? Not a problem.

Is it a problem with the GOP elsewhere? Possibly, although I don't have the stats at my fingertips. I will say it's possible it may have been more of a problem if Romney had been in a more competitive field of candidates, but he got lucky in his GOP opponents this time around. With apologies to Santorum and Paul supporters, at this point it's between Romney and Gingrich. While you can't count Gingrich out unless you stake his heart, chop off his head, fill his mouth with garlic and bury him at a crossroad, I think most GOP voters realize at this point that the vampire treatment is exactly what Obama would do to Gingrich in the general election. There's also the very real possibility that in going down, Gingrich would take all of the modern GOP with him, on the thinking that as he was the one who birthed it, he might as well kill it off, too. Romney, whatever his other flaws or advantages, at least won't immolate his entire party if he loses the election.

At the end of the day, Romney has consistently been the GOP front-runner in this election cycle. Gingrich spikes up past him now and then, but that's just it: He spikes. Then people remember Gingrich is Gingrich (Romney spending millions in attack ads helps) and then it's back to status quo. I know of grumbles of Romney's LDS affiliation among some evangelical GOP voters, but it seems like it's been just that: grumbles. There's also this: When it comes right down to it, do these evangelical GOP voters dislike the idea of an LDS member in the White House *more* than they dislike Obama? I'm gonna go with a "no" here.

Regarding the general election, I think Romney's major problem is not his religious belief but everything else about him, starting with the fact he's socially clueless about how obnoxious he is about his wealth, and (conversely) how much the electorate is becoming sensitized to the fact he's a clueless rich dude. I'm not going to suggest his LDS affiliation won't matter to some voters; it will. I just don't think it's going to land in the top five concerns that most voters have about him.

Does Romney being a member of the LDS church concern me personally? No. Readers here will recall that of all the GOP candidates this cycle, the one I liked best (and even sent money to) was Jon Huntsman, who is also a member of the LDS church. So my recent track record on this particular aspect of a candidate's profile is at the very least neutral.

In a larger sense, on a purely personal and anecdotal level, my overall feelings about LDS church members defaults to vaguely positive. This is mostly because I know a fair number of LDS folks, and the ones I know personally tend to be good people whose company I enjoy. I allow that this may have less to do with their church affiliation and more to do with the fact I like good people and don't tally church affiliation of any sort as an automatic negative. Good people you like are hard to find and you should cherish them without the use of a checklist. Be that as it may, that's my initial default, so it doesn't hurt Romney any.

Regarding the LDS Church as an entity, there's a lot about its political and social positions I dislike and disagree with, and I think its theological underpinnings are a heaping stack of nonsense. This puts it on a par with a number of churches, including the Catholic church, a whole pile of protestant churches (particularly evangelical churches), and pretty a fair number of non-Christian religions (and/or their various sects) to boot. I certainly could not be an LDS church member now; if I were born into it I'm pretty sure I'd be apostate. But again, that'd be true regardless of church. Luckily for me, aside from a baptism I didn't have a vote on and wasn't followed up on in any event, I've never had a church affiliation. I don't have to be apostate; I can just be not religious.

I don't automatically hold official church positions against church members, regardless of religion. I assume individual church members have brains and agency and may or may not agree philosophically with every single proclamation that comes out of their particular hierarchy. People who assume that Romney will take orders from Salt Lake City are on par with the voters of 1960 who assumed that Kennedy would take orders from Rome. I have no intention of voting for Romney in the general election. But when I don't vote for him, his being a member of the LDS church won't be a part of it.

Would I ever vote *for* a member of the LDS church for public office? Sure, if their political positions were aligned with mine for the office they were seeking. Romney's don't, which is why he won't get my vote in November.

The Santorum Solution

Feb
8
2012

Wow, I gotta tell ya, I really suck at prognosticating this GOP primary season. Just this weekend I mentioned how it was a two-man race between Mitt Romney and Newt Gingrich, and here it is Wednesday and Rick Santorum has just won the caucuses in Minnesota and Colorado as well as the Missouri primary, with Mitt a distant second in Missouri and Colorado and third in Minnesota (with Ron Paul second!), and poor angry Newt third in CO, fourth in MN, and not even on the ballot in MO at all. If predicting GOP results were my job, I would totally fire me. But then again, after last night I would not be the only person who would have to be fired. There would be a lot of unemployed people today. Which would drive down employment numbers! And that's good for the GOP's chances this year. Sorry, I'm rambling.

I also have to tell you that I *like* this GOP primary season. It's *exciting*. By this time Romney was supposed to be blandly cruising his way to the nomination, held aloft by large stacks of money and the air of inevitability cash manufactures, but here on February 8, Santorum has won more states than Romney has, and while Romney has twice the delegates as Santorum (thanks to Florida's "winner take all" primary), his lead is not unassailable. Now Romney will have to spend even *more* money! To fight off *Rick Santorum*. Who in a *rational* universe would have been packed away long before now.

Meanwhile: Newt Gingrich, who at this point is not in the race to win it but to hurt Mitt Romney as much as possible between now and the day, hopefully in the late spring, when Romney drags his battered carcass over the 1,144 delegate line he needs to take the nomination. Newt will be sniping Mitt all the way, and Mitt will be distracted by having to deal with Santorum while he does so. This is my new scenario. Because why not.

And yes, I still think Romney's going to take it, eventually (and yes, probably sooner than later). But, hey, who knows, right? It *could* be Santorum! I find him a querulous bigot, but apparently "querulous bigot" in Scalzi World equates to "genuine conservative" in GOP Land, and the genuine conservatives out there apparently aren't happy with Romney and his actual governing track record in Massachusetts. Could Santorum capitalize on his victories last night? Sure. Could GOP voters become increasingly disenchanted with Romney? Absolutely. Will Gingrich stay on mission to stab Romney through the eyeballs at every possible opportunity? You know he will. Santorum could drag it out! And pick up delegates! And win the nomination!

And then get *slaughtered* in the general election, since outside of GOP circles, querulous bigots are probably bad presidential candidates here in 2012. But if the GOP wants to try the Santorum Solution, then I wouldn't be the one to try to stop them. Please, GOPers, run Rick Santorum for president. Indeed: Santorum/Bachmann 2012. It would be the best ticket ever. For values of "best" that don't mean what "best" usually does, mind you; even so.

Anyway, as I said: *exciting*. Good for the GOP or the nation? Probably not so much. But this is where we are at the moment. I couldn't tell you where we go from here. The suspense is killing me! I hope it will last!

Scalzi Shakes His Cane At The Kids' Music Today

Apr
5
2012

The song in question: "Ass Back Home" by Gym Class Heroes. It's a song in the genre of "Musician pines for his woman back home while he's out on the road, totally not partaking in groupies," the most famous of which for my generation is Journey's lighter-launcher "Faithfully." The song itself is actually not bad, although it's another example of Gym Class Heroes relying on a guest vocalist to lay down a tasty chorus to prop up GCH's bland rap verses (previous example: "Stereo Hearts"). But what *does* bother me are the lyrics of the chorus, in which the unfortunately-named Neon Hitch sings:

> *I don't know where you're going/Or when you're coming home/I left the keys under the mat to our front door*

The song and the video both establish that the two vocalists of the song are in some sort of long-term, co-habitating relationship; good for them. It also establishes that he's on the road for a tour while she's back at home. Fine.

But if all that's the case, really? She's doesn't know where he's going, or when he's coming home? Did he not provide her with a tour schedule? Because, you know, when *I* go out on tour, I make sure my longtime companion, the lovely and effervescent Mrs. Scalzi, has the itinerary in her possession. But even if I or the Gym Class Heroes dude didn't drop that knowledge on the respective loves of our lives, the fact is most entertainers who tour make that information public. If she didn't know where he was going or when he was coming home, she could just go to the band web site and click into the tour area. Where's he going? Athens, Georgia, on April 10! When's he coming home? Probably May 4th or 5th, by the looks of things. Then he goes out again! Look, it's all there.

(Not to mention, as the video shows them on the phone to each other, she could just ask, *hey, what's the next stop after this one?* Admittedly, the lyrics note that sometimes he doesn't know where he is, or what day it is, but most modern phones have GPS and a calendar app, so that's easily solved. There are *a lot of options* here for access to accurate information.)

Likewise: She leaves a key under the mat to their front door? Why? Doesn't he have a key of his own? Does he not live there when he's not on tour? The possessive plural nature of the pronoun in this sentence rather strongly suggests so. Can he not be trusted with his own key? Is he always losing them in hotel rooms? Do the key gnomes have a vendetta of long standing against this poor man? These seem doubtful. He's driving home a motorcycle at the end of the video; clearly he didn't lose the keys to that. I'm guessing the house key's on the same ring.

Yes, I know. I've *drastically* overthought this. But come on. These are not lyrics filled with metaphor or allusion; they're pretty straightforward declarative statements that individually parse perfectly well but which in context don't make a damn bit of sense. Drives me nuts. I'm glad these two people in the song are in love, but clearly they need to a) work on their communication skills, b) learn to use the Internet to find things, c) go down to the end of the street and have a couple of spare keys made. None of this is hard.

I'm just saying.

(shakes cane)

Done.

A Self-Made Man Looks At How He Made It

Jul
23
2012

To begin, my mother and father are responsible for me existing at all, so I suppose the first round of "How I made it to where I am" begins there.

I was born at Travis Air Force Base in Fairfield, CA, and as I understand it I was not the easiest of births, taking on the order of three days to be evicted from the womb. That couldn't have been comfortable or safe either for my mother or for me, so thanks go to the medical team of doctors and nurses who helped with my birth. Likewise, the fact I was born at an Air Force base means that I owe a thanks to America's military for offering medical care to my mother (based on her relationship to my father, who was in the military at the time), and indirectly to America's taxpayers, whose dollars went to supporting the military, and thereby those doctors, nurses, my father's paycheck and my mother's medical care.

My parents' marriage did not last particularly long and in the early seventies—and off and on for the next several years—my mother found herself in the position of having to rely on the social net of welfare and food stamps to make sure that when she couldn't find work (or alternately, could find it but it didn't pay enough), she was able to feed her children and herself. Once again, I owe thanks to America's taxpayers for making sure I had enough to eat at various times when I was a child.

Not having to wonder how I was going to eat meant my attention could be given to other things, like reading wonderful books. As a child, many of the books I read and loved came from the local libraries where

I lived. I can still remember going into a library for the first time and being amazed—utterly amazed—that I could read any book I wanted and that I could even take some of them home, as long as I promised to give each of them back in time. I learned my love of science and story in libraries. I know now that each of those libraries were paid for by the people who lived in the cities the libraries were in, and sometimes by the states they were in as well. I owe the taxpayers of each for the love of books and words.

From kindergarten through the eighth grade, I had a public school education, which at the time in California was very good, because the cuts that would come to education through the good graces of Proposition 13 had not yet trickled down to affect me. My schools in the cities of Covina, Azusa and Glendora all had "gifted and talented" programs that allowed me and my other classmates extra opportunities to expand our minds, aided by excellent teachers, most of whose names I can still rattle off after 30 years: Mrs. Chambers, Mrs. Fox, Mrs. Swirsky, Mr. Johnson, Mr. Kaufman, Ms. Morgan. Through much of this time I was fed through school lunch programs which allowed me a meal for free or reduced rates. In the sixth grade, when again my mother and I found ourselves poor and briefly homeless, and I began feeling depressed, the school's counselor was there to do his best to keep me on an even keel. These schools and programs were funded locally, through the state and through the federal level. The taxpayers helped me learn, kept me fed, and prevented despair from clouding up my mind.

By the eighth grade it became clear public education in California was beginning to get stretched by shrinking budgets, and my mother went looking for a private high school for me to attend. She called up the Webb School of California, and found out it cost more to attend than she made in a year. But she was convinced it was the right place. I went and took the entrance test and had my interview with a teacher there, named Steve Patterson. I don't remember what it was I said during the interview; I have almost no memory of that interview at all. But I was told years later by another teacher that Steve Patterson said that day to the Webb admissions people that if there were only one child who was admitted to Webb that year, it should be me. His argument must have been convincing, because Webb admitted me and gave me a scholarship, minus a small parental contribution and a token amount which I would be responsible for after I left college, because the idea was that I had to be in some way responsible for my own education. I don't know if I would have made it into Webb without Steve Patterson. I owe that to him.

I received a fantastic education at Webb, although there were many times while I was there that I did not appreciate it in the moment. Regardless, the teachers there taught me well, whether I appreciated it or not. As with earlier teachers, the names of these teachers remain in my mind: John Heyes, Art House, Dave Fawcett, Laurence MacMillin, Chris Trussell, Joan Rohrback, Roy Bergeson among many others. I learned of the world beyond my own immediate life from them, and that my life would be better thinking about things beyond its own limited scope.

When it came time to choose college, I had my heart set on the University of Chicago but I was a borderline case: The tests and essays were there, but the grades? *Meh* (I was one of those people who did well in the things he liked, less so in the things he did not). University of Chicago Admissions dean Ted O'Neill called Marilyn Blum, Webb's college counselor, and asked her for her opinion on whether I would be a good fit for Chicago. She told O'Neill that I was exactly the sort of student who would benefit from Chicago, and that he would never regret admitting me. O'Neill told me this years later, after I had been Editor-in-Chief of the *Chicago Maroon* and the Ombudsman for the University, by way of letting me know in his opinion Blum had been correct. I owe Blum for being my advocate, and O'Neill for believing her.

The University of Chicago is one of the best universities in the world, and it is not cheap. I was able to attend through a combination of scholarships, government Pell Grants and work study jobs and bank loans. I owe the alumni of the University of Chicago who funded the scholarships, the taxpayers who paid for the grants and subsidized the work study jobs, and, yes, the banks who loaned me money. When one of my expected payment sources for school disappeared, my grandfather told me he would replace it—if I sent him a letter a month. I did. He did. This lasted until my senior year, when I was making enough from freelancing for local newspapers that I could pay for much of my college education myself.

Speaking of which, I owe *Chicago Sun-Times* editor Laura Emerick for reading the articles I wrote for the *Chicago Maroon* and during my internship at the *San Diego Tribune* and deciding I was good enough to write for an actual professional newspaper, and for giving me enough work (at a decent enough payment scale) that I could pay rent on an apartment and school fees. *The San Diego Tribune* internship I got not only through my clips from the *Maroon* but also because I mentioned to a friend that I was looking around for an internship and he said, well, my dad is a friend with the editor of the *Trib*, why don't I ask him to make a call? This was my first but not last experience with the value of connections. I owe that friend, his father, and the editor.

My experience as a freelancer for the *Sun-Times* and the fact that I had a philosophy degree from Chicago were impressive to the Features Editor of the *Fresno Bee*, who gave me a plum job right out of college, for which I had almost no practical experience: Film critic. I owe Diane Webster, that editor, for having the faith that a kid right out of college would live up to the clips he sent. I owe Tom Becker, the Entertainment Editor, as well as a raft of copyeditors and fellow staff writers at the *Bee*, for helping me not make an ass of myself on a day-to-day basis, and to guide me through the process of becoming a pro journalist and newspaper writer.

Because of the *Bee* I did a story on a local DJ, Julie Logan, who did an event at a bar in Visalia. While I was there the most gorgeous woman I had ever seen in my life came up to me and asked me to dance. Reader, I married her (although not at that moment). This woman, as it turns out, had an incredibly good head on her shoulders for money management and had a work ethic that would shame John Calvin. Since Kristine Blauser Scalzi came into my life we have as a couple been financially secure, because she made it her business to make it so. This level of security has afforded me the ability to take advantage of opportunities I otherwise would not have been able.

Eventually I left the Bee to join America Online in the mid-90s, just as it was expanding and becoming the first Google (or Facebook, take your pick). My job there was to edit a humor area, and the practical experience of helping other writers with their writing made me such a better writer that it's hard for me to overstate its importance in my development. I owe Katherine Borsecnik and Bill Youstra for hiring me and handing me that very odd job.

I lasted two years at AOL, at which point I was laid off and immediately rehired as a contractor, for more money for less work. By this time AOL was shedding talent to other startups, many of whom hired me as an editorial contractor because a) They had seen my work and knew I was good, b) I was the only writer they knew. I am indebted to America Online for hiring so many bright, smart people the same time I was there, and then shedding them to go elsewhere, and for all those bright, smart people for remembering me when it came time to look for writing work.

One of those contracts I had included writing a financial newsletter. In 1999, my non-fiction agent Robert Shepard was on the phone with the editor of Rough Guides, who mentioned to him that they were looking for someone to write a book on online finance. My agent said, hey, I have a guy who writes a financial newsletter for AOL. The Rough Guides people said, great, ask him if he wants to write this book. I did. It was my first published book, and it led to two more books by me for Rough Guides. I owe Robert for being proactive on my behalf when he could have let that opportunity swing past him, and I would have been none the wiser.

In 2001 I wrote a novel I intended to sell but then didn't. I decided to put it online on Whatever in December of 2002. Patrick Nielsen Hayden, the senior editor of science fiction at Tor Books, read it and decided to make me an offer on it, which I accepted. If Patrick hadn't read it (or alternately, had read it and did nothing about it because I hadn't formally submitted it), then it's deeply unlikely I would have the career I have now in science fiction.

When that book, *Old Man's War,* came out in 2005, it was championed by Glenn Reynolds of Instapundit to his readers, and by Cory Doctorow of Boing Boing to his. Because of their enthusiasm, the first printing disappeared off the shelf so quickly that it became clear to Tor that this was a book to watch and promote. Glenn and Cory made a huge difference in the early fortunes of that book. In 2006, Neil Gaiman was informed that his book *Anansi Boys* had been nominated for a Hugo in the category of Best Novel and asked if he would like to accept the nomination. Neil, who won a Hugo a year for the previous three years, politely declined, believing (he told me later) that someone else might benefit from that nomination more than he. The nomination he declined went to the next book in the nomination tally: *Old Man's War.* And he was correct: I benefited immensely from the nomination.

The publicity *Old Man's War* gained from the Hugo nomination, among other things, took the book far and wide and brought it to the attention of Scott Stuber and Wolfgang Petersen, who optioned the book to be made into a film, and to Joe Mallozzi, a producer on *Stargate Atlantis,* and who (with Brad Wright) eventually hired me to be the Creative Consultant to the *Stargate: Universe* series. The latter experience was huge in helping me learn the day-to-day practicalities of making television, and having the chance to intensively study scriptwriting; the former has helped me get my foot in the door in terms of having my work seen in film circles. Its success has also made it easier for my fiction agents Ethan Ellenberg and Evan Gregory to sell my work overseas; they've sold my work in nineteen languages now, none of which I would have been able to do on my own.

And so on. I am eliding here; there are numerous people to whom I owe a debt for the work that they have done on my behalf or who have done something that has benefited me, who I am not calling out by name. Some of them know who they are; many of them probably don't, because most of them haven't met me.

There is a flip side to this as well. I have helped others too. I am financially successful now; I pay a lot of taxes. I don't mind because I know how taxes helped me to get to the fortunate position I am in today. I hope the taxes I pay will help some military wife give birth, a mother who needs help feed her child, help another child learn and fall in love with the written word, and help still another get through college. Likewise, I am in a socially advantageous position now, where I can help promote the work of others here and in other places. I do it because I can, because I think I should and because I remember those who helped me. It honors them and it sets the example for those I help to help those who follow them.

I know what I have been given and what I have taken. I know to whom I owe. I know that what work I have done and what I have achieved doesn't exist in a vacuum or outside of a larger context, or without the work and investment of other people, both within the immediate scope of my life and outside of it. I like the idea that I pay it forward, both with the people I can help personally and with those who will never know that some small portion of their own hopefully good fortune is made possible by me.

So much of how their lives will be depends on them, of course, just as so much of how my life is has depended on my own actions. We all have to be the primary actors in our own lives. But so much of their lives will depend on others, too, people near and far. We all have to ask ourselves what role we play in the lives of others—in the lives of loved ones, in the lives of our community, in the life of our nation and in the life of our world. I know my own answer for this. It echoes the answer of those before me, who helped to get me where I am.

A Small Meditation on Art, Commerce and Impermanence

Jan
30
2012

I'm going to touch on something that I've discussed briefly before but which I think is worth reheating into its own post. Here are the best selling books in the US from 1912, which is (for those of you for whom math is not a strong suit) 100 years ago.

1. *The Harvester* by Gene Stratton-Porter
2. *The Street Called Straight* by Basil King
3. *Their Yesterdays* by Harold Bell Wright
4. *The Melting of Molly* by Maria Thompson Davies
5. *A Hoosier Chronicle* by Meredith Nicholson
6. *The Winning of Barbara Worth* by Harold Bell Wright
7. *The Just and the Unjust* by Vaughan Kester
8. *The Net* by Rex Beach
9. *Tante* by Anne Douglas Sedgwick
10. *Fran* by J. Breckenridge Ellis

Questions: How many of these have you read? How many of the author names do you recognize? How influential have these books been to modern literature, or at the very least, the literature you choose to read? Do you think these authors believed that their works would, in some way, survive them? I think it's fair to say that outside of a small group of academic specialists or enthusiasts, these books and their authors don't have much currency.

This isn't a slight on the authors or their works, mind you. If you look up some of these authors, they're pretty interesting. Gene Stratton-Porter was an early conservationist and owned her own movie studio.

Meredith Nicholson was a US diplomat to several countries in South America and central America. Howard Bell Wright was reportedly the first author to make more than a million dollars writing fiction, and this was back in 1912, when a million was worth more than $22 million today. I don't doubt at least some of these books were well-regarded as art. And I would imagine, author egos being what they are, that at least a couple of them imagined that we would be talking about their works today, a hundred years later, as influences if nothing else.

We're not. Now, I imagine there's at least a couple people out there shaking their fists at me, wondering how I could not see Stratton-Porter (or whomever) as a towering figure in American literature. As noted above, I cede there is possibly academic or specialized interest. I'm talking about everyone else. I feel pretty confident of my basic knowledge of early 20th century literature, if nothing else than through my interest in HL Mencken, who was one of the preëminient literature critics of the day. If I'm coming up blank on these names and books, I feel reasonably confident in suggesting most readers these days—even the well-read ones—will do similarly.

If you're a writer, this might depress you. If the best-selling books of 1912 are largely forgotten, what chance do *your* books have in 2012, especially if they don't scale the heights of sales these books have? Surprise! Probably little. I mean, it's certainly possible they will survive: Neither Theodore Dreiser nor Sherwood Anderson got near the year-end best-seller lists between 1910 and 1919, but they are still taught and discussed, and in their way influence literature today. But, yeah. Don't count on it.

And that's fine. Relieve yourself of the illusion that you're writing for the ages. The ages will decide who is doing that on their own; you don't get a vote. I understand the temptation is to try to write something that will speak to the generations, but, look, in 1912 they hadn't even yet invented pre-sliced bread. If you aim for being relevant to the future, you're probably going to fail because you literally cannot imagine it, even if you write science fiction.

Forget even sliced bread; you can't imagine the values or interests or views on the world that people might have a century from now. Human nature as defined by biology doesn't change much over decades or centuries but the culture sure does, and it's a moving target in any event; there's no end point in attitudes and opinions. If I tried to explain a woman's place in 1912 United States to my daughter, she would *explode with outrage*. If a writer in 1912 tried to write specifically to my daughter (or anyone's daughter) 100 years hence, the disconnect would be impressive. If I tried to write for a thirteen-year-old girl in 2112, the same thing would happen.

If you *must* aim for relevance, try for being relevant *now*; it's a context you understand. We can still read (and do read) Shakespeare and Cervantes and Dickinson, and I think it's worth noting Shakespeare was busy trying to pack in the groundlings *today*, Cervantes was writing in no small part to criticize a then-currently popular form of fiction, and Dickinson was barely even publishing at all, i.e., not really caring about future readers. In other words, they were focused on their *now*. It's not a bad focus for anyone.

Will your work survive? Probably not, but so what? You won't survive, either. 100 years from now you're *very* likely to be dead. Even if your work survives, it won't do *you* much good. In the meantime that still leaves lots of people *today* to potentially read your stuff, argue about it, be inspired by it (or react against it) and generally make a lot of noise about it. You might even make a living at it, which is a bonus. Focus on those people today, and on today's times. Enjoy it all now. Enjoy it while it lasts. Then when it's over, you can say you had fun at the time.

A Small Rant About The Things I Might or Might Not Know Which I Might or Might Not Tell You About

Spin magazine had up a piece on Amanda Palmer and Neil Gaiman performing a benefit gig the other night, in which it revealed that the two of them revealed to the audience that they were dating. Good for them. But the news of their dating prompted someone to send me an e-mail, asking me why *I* had never mentioned that Palmer and Gaiman were dating and suggesting that it was somehow my duty to keep people informed about such things.

E-mail being the emotionally flat medium that it is, I was not entirely sure that this person was joking, but the more I re-read it the more I became convinced that this person was at least mildly piqued that they thought I was holding such a choice tidbit of quasi-celebrity news from them, and did believe I was obliged to spill about people of fame they assumed that I knew personally.

Assuming that I am in fact not being hypersensitive, two points here:

1. How was *I* supposed to know this? I'm an admirer of both Miss Palmer's music and her crazy eyebrows, but I don't know her and have never met her. Seems unlikely I would be her bosom confidant. Likewise, while it may seem to some outside observers that I *should* know Neil Gaiman, we've only ever exchanged a few brief e-mails, mostly about the recent Hugo Voters Packet. I've spoken to him once, but that was in 1992, when I called him up to interview him for a newspaper article I was doing on graphic novels. At no time in our conversation did Gaiman ever say "Hey, anonymous newspaper reporter whom I shall probably never speak with again, seventeen years from now I plan to date a very cute and talented musician. Please keep this news in the strictest of confidence, unless at such time you happen to own a blog, which right now sounds like a disease involving phlegm, but which in the future will mean something else entirely, in which case you may write about it there." At which point I suspect I would have thought to myself, *hmmm, this guy's been drinking too much cartoonist's ink.*

Well, you say, you know lots of people who know Gaiman (and now, presumably, Miss Palmer). That's almost like knowing them! Well, no, not really. Look: One of the people who is close enough to me that I consider them family is close enough to Brad Pitt that they went to each other's weddings. I do not know Brad Pitt. Someone I was a friend of in college was for years a close confidant of Hillary Clinton. I do not know Hillary Clinton. As recently noted, people I know can get on the phone and talk to Harlan Ellison any time they want. I do not know Harlan Ellison. I could amaze and delight you with the list of all the notable people I *almost* but in fact *don't* know personally.

Now, perhaps one day I shall meet Mr. Gaiman and Miss Palmer; seems a reasonable bet I'll see at least one of them this August. And perhaps on that day we'll experience the sort of immediate and massive friendcrush that leads each of us to reveal all sorts of secrets to one another in long intimate conversations that will instantly cement our new status as *ZOMG totally BFFs*. Hey, I'm somewhat personable; it could happen. And then in fact I *will* know everything there is possibly to know about Mr. Gaiman and/or Miss Palmer. Which leads to the next point:

2. Even if I *did* know personal information about Gaiman or Palmer, why would any of you be under the impression I would tell *you*? I already have enough problems with people who *don't* know me assuming that every single thing that I ever do or learn about in my personal life is going to get plastered up on Whatever in an orgy of attention-seeking indiscretion. The last thing I need to do is to actually *prove them right*.

This may be hard for some folks to believe, but my default assumption when someone mentions something about themselves to me is *to tell no one else*. Before anything else, this is simply the polite thing to do, and what I would hope others would do for me if the situations were reversed. But more than that, there's the fact that somewhere along the way I realized it's better to have the sort of friends who know they can trust you, than the sort of friends who value the entertainment value of your inability to keep a confidence. I want *friends*, not an audience.

If I meet Neil Gaiman/Amanda Palmer/Whomever and we decide we're gonna be pals and share each other's *unmentionable, career-damaging secrets* in the creative person's drunken equivalent of becoming blood brothers, here's probably what I'd mention about it here: "Hey, so I met Neil Gaiman/Amanda Palmer/Whomever, and they were very cool once I got all my squeee over and done with." Because—no offense—that's about all you need to know about that. Everyone's personal life is personal until and unless they choose to make it otherwise. Even the people you like and admire and may in some way, and against all reason, feel you own.

Snark and Insult

Mar 19 2012

Let's go ahead and get Reader Request Week started, shall we? To begin, this question from SMQ:

> *You have a well-earned reputation for snark and the art of the thought-out-but-blistering retort, but unlike many you usually seem to avoid crossing the line too far into personal attacks (and are even quick to mallet those who do so in comment threads). Where do you see the line between snark and ad hominem? Is it a sharp line or a fuzzy one? Other than raw talent, how do you personally maintain that balance?*

First, to be pedantic, an *ad hominem* argument is different than a personal attack. Here's a personal attack: "You're a worm." Here's an *ad hominem* argument: "You're a worm, therefore your opinion on the Republican primaries is worthless." You may or may not be a worm of a person, but it does not follow that *because* you're a worm, your opinion on the GOP primaries is invalid; it may be that you're extraordinarily versed on the Republican candidates, their positions and their relative strengths in each primary, and that, independently, you have worm-like personal qualities that mean you're not worth spending time with on a regular basis. It's also the case that not every *ad hominem* argument is a poor one, to wit: "You're appallingly ignorant, therefore your opinion on the Republican primaries is worthless." If one is indeed appallingly ignorant, particularly on political matters, it may put one in a poor position to have a worthwhile opinion on the GOP primaries. That said, most people don't employ *ad hominem* arguments in this fashion.

Pedantry aside, I think what's being asked here is how do I keep a written piece involving a person from crossing over from legitimate criticism to simple (and mere) insult. I don't have an actual checklist for these things, but when I'm writing an entry, here are some of the things I think about.

1. Public or private figure: I'm more likely to be more free with my snark if the person at whom it is aimed is a public figure—a politician, celebrity, writer, etc—than I am if it's just some person. This is partly years of working as a professional journalist inculcating the practical aspects of *New York Times v. Sullivan* into my brain, and partly a recognition that I natively have tens of thousands of daily readers and can on occasion, with the right topic, produce an exponentially larger number of readers through links, reposting, and media coverage, thus making it easy for me to really mess up someone's day. So I do choose my targets.

For example, when Kirk Cameron shows up on Piers Morgan's talk show and expounds on his views regarding homosexuality, he's doing so in his capacity as a public figure: he was on the show promoting his latest work, he's a person who actively courts the public eye to express his religious and social views and the show is broadcast to a national audience. An example of the opposite end of things: A teenage girl writing in her blog criticizing something I wrote, which I felt could use a response. This was a private individual expressing her view on a blog which while ostensibly public was not at all well-trafficked and for which there was no expectation that the opinion would circulate beyond her own personal circle of friends and readers.

Do I treat both equally? Of course not. Kirk Cameron is an adult and a public figure and however much he whines about how it's unfair that people are mean to him, is eminently capable of handling criticism of any sort. The teenage girl was not courting the public with her commentary, and would likely have been embarrassed by an influx of visitors to her site wanting to engage her on the topic. So Kirk Cameron I feel fine unloading on; the girl I was careful not to, up to and including *not* linking to her site (or quoting her directly, which would have made it easy for the ambitious to find her).

Mr. Cameron's indubitably a public figure, and the anonymous teenage girl is indubitably a private figure, but what about, say, Lori Jareo, who several years ago tried to sell her Star Wars fanfic on Amazon? Or Judith Griggs, former editor of *Cooks Source*? A not unreasonable number of people who I comment on fall somewhere in the middle of the line and my choice to comment on them or not—or to publicly identify and link to a comment—really is a judgment call. Whether I make that call correctly in every case is open to question.

2. On point vs. pointless: Let's go back to Kirk Cameron, as I have discussed him most recently, when he described homosexuality as "unnatural" and detrimental to civilization. Quiz for you: Which of the following do you think I think is legitimate to call him, and which do you think is less so?

a) "Ignorant bigot"

b) "Pestilent toad"

The answer: a). It's legitimate to suggest Mr. Cameron's an ignorant bigot because one, he doesn't appear to know that homosexuality is in fact totally natural and well-documented as occurring in the natural world (thus, "ignorant"), and two, he believes that homosexuality is detrimental to civilization, and also that "unnatural" is a negative thing in his assessment (thus "bigot"). And call Mr. Cameron an "ignorant bigot" I did.

(I'll note here that in the comments thread to the piece, some folks offered a number of defenses for use of the word "unnatural," among them theological and philosophical concepts reaching back to Aquinas. In my opinion that gives Mr. Cameron, champion of the Crocoduck, rather a lot of unearned credit, but even if it's true what it essentially means is that Cameron's using "unnatural" in the sense of "opposed to a philosophical construct of the concept of 'natural' which in itself has no rigorous scientific relationship to what occurs in the natural world." Which to my mind does not improve things dramatically for him.)

It's rather less legitimate to label Mr. Cameron a "pestilent toad," because, well. He seems pretty clean. But more to the point, calling him a pestilent toad doesn't really do much other than call him a name. One may argue that he spreads the pestilence of intolerance and that his antipathy toward gays is positively amphibian, but you have to explain it and it seems the long way around, sort of like suggesting how "unnatural" really refers to philosophical concepts pioneered by Aquinas. It might be better to keep things simple, or if not simple, then immediately relatable to the subject on hand.

Now, ironically, should Mr. Cameron ever attempt to sue me for libel, my defense would be marginally better if I did refer to him as a pestilent toad rather than an ignorant bigot, because I could claim "pestilent toad" as an example of hyperbole, since I don't really believe he's an *actual* pestilent toad, whereas I suspect he may be an *actual* ignorant bigot. But this goes back to the whole "public figure" thing.

3. The whole "there's a person there" thing: Public figure or not, Mr. Cameron's a human being and I suspect on a day-to-day basis he's perfectly nice to his wife, family members, etc, as are other people who have particular opinions or actions I might disagree with or oppose (Note: this is *not* your cue to haul out stories of Mr. Cameron being a terrible person from his *Growing Pains* days, or to remind me that Hitler surely loved his dogs). And while the Internet does make it easy to forget that you're responding to or about an actual human being rather than a bunch of words on a screen, that's all the more reason to remember there's a person there. So I do operate on the principle of not saying about others that which I would not have said about me. This fact must necessarily be tempered with the understanding that I am someone who gleefully collects one-star reviews and sends back hate mail for being insufficiently creative, with the demand that the writer revise and do it better.

Even so, it makes me less inclined to go head-hunting just for the thrill of head-hunting. That was fun once, but now I'm in my forties and the thrill of pounding on someone just to pound on them has lessened considerably. I do try to have a *point* to it.

Which brings us to the final point:

4. Having a point: When I bang on someone, it's usually not just to bang on them for existing but to talk about something they said/did/believe. Also, when I bring them up, generally I'm not talking to that person specifically; I'm talking to the people who are reading here. And while I know everyone loves watching me get my snark on, I flatter myself—and my readers—in supposing they are not just here to watch me explode; they want a cogent point in there somewhere. That being the case, there's a point at which any snark aimed at the person stops being a persuasive part of the argument and starts being its own thing to the detraction of the larger argument. The trick is staying on the right side of that. The three points above help me make that determination, but it's also the experience of writing this sort of way that helps me know where that line is.

And, you know, sometimes I *don't* know—sometimes I screw up and make an ass of myself unintentionally. Sometimes I might decide I don't want to be constructive and just want to vent, in which case I may make an ass out of myself *intentionally*. Sometimes I'll think I've toed the line perfectly but any one of you (or more) will decide that I've gone too far—this is often but not always correlative with whether the person or subject I'm going off on is one you're passionate about. Toeing the line isn't an exact science. Fortunately, I don't have problems apologizing when it's obvious that's what needs to be done.

Which is another topic entirely, so let's end this piece here.

Sociopathic Corporations

Mar
17
2011

Arrow Quivershaft asks:

How can we justify treating multinational corporations as people, despite the fact that most of them act like clinical sociopaths in general action?

Well, the *FCC v. AT&T* ruling suggests that in fact there's a very long way to go before we do in fact treat them as people, so I'm not in agreement with the assertion that we do. That corporate "personhood" exists is non-controversial, but their "personhood" is not of a manner that tracks precisely with being a real, human person. This being the case I don't think it's accurate or useful to describe their behavior with reference to the behavior of real live individual humans.

In particular, I disagree with the notion that most of them act like clinical sociopaths. Rather, I think the majority of corporations act logically and rationally and in a manner consistent with the general reason for their existence. And the reason most corporations exist—and most large multinational corporations in particular—is simple: To maximize shareholder value. There is also a general need to do so on a regular schedule; the one that is most familiar is a quarterly one, consistent with the SEC requirement that publicly-held corporations must file 10-Q forms. There may be other goals or aspirations a publicly-held corporation might have, but when it comes down to it, those are the two that count.

If you acknowledge that in the final analysis the purpose of a corporation is to maximize value to the shareholders, and make sure that each quarterly report shows such value maximization as its trend line, then their actions make perfect, reasonable sense—and might even if you employed them on a human scale. Why do corporations avoid paying corporate taxes whenever possible? Because that maximizes shareholder value—and don't *you* take every possible tax deduction you can? Why do corporations lay off workers in the US and hire them in cheaper countries? Because that maximizes shareholder value—and might not *you* switch from a more expensive name brand to a store brand to save a little money? Why do corporations lobby governments for tax breaks and credits—and bail-outs, when it comes to that? Because that maximizes shareholder value—and don't *you* vote your self-interest and ask the government for help when you're in trouble? And so on.

But, you may say, there's a *difference* between when I buy a store brand, and when a corporation lays off thousands of workers. Well, yes. Corporations aren't people. As I was saying earlier. But just as your buying a store brand is not evidence of sociopathic behavior, neither is a corporation laying off thousands and hiring cheaper labor elsewhere. You're both staying consistent to ground level economic imperatives, but your ground level economic imperatives are different, because you are fundamentally different entities.

But! You say! Like Soylent Green, corporations are made of people! If they are made of people, should they not then at least keep the interests of people at heart? Well, you tell me: When you pay a CEO $80 million (or whatever) and tell him his single job is to maximize shareholder value, where do his interests lie? People, bless our black little hearts, are selfish and self-justifying primates, and we can excuse—nay, justify—nay, *celebrate*!—a lot of behavior in ourselves if the compensation is high enough. If a CEO needs to cut $80 million from his company to increase shareholder value, he's going to figure it'll be more useful to slice off a thousand workers than to fire himself. He may not even be wrong, since the next CEO they hire will cost just as much, whereas the work those 1,000 workers did can be dumped on their colleagues who were happy to have survived the axe.

Here's the deal: In order to change corporate behavior, you have to change the underlying goals of the corporation. If for example the reason for the existence of the corporation was not to maximize shareholder value but instead to offer steady, well-compensated employment to its workers here in the US, would that have a significant impact on how the corporation acted? It might, although from the outside it might be difficult to see (it would still likely try to avoid taxes, lobby governments, etc). But in a general sense, if you change why the corporation exists, it's possible you'll see a change in what it defines as logical and rational behavior.

Short of that you have to make sure that corporations are subject to laws and limits on their behavior—and of course they'll fight that every step of the way because it impedes their goal of maximizing shareholder value. But the magic of corporations, if you want to call it that, is that regardless of the economic or social milieu you put them in, they will do what they do—maximize shareholder value!—as well as they can possibly do it. US corporations did fine in eras where their taxes were higher than they are now, so the various hand-wringing about the onus those taxes place on corporations doesn't particularly *move* me, I have to say.

I don't think you have to change the fundamental nature of corporations, personally, even if I think they're stupid to think in quarterly terms rather than focus on longer-term strategy. What I do think you need to do is let their single-minded focus on maximizing shareholder value work for the overall benefit of the country. How you do this is of course a matter of some debate, and where I am fairly sure I fall out with conservatives on strategy, since among other things I wouldn't be at all opposed to hiking (or closing loopholes in) both corporate and capital gains taxes in a manner that protected the rather meager middle-class investment in both. I understand these days that a belief in the value of a progressive taxation schedule makes me a dirty communist fit only to be set on fire, but you know what, you go ahead and bring that gasoline. Speaking of sociopaths.

The Sort of Crap I Don't Get

Aug
31
2011

Over at Twitter, author Adrienne Martini asks me if I get the sort of jackassed comments and e-mails that Shawna James Ahern, a female food blogger, talks about in a recent post, and wonders if it's a gender-related thing.

The short answer: No I don't get those, and yes, I think it's substantially gender-related.

The longer answer: I do of course get hate mail and obnoxious comments. The hate mail gave me a title for a book, after all, and the obnoxious comments on the site are just part of doing business as a Public Internet Figure™. This is why I have a robust commenting policy and am not afraid to follow up on it. Whenever jackholes pop up, I mallet them down, and that's the way it should be.

What I don't have, however, is the sort of chronic and habitual stream of abuse this blogger describes. There are constantly people annoyed with me (go search "Scalzi" on Twitter today and you'll see some fellows mewling plaintively about me, for example; it's darling), but it doesn't appear anyone makes a *hobby* out of it. It's all situational, in that I'll write something that annoys someone, they'll be annoyed and write about it, and then it all goes away. There are additionally and quite naturally people who seem to have a default dislike of me. So perhaps they are more inclined to be annoyed with me and they'll become so quicker than the average person might, and thus be publicly annoyed with me at a higher frequency.

But again, they don't do it all the time; they're not making it their mission in life to ride me. And to be clear, people are *annoyed* with me, or may mock me, or may even call me names. But these people are not fundamentally (or, generally speaking, not even *slightly*) hateful or hurtful people and it would be wrong to characterize them as such. What I *don't* receive, other than exceptionally rarely, is what I consider to be actual abusive commenting, where the intent is to hurt me, from people who are genuinely hateful.

What follows is my own anecdotal experience, but it's also the anecdotal experience of someone blogging for 13 years and having been engaged in the online world for almost 20, i.e., decently knowledgeable. In my experience, talking to women bloggers and writers, they are quite likely to get abusive comments and e-mail, and receive more of it not only than what *I* get personally (which isn't difficult) but more than what men bloggers and writers typically get. I think bloggers who focus on certain subjects (politics, sexuality, etc) will get more abusive responses than ones who write primarily on other topics, but even in those fields, women seem more of a target for abusive people than the men are. And even women writing on non-controversial topics get smacked with this crap. I know knitting bloggers who have some amazingly hateful comments directed at them. They're blogging about *knitting*, for Christ's sake.

Why do women bloggers get more abuse than male bloggers? Oh, I think for all the stereotypical reasons, up to and including the fact that for a certain sort of passive-aggressive internet jackass, it's just psychologically easier to erupt at a woman than a man because even online, there's the cultural subtext that a guy will be confrontational and in your face, while a woman will just take it (and if she doesn't, why, then *she's just a bitch* and deserves even more abuse). Cowards pick what they consider soft targets and use anonymity and/or the distancing effect of the Internet to avoid the actual and humiliating judgment of real live humans that they'd have to receive out in the world.

There's also the fact that culturally speaking, women are burdened with a larger number of things they are made to feel bad about, things that men don't have to bother with. Notes Ms. Ahern, about a recent trip to New Orleans:

From those brief 25 hours, I received emails that said, "Don't you know that processed food is killing Americans? How could you have posted a photo with Velveeta cheese?" or "What kind of a mother are you, leaving your child for another trip? Selfish bitch." or "Sausage? Andouille sausage? You don't think you're fat enough already, you have to stuff more sausage in your mouth?" There were complaints about where I ate, how much I ate, how happy I was to be with the people I sat with, that I was bragging by listing the people with whom I had dinner. There were comments about my weight, comments about my parenting, comments about the way I spend money, comments about the farce of gluten-free, comments about my photographic skills, and comments about how often I posted on Twitter (for some, that answer was: too much). Nothing goes undiscussed as being disgusted in my online world.

I can contrast this with how people approach me on similar topics. When I post photos of processed cheese, I don't get abused about how bad it is and how bad I am for posting about it. People don't abuse me over my weight, even when I talk explicitly about it. I go away from my family for weeks at a time and never get crap about what a bad father that makes me, even though I have always been the stay-at-home parent. Now, it's true in every case that if I did get crap, I would deal with it harshly, either by going after the commenter or by simply malleting their jackassery into oblivion. But the point is I don't *have* to. I'm a man and I largely get a pass on weight, on parenting and (apparently) on exhibition and ingestion of processed cheese products. Or at the very least if someone thinks I'm a bad person for any of these, they keep it to themselves. They do the same for any number of other topics they might feel free to lecture or abuse women over.

It's this sort of thing that reminds me that the Internet is not the same experience for me as it is for some of my women friends, and why I've spent a substantial amount of time drilling into Athena's head that the Internet is full of assholes who like to void themselves all over the women they find. I'm sad this is still the case. But being sad about it isn't going to keep me from trying to build those defenses into her, so that when inevitably she runs up against these people, she can deal with them properly, with a sound that approximates that of a flushing toilet.

That this will outrage them and make them more inclined to rail at her doesn't negate the necessity. It makes it more of a necessity, alas.

Speech and Kirk Cameron

Mar
7
2012

Kirk Cameron, former child star and current subscriber to an apparently particularly uneducated brand of evangelical Christianity, is shocked and appalled that when he makes public statements on a nationally-televised talk show about homosexuality (and thus, the people who are homosexual) being "unnatural" and detrimental to civilization, there are a large number of people who will react to such a public statement by taking it upon themselves to mock him for it. He says:

> *I should be able to express moral views on social issues, especially those that have been the underpinning of Western civilization for 2,000 years—without being slandered, accused of hate speech, and told from those who preach 'tolerance' that I need to either bend my beliefs to their moral standards or be silent when I'm in the public square.*

Well, Kirk Cameron, here's the thing. You are correct when you say you should be able to express your moral views on social issues, and as a staunch defender of the First Amendment, I will defend to the death your right to say whatever ridiculous, ignorant and bigoted thing that has been fermenting in that cracked clay pot you call a brain pan. But the First Amendment also means that when you say such things, other people have the a right to mock you and the silly, stupid words that have dribbled out of your skull through that word hole above your chin. If you call someone "unnatural," they might call you an "asshole." That's the deal.

To put it another way: The First Amendment guarantees a right to speech. It does not guarantee a right to *respect.* As I am fond of saying, if you want people to respect your ideas, get better ideas. Likewise, freedom of speech does not mean freedom from consequence. If you're going to parade around on television engaging in hateful bastardry, then, strangely enough, people will often call you out on it. They may also call you out on the hypocrisy of maintaining that when *you* say that the way someone else lives is unnatural and detrimental to civilization, you mean it with *love,* but when *they* call your words bigoted trollspeak, they're crossing a line or engaging in slander—the legal concept of which, incidentally, you don't appear to understand very well, nor libel, which generally speaking is probably more applicable in this case, you crazy public figure, you.

(You're also wrong about homosexuality being unnatural—birds do it, bees do it, even educated fleas do it!—not to mention, of course, that the imputation that "unnatural" means "wrong" is one of those stupid things people say when they haven't thought through the implications of the assertion. I mean, you're aware *television* is "unnatural," right? So are *pants.* So are eyeglasses, cell phones, indoor plumbing, the *Growing Pains* complete second season on DVD, and just about any weapon more complicated than a rock. The rule I would like to apply moving forward is that anyone using "unnatural" as an intrinsic reason for something being bad or wrong must commit to a life of Rousseauean simplicity in a location untrammeled by the unnatural accoutrements of human civilization. I recommend the forests of Papua New Guinea or any place in Siberia, so long as it is above the Arctic Circle.)

Kirk Cameron, I fully support your right to speak your mind about moral views. I also fully support the rights of other people to criticize you and those views, and also their right to be *mean* to you while doing so, and not *just* because, in my opinion, it's mean and not in the least bit *loving* to suggest gays are detrimental and destructive, simply by existing and loving who they choose to love and refusing to accept your desire for them not to be who they are. You're entitled to your stupid, petty, awful, hateful bigoted opinion. Everyone else is entitled to call it exactly what it is.

Spoiler Statute of Limitations

Mar
6
2009

Last night I decided to annoy some geeks, so I wrote on Twitter: "Note to *Watchmen* fans: THERE IS NO CONSPIRACY. THE COMEDIAN JUMPED." Which immediately returned a series of death threats and furious rebukes, so, you know, mission accomplished (note: no, I don't think any of those people were actually upset). But along with those were a couple of people who twittered back, "Uh, dude? Did you just, like, do a *spoiler*? 'Cause that's not cool."

It's not a spoiler, since, among other things, within the first three pages of the comic it becomes evident that jumping is not precisely what the Comedian did. Also, given the placement of the Comedian's death in the novel (i.e., right at the beginning), and its being highlighted in the various movie trailers, discussing it is no more spoiling *Watchmen* than noting that, say, Marley was dead, to begin with—or, alternately saying that Marley *wasn't* dead to begin with, he just moved to Jamaica and picked up the guitar.

That said, even if it *were* a spoiler, the thing is: Look, *Watchmen* is twenty-three years old. Surely the statute of limitations on spoiling the book has run out by now. SPOILER ALERTS should not be in effect forever. Yes, they have their place: If I had run out of *The Crying Game* screaming "The chick's a *dude!*" as people were waiting to see it for the first time, it would be a case of justifiable homicide. But now, in 2009? Sorry, man. You missed your window to be outraged.

(Funny story about that particular movie is that I actually first saw it at home: I was a movie critic and Miramax sent me a screener on tape.

I remember getting to that part and going "wait, *what?*" and actually rewinding. And then I remember writing a *very careful review.*)

If there is, in fact, a spoiler statute of limitations, the question then becomes, well, how long is it? I throw that question open to the crowd, but here are my suggestions:

Television: One week (because it's generally episodic, and that's how long you have until the next episode)

Movies: One year (time enough for everyone to see it in the theaters, on DVD and on cable)

Books: Five years (because books don't reach nearly as many people at one time)

So, for example, the big spoiler in *Old Man's War* (gung Wnar Fntna vf Wbua Creel'f qrnq jvsr'f pybar!—that's ROT-13 encoding, by the way, if you're inclined to decode it) should probably remain a spoiler until next January, the five-year anniversary of OMW. But the big spoiler of M. Night Shyamalan's *The Sixth Sense* (Oehpr Jvyyvf vf gbgnyyl qrnq!) expired on August 6, 2000, and the big spoiler of the same director's *The Happening* (Z. Avtug Fulnznyna'f fugvpx unf orra fhpxrq qevre guna n urzbcuvyvnp ng n inzcver pbairagvba!) runs out next June 13, although in that case, it won't be that much of a surprise to anyone.

Status Check, Re: USA

Jul
4
2010

The 234th birthday of the United States of America is a fine time to check in with one's self about how one feels about being a citizen of this country, so today's question: Am I proud to be an American?

I am. The United States, like so many things, is better as an idealized concept than it is as an actual entity, on account that the nation is made up of people, and while most people mean well, in a day-to-day sense they struggle with their ideals, which are often so *inconvenient* to their desires. And so, like a married family-values politician with a Craigslist personal ad, or a vegan Febreezing the apartment so no one will catch the smell of bacon, America often finds itself failing its own expectations for itself and others.

In times like this what I remember is that while people (and countries) fail their expectations and ideals, those expectations remain, and even when failing them, people and countries find those expectations and ideals to be powerfully attractive. Despite sidesteps, backtracks and inactions, over time—over the long haul—we move toward our ideals. Martin Luther King famously noted that the arc of history is long but bends toward justice. He was correct, but only to the extent that justice is in itself genuinely held as a goal.

As Americans, we do hold it so: It's right there in the preamble of the Constitution of the United States, along with other laudable goals. And I do believe that despite whatever day-to-day failings our nation has, however we are on this particular day struggling to live up to our ideal of ourselves, nevertheless over the arc of history we are bending toward justice, and are forming that more perfect union we imagined ourselves having more than two centuries ago. It is this commitment to justice and a more perfect union, written into our country's genetic code, that makes me proud to be an American, and inspired to make sure that I do my part to get us there.

Will we get there? Not in my lifetime, and perhaps not in any lifetime; people stubbornly remain people, and heir to weakness, desire, self-absorption and stupidity. The Founding Fathers were wise to note we were working on a "more perfect" union, not a "perfect" one, because perfection is hard with actual humans involved. But I believe we can get closer to perfect, and then closer than that, and then closer still. It's like approaching the speed of light: the closer you want to get to it, the more energy you have to put in to get to it. You'll never get all the way to it. But you can get close enough to get to where you want to go, in time, with effort.

So happy birthday to the United States of America. I'm glad to be a part of it, and glad to be working on it.

Steve Jobs and Me

Oct
5
2011

The Macintosh was not the very first computer I remember working and playing on—that honor would go to the Radio Shack TRS-80—but I wrote my very first story ever on a Macintosh. In fact, I wrote it on the very first generation of the Macintosh. My friend Ezra Chowaiki had one when we were in high school, and as a result, I think I spent more of my freshman year in high school in his room than I spent in my own, banging out stories (in eight-page chunks, as that was the file size limit at the time) and playing with the paint program. Occasionally I would have to borrow someone else's computer (I didn't have my own), and then I would end up being confused and frustrated that whatever PC I was on was not nearly as simple to write on. I was spoiled by the Macintosh at the very beginning of my writing career; simply put, it was the way writing was supposed to have been. It would be wrong to say I would not be a writer if the Macintosh did not exist; it is accurate to say that the Macintosh made it so much *easier* for me to be a writer that I never seriously entertained being anything else.

I didn't own a computer of my own until just before my senior year of college, when I bought a surplus Macintosh SE from my college newspaper. It was with this computer that I first went online outside of a business setting—I got myself a modem and a disc with the Prodigy online service and I was off to the races. With my next computer—a Mac Quadra—I logged onto the Internet proper, got myself Mosaic, went to Yahoo, hit its "random site" button and kept hitting it for just about 72 hours straight. Very shortly thereafter my I coded my very first personal

Web Site on a local internet provider. The very first iteration of my Web presence was made on a Mac.

Which is not to say I am a card-carrying member of the Cult of Apple; indeed, there is some evidence to the contrary. But I am an admirer of technology that gets it right, and say what you will about Apple as a corporate entity and Apple products as fetish objects, the fact is the company makes some really excellent things. I've owned non-Apple mp3 players and I've owned iPods; iPods have generally been better. I've owned tablet computers and an iPad; the iPad is better. I've owned several laptops; the Mac Air I'm writing this on is hands down the best laptop I've ever owned. To admire the technology is to in some way admire the ethos behind it, which is even more indirectly to admire the man who inspired the ethos.

Which brings us to Steve Jobs, who I am sure almost all of you know passed away earlier today. Jobs was the man behind the Mac, the computer which made it easy for me to be a writer and to find my way online, two things which have shaped my life so significantly that I would literally be a different person without them. The Mac works the way it does because Jobs made it his business to make it work like that. For that, I owe him a rather large debt of gratitude. The iPods and iPads and ginchy thin laptops are all just icing on that substantial slice of cake.

I cannot of course speak of Jobs as a human; I didn't know him, never interacted with him, and most of what I knew of him came through the technology press, with which he seemed to have contentious relationship at best. All that I can speak about is how what he *did* affected me. Simply put, it affected me by helping me to *become* me—to express myself easily, fluidly and to people all over the world, and in doing so, end up as the person I am today. This is important. I won't forget it.

For it, and for everything that's come because of it, I say: Thanks, Steve. You will be missed.

Straight White Male: The Lowest Difficulty Setting There Is

May
15
2012

I've been thinking of a way to explain to straight white men how life works for them, without invoking the dreaded word "privilege," to which they react like vampires being fed a garlic tart at high noon. It's not that the word "privilege" is incorrect, it's that it's not *their* word. When confronted with "privilege," they fiddle with the word itself, and haul out the dictionaries and find every possible way to talk about the word but not any of the things the word signifies.

So, the challenge: how to get across the ideas bound up in the word "privilege," in a way that your average straight white man will *get*, without freaking out about it?

Being a white guy who likes women, here's how I would do it:

Dudes. Imagine life here in the US—or indeed, pretty much anywhere in the Western world—is a massive role playing game, like World of Warcraft except appallingly mundane, where most quests involve the acquisition of money, cell phones and donuts, although not always at the same time. Let's call it The Real World. You have installed The Real World on your computer and are about to start playing, but first you go to the settings tab to bind your keys, fiddle with your defaults, and choose the difficulty setting for the game. Got it?

Okay: In the role playing game known as The Real World, "Straight White Male" is the lowest difficulty setting there is.

This means that the default behaviors for almost all the non-player characters in the game are easier on you than they would be otherwise. The default barriers for completions of quests are lower. Your leveling-up thresholds come more quickly. You automatically gain entry to some parts of the map that others have to work for. The game is easier to play, automatically, and when you need help, by default it's easier to get.

Now, once you've selected the "Straight White Male" difficulty setting, you *still* have to create a character, and how many points you get to start—and how they are apportioned—will make a difference. Initially the computer will tell you how many points you get and how they are divided up. If you start with 25 points, and your dump stat is wealth, well, then you may be kind of screwed. If you start with 250 points and your dump stat is charisma, well, then you're probably fine. Be aware the computer makes it difficult to start with more than 30 points; people on higher difficulty settings generally start with even fewer than that.

As the game progresses, your goal is to gain points, apportion them wisely, and level up. If you start with fewer points and fewer of them in critical stat categories, or choose poorly regarding the skills you decide to level up on, then the game will still be difficult for you. But because you're playing on the "Straight White Male" setting, gaining points and leveling up will still by default be easier, all other things being equal, than for another player using a higher difficulty setting.

Likewise, it's certainly possible someone playing at a higher difficulty setting is progressing more quickly than you are, because they had more points initially given to them by the computer and/or their highest stats are wealth, intelligence and constitution and/or simply because they play the game better than you do. It doesn't change the fact *you* are still playing on the lowest difficulty setting.

You can lose playing on the lowest difficulty setting. The lowest difficulty setting is still the easiest setting to win on. The player who plays on the "Gay Minority Female" setting? *Hardcore.*

And maybe at this point you say, hey, I like a challenge, I want to change my difficulty setting! Well, here's the thing: In The Real World, you don't unlock any rewards or receive any benefit for playing on higher difficulty settings. The game is just *harder,* and potentially a lot less fun. And you say, okay, but what if I want to replay the game later on a higher difficulty setting, just to see what it's like? Well, here's the *other* thing about The Real World: You only get to play it once. So why make it more difficult than it has to be? Your goal is to *win* the game, not make it difficult.

Oh, and one other thing. Remember when I said that you could choose your difficulty setting in The Real World? Well, I lied. In fact, the computer chooses the difficulty setting for you. You don't get a choice; you just get what gets given to you at the start of the game, and then you have to deal with it.

So that's "Straight White Male" for you in The Real World (and also, in the real world): The lowest difficulty setting there is. All things being equal, and even when they are not, if the computer—or life—assigns you the "Straight White Male" difficulty setting, then brother, you've caught a break.

Straight White Male Follow-up: A Child's Treasury of Deletions

May 16 2012

Yesterday's post garnered 800 comments before I put it to bed and I ended up deleting a record number of comments out of it, largely from presumably straight white men enraged at the idea their life doesn't necessarily suck as much as other folks' and/or because they ate lead paint chips as children and have impulse control issues (plus a couple from other, calmer folks following up on posts I later deleted, so theirs needed to be deleted too). Whatever the reason, I thought it would be fun to post a compendium of Malletings here for your enjoyment.

So without further ado: The Deletions of May 15, 2012!

Warning: Intemperate language follows.

[Deleted because inasmuch as the author of it admits to not reading the entry at all, anything he has to say will be aside the point for the thread—JS]

[Deleted for pointlessness. Did some site with exceptionally stupid readers just link in?—JS]

[Deleted because being a troll isn't merit badge-worthy—JS]

[Deleted for garden variety racism, misogyny and assholishness—JS]

[Deleted for trollage—JS]

[Deleted because That Guy is a homophobic moron—JS]

[Deleted because Scorpius was already told he was off the thread—JS]

[Aaaand now Scorpius has earned a place in the moderation queue. Enjoy it, Scorpius! You'll come out again when I decide you're not trolling—JS]

[Further deleted because That Guy is nowhere as clever as he seems to believe he is—JS]

[Deleted because That Guy is tiresome—JS]

[Contentless troll deleted—JS]

[People who comment to tell me that they didn't read get deleted! Because they're jackassed trolls who have nothing to add to the conversation!—JS]

[Deleted for pointlessness—JS]

[Speaking as a white male, I have deleted the comment because of its abject stupidity—JS]

[Deleted for spittle-flinging assholishness—JS]

[Jackassed homophobia deleted—JS]

[Deleted for teh stupid—JS]

[Deleted for not being clever—JS]

[Deleted for being wrong—JS]

[Deleted for stupidity. Also, to the idiot white guy who posted this to see whether or not I would delete a comment by "beautiful strong black lesbian," whose previous stupid comment I also deleted, nice try.—JS]

[Deleted because it's responding to a post I deleted. Xopher, dude. Do you really think I was going to let that comment stay up?—JS]

[Name of commenter changed because pointlessly homophobic; comment deleted because 20 years of being a professional writer makes me laugh at this guy—JS]

[Jackassed assertion presented without shred of proof deleted—JS]

[pointless nonsense deleted—JS]

[Hey, you know what? Enough people responded to Don's last stupidly sexist post that I didn't want to delete it. But I can delete *this* stupidly sexist post!—JS]

[Deleted again for ridiculous misogyny. Don, consider a break from the thread, please—JS]

[Don, if you really have to ask how your posts are misogynistic, it's probably for the best I'm deleting them as I go along—JS]

[Wow, I'm really getting tired of deleting misogyny in this thread—JS]

[Racist dipshittery deleted—JS]

[Hey, look! I've malleted this asshole twice!—JS]

Yes, yes. A busy day for the Mallet of Loving Correction, *indeed.*

Teabaggers and Puppetmasters

Apr
21
2009

(Note: This article written before Tea Party folks figured out what "teabagging" meant in a slangy sense, and therefore were still calling themselves "teabaggers." Yes, I found it amusing—JS)

In e-mail today, which I suspect is tongue-in-cheek, but which actually is worth making a point about:

Why do the teabaggers and their puppetmasters hate America so much?

Well, in terms of the teabaggers, of course, they *don't* hate America. They love America, and no, I'm not being arch and sarcastic. They do. Deal with it. The problem is that as much as they love America, they love an alternate history version of America *more,* the one in which someone other than Barack Obama won the presidency, the Republicans aren't the minority in Congress, and where they can not worry overly much about the excesses of big government because at least it's *their* big government.

They love it so much that they are having a hard time grasping that it *is* an alternate history version of America, partly because where they live, it doesn't seem like alternate history. Dayton, Ohio had one of the largest teabagger turnouts in the nation, and if you look the county election map for 2008, it's easy to see why: Because Dayton's Montgomery county is an island of blue surrounded by a sea of red, including my own county, Darke, which is incidentally represented by the GOP's top congressman, John Boehner. When you live in counties that went 60% or more for McCain (Darke was at 68%), you have a hard time believing your vision of the US is the alternate one.

If you don't want to believe this, I ask you to cast your mind back to, oh, say, November 3, 2004 and check in with how liberals and Democrats were feeling that day, and indeed additionally for much of the time between then and November 4, 2008. Well, you say, at least *we* never threatened to secede. To which I say: Oh, I don't know about that. Granted, it wasn't the governor of one of those blue states getting himself all hopped up on secession fumes and blurting stupidities on national television. But this is neither here nor there regarding a chunk of the electorate being in shock and denial about how another, larger portion of the electorate voted.

So that's the teabaggers. What about their puppetmasters—most specifically Rupert Murdoch and his minions at Fox News, Rush Limbaugh and the various other contributors to the whipping up of these alternate America lovers? You know, the ones that the teabaggers are adamant aren't their puppetmasters, because no one tells *their* grassroots movement what to do?

Well. Rupert Murdoch doesn't actually give a shit about the teabaggers one way or another, save retaining them as eyeballs for his advertisers. Murdoch understands the dynamics of American political opinion, and that outside the sixty percent of the US electorate that constitutes the fuzzy, unpredictable political middle, there's a hard-edged twenty percent on either side that is reliable, predictable and loyal to its politics, and to those who support them. Murdoch long ago staked out one of those twenty percent for his own benefit and enrichment, and now maintains it assiduously. Done and done.

Limbaugh's the same, although I suspect he's less dispassionate about it than Murdoch; he's enjoying the fact that for now, fortune has crowned him the right's unofficial policymaker. Between Limbaugh and Murdoch and the teabagging rabble is a middle class of opinionators and politicians who may believe what they expound to a greater or lesser degree but who equally see themselves as chessplayers, moving the teabagging public into position for the next game, i.e., 2010.

Will any of it work? Doubt it in the short run; President Obama is being tricky by not actually playing their game and instead focusing on his own plans, carving out a constituency in the middle of the road and generally being successful at it, leaving the teabagging right, which will never support him regardless of what he does, to spin in tight, isolated circles and do its own thing—except when from time to time he reaches out to them. Which they reject, which allows him to say "well, I tried," and then do what he was going to do anyway, with the added benefit of making the right look petulant and insular. He's already done this a time or two, with excellent effect, politically speaking. This is not to suggest Obama is an Ultimate Political Jedi Master. He screws up enough. But at the moment he is better at politics than his opponents, which is sufficient for his purposes.

Also, I doubt any of it will work in the long run, either. Not because conservativism is doomed—it's not. But the current iteration of it—the socially fundmentalist, expansive government, rights grabbing, it's-right-if-we-say-it's-right-because-*we're*-right version—almost certainly is. The smart conservatives (and the younger ones, not necessarily always the same) have already started to separate themselves from this dried-up conservatism, particularly its social fundamentalism: Note the recent appearance of Steve Schmidt and Meghan McCain at the Log Cabin Republicans convention, banging on the old guard for being clueless (or as McCain noted, for being "scared shitless"). These folks aren't living *in* an alternate America, the one that denies that it's lost the argument; they know the score well enough. They're living *for* an alternate America, one in which they win because they have a *better* argument.

They know what most of the teabaggers don't (and what their puppetmasters don't seem to care about): No amount of hopping up and down about taxes or secession or same-sex marriage or whatever will mean anything if the majority of Americans have already rejected your message and see you as embarrassingly clueless about not getting the memo. So, no. The teabaggers don't hate America. They love America. It'd be nice if they started living in the real one.

Tax Frenzies and How to Hose Them Down

Sep 26 2010

A question in e-mail based on all the recent "rich people feeling not rich" nonsense, and the associated commentary online:

Why is it that the people freaking out the most about taxes on the rich are the ones who don't seem to know how the tax code works?

The answer is in the question: Because they don't know how the tax code works. The major failing seems to be an incomprehension regarding marginal tax rates, but people also seem to fall down on the matter of taxable income vs. gross income (i.e. how deductions can work for you!), how to apply tax credits, and other various and fairly basic aspects of the tax code here in the US.

If you don't know that stuff—if you basically wander through your life thinking the government taxes all of your income based on the highest possible percentage—then I suppose it's no wonder you freak out. But it also kind of makes you the financial equivalent of the people who think that Darwin said we are all descended from monkeys, or that the Bible says "God helps those who help themselves." In short, it means you're a bit ignorant. You should stop being that. It's easily correctable. In any event, at some point in time, real live grown-ups should understand the concept of marginal rates. It's not that difficult to grasp.

There is another answer as well, which can be paired with the above or stand on its own, and it's that there's a certain sort of person who believes that all taxation (or all taxation outside of one or two very specific things of which they approve) is theft. Naturally that sort of person will fly to the defense of any who bleat about their taxes being too high, even if in point of fact, the wealthy in the US are currently being taxed at historically low rates ("but they're still too high!").

I really don't know what you do about the "taxes are theft" crowd, except possibly enter a gambling pool regarding just how long after their no-tax utopia comes true that their generally white, generally entitled, generally soft and pudgy asses are turned into thin strips of Objectivist Jerky by the sort of pitiless sociopath who is actually prepped and ready to live in the world that logically follows these people's fondest desires. Sorry, guys. I know you all thought *you* were going to be one of those paying a nickel for your cigarettes in Galt Gulch. That'll be a fine last thought for you as the starving remnants of the society of takers closes in with their flensing tools.

Getting back to the real word for a bit, I'll be the first to admit that while understanding the basics of the US tax code is useful for not irrationally freaking out when there is talk of raising the marginal rates of the top few percent of income earners in the United States, in point of fact, unless all one is doing is filling in a 1040 A or EZ form, on a practical level the US Tax Code quickly becomes too complicated for most people to deal with, especially when the only time they deal with it is between April 10 and April 15 every year. This is why probably the single most important thing you can do for yourself financially, the moment your tax profile outgrows the 1040 A or EZ, is to *get yourself an accountant*. Because it's the accountant's job to know the tax code—not just a half a week a year but all year long.

In the now-long-gone blog entry of Professor Todd Henderson's that started off this entire recent round of income-related nonsensery, the one thing in it that actually gave me pause—and which convinced me the man was something of a fiscal naif—was when he revealed that a) he didn't have an accountant and b) that he was still using TurboTax for his taxes. And I was all, like, *what*? Dude, you can pay for a *gardener* but then cry that paying for an accountant is too dear? No wonder you're all worked up.

I very specifically don't want to start another round of Henderson-whacking—the man's been whacked enough—but I will say that after a certain level rather below Professor Henderson's income and taxation situation, you should recognize that what you don't know about the US tax code is probably making you pay more than you have to and/or making you miss something you shouldn't. Which will come back to bite you in the ass in the form of an audit, followed by late payment penalties and fees.

My own moment of clarity on this score came in 2001, when we moved to Ohio; we became landlords and I also started my own company. Both of these things, and other financial events, caused me to look at my tax profile and go, *oh, man, I am so very over my head right now.* Bear in mind that I said this when I had written a book on finance, and when I was currently writing a finance newsletter for AOL, and also working as a consultant for a number of financial services companies. I was not exactly innumerate. But then maybe that was the thing: I knew enough to know I didn't know nearly enough. So we got ourselves an accountant, and she was (and is) very good at what she does, and her competence at her job means our tax situation is both well-managed and never a surprise.

So. If you're freaked out about taxes, please make sure you actually know what you're talking about when it comes to taxes. If you are a high-income earner and/or have a complicated tax profile, invest in an accountant. Either or both should help to calm your tax frenzy a bit. And if they don't, accept that the reason you're in a frenzy is probably because you want to be, rather than because the situation genuinely warrants it.

That Obama Speech, or, Expunging the Stupid Use of Words

Sep
9
2009

Wow, that was sure some *socialist* speech Obama gave yesterday to those schoolkids, huh? I went to pick up Athena from school, and all the kids marched out of building, singing "The Internationale" and clutching copies of the children's illustrated edition of *Das Kapital*, distributed by smiling members of Young People's Socialist League. Truly, it's a new day in America, comrades!

Alternately, Obama gave a pleasant, platitudinous and largely bland speech exhorting the kids to, you know, stay in school and study hard and respect their teachers, and everyone who got all wound up that the President of the United States would have the *gall* to address the nation's school children *when he's a socialist* now looks like a complete jackass.

To be sure, they looked like complete jackasses *before* the speech, but now that the man's actually done the deed, people feel more comfortable saying so. One wonders why they felt they had to wait; perhaps they were expecting this least spontaneous of all recent presidents to have the head of Eugene Debs erupt from his collarbone, take control of his body, and snatch and bloodily consume members of the audience while howling about the Pullman Strike. It did not happen, unless the live television cameras of the liberal media were somehow able to mask the gory sight of Obama Possessed By Undead Eugene Debs feasting on the tender young bodies of our nation's youth. *WHICH THEY MIGHT HAVE.*

Seriously now, how much longer do any of us have to pretend that the sort of people bleating about Our Socialist President aren't, in fact, ignorant as chicken, or mad as hatters, or as madly ignorant as chicken hatters? I've already noted that we're well past the point where anyone still barfing up the "Obama is a Socialist" meme deserves a "tool" sign over their head; I propose we go further and call them morons. Because, at this point, if you're still calling the man a "socialist," that's what you are. Want to call Obama a Democrat? Well, that's what he is. Want to call him a liberal? It's not out of line to do so, although I suspect he's closer to what we'd call moderate these days. Want to call him a progressive? Actual progressives will argue the point with you, but if you're on the right, anything left of John McCain counts as progessive, so, fine.

Call Obama a socialist? You're a fucking moron.

You know who don't think Obama is a socialist? Socialists, that's who. "We know, of course, that Obama is not a socialist, and that he is not a radical," wrote Dave McReynolds, in the pages of *The Socialist*, which, if you don't know, is the magazine of the Socialist Party USA, and McReynolds a two-time presidential candidate for that party. Yes, I know, it's wacky to rely in this matter on the assessment of someone who is both a socialist and a Socialist, rather than, say, someone belonging to a tribe of political thinkers whose understanding of socialism is so screwed up that many of them apparently can't tell the difference between socialism and fascism. But you know what, I think I'm going to do that *anyway*. Words actually mean things, and despite persistent attempts by many on the right to make it so, "socialism" does not mean either "any government activity that is not a tax cut or an attempt to kill swarthy people with weapons" or "whatever it is Obama happens to be doing at the moment."

Now, I may not be able to do anything about anyone else tolerating the "Obama is a socialist" canard elsewhere, but I can do something about it here. So: Henceforth, anyone who comes around here blathering about how Obama is a socialist (or any of its various cognates) is signaling to me that they're either ignorant or a troll. If it's the former, I may give them a small bit of leeway to learn their terms; if it's the latter, however, well then. They run the risk of what I do to trolls, which is that I delete them for trolling, and make fun of them while I do it.

This is *not* to say that one is no longer allowed to criticize Obama or his policies here—really, please do. Nor is it to say one can't speak of (or criticize) socialism here. But playing the "Obama = socialist" card is your sign to me that in fact, you're *not* serious, nor are you interested in the exchange of ideas—what you're interested in doing is crapping out an idiotic talking point that has no basis in reality, because someone who is either ignorant or deceiving told you so, and you feel you must further spread the ignorance. And you know what? I don't have time for that right now.

So, Obama opponents, either find a better and more accurate way here to voice your opposition to the president and his policies than diving for the "socialist" button, or run the risk of being expunged for being a moron, and having me laugh at you while I do it. I'm tired of it, here and everywhere else, but especially here. Please, Obama opponents, be *smarter.* The nation, its president, its people and its discourse, deserve better.

THESE THINGS I BELIEVE

Jun
14
2008

One of the more amusing comments about my recent "Baby Mama" rant (or at least amusing to me, anyway), came from over on Daily Kos, when someone there wondered whether if I was on their side, politically speaking. Because, I guess, if I'm *not*, then it's not okay to enjoy the snark for its own sake. Or whatever.

Well, I don't want my political proclivities to be in doubt, so let me be *absolutely crystal clear* where I stand:

I support the right of same-sex married couples to carry concealed weapons.

I hope this explains *everything.*

Thank you for reading.

The Thing About "Rock Stars"

Sep 5 2008

For all the Republicans who are exulting that there's now a "rock star" on the GOP ticket (and all the Democrats who are freaking out about it), there is one minor detail that's worth considering in the days and months ahead. And that is that the "rock star" on the Democratic ticket is actually the person who is running for president, while the "rock star" on the GOP ticket...*isn't*. At the top of the GOP ticket is a 72-year-old man who just gave a mediocre speech that served primarily as an attempt to suggest that a fellow who's spent two and half decades in Washington and voted with the extremely unpopular current president 90% of the time somehow represents change. *That's* the guy going up against the Democratic rock star.

And to the surprise of absolutely no one, the Democratic rock star knows this perfectly well. This is why yesterday when reporters tried to get Obama to react to Palin's attacks on him, his response was to say, more or less, "whatever," and to note his presidential opposition was McCain, not Palin. This is also why outside of the hothouse atmosphere of a political convention, Palin's sniping at Obama is likely not to hit the radar screens, because when all is said and done, she's the VP candidate, and the press is covering a presidential election, not a vice-presidential one.

Obama's already signaled he's not going to bother with her; she'll be shopped out to Biden—or even better, Hillary Clinton, who I would expect is privately fuming that the McCain and the GOP think so little of her positions and personality that they expect her supporters to be swayed by someone who holds antithetical political positions, simply because that person's got fallopian tubes. If the GOP wanted to keep the Clintons on the sidelines this election, this was not the way to do it.

Beyond this we'll see what value being a "rock star" really brings to the table, which I suspect is rather less than what people suppose. The GOPers ecstatic over their new star might remember that **a)** Obama's rock star status hasn't kept this election from being reasonably close so far, and **b)** that Palin's "rock star" status is not yet two days old, based on a speech written for a generic GOP VP candidate with some personal touches bolted on. Two and a half days ago people were wondering if she would have left the ticket by today. It's fair to say Palin's been up and been down. And starting today she and Joe Biden begin their descent into the shadowy netherworld of VP candidates on the campaign trail, to be largely ignored save for the occasional snipe or screw-up. It's nice to be a "rock star" politician, but let's just say I'm not 100% convinced the "rock star" shine is all that it's cracked up to be, especially when at the end of the day you're the political equivalent of the opening act.

And at the end of the proverbial day, this election is the guys who are the headliners: about McCain and Obama, and their policies and plans, or lack thereof. One of these guys is a rock star, and the other isn't—and to be honest, I hope *that* doesn't matter, either. What *should* matter, and what I hope will matter, is the substance of the two candidates. Substance is not what people come to "rock stars" for. But it should be what we look for in a president.

THINGS I DON'T HAVE TO THINK ABOUT TODAY

Oct

18

2010

Today I don't have to think about those who hear "terrorist" when I speak my faith.

Today I don't have to think about men who don't believe no means no.

Today I don't have to think about how the world is made for people who move differently than I do.

Today I don't have to think about whether I'm married, depending on what state I'm in.

Today I don't have to think about how I'm going to hail a cab past midnight.

Today I don't have to think about whether store security is tailing me.

Today I don't have to think about the look on the face of the person about to sit next to me on a plane.

Today I don't have to think about eyes going to my chest first.

Today I don't have to think about what people might think if they knew the medicines I took.

Today I don't have to think about getting kicked out of a mall when I kiss my beloved hello.

Today I don't have to think about if it's safe to hold my beloved's hand.

Today I don't have to think about whether I'm being pulled over for anything other than speeding.

Today I don't have to think about being classified as one of "those people."

Today I don't have to think about making less than someone else for the same job at the same place.

Today I don't have to think about the people who stare, or the people who pretend I don't exist.

Today I don't have to think about managing pain that never goes away.

Today I don't have to think about whether a stranger's opinion of me would change if I showed them a picture of who I love.

Today I don't have to think about the chance a store salesman will ignore me to help someone else.

Today I don't have to think about the people who'd consider torching my house of prayer a patriotic act.

Today I don't have to think about a pharmacist telling me his conscience keeps him from filling my prescription.

Today I don't have to think about being asked if I'm bleeding when I'm just having a bad day.

Today I don't have to think about whether the one drug that lets me live my life will be taken off the market.

Today I don't have to think about the odds of getting jumped at the bar I like to go to.

Today I don't have to think about "vote fraud" theater showing up at my poll station.

Today I don't have to think about turning on the news to see people planning to burn my holy book.

Today I don't have to think about others demanding I apologize for hateful people who have nothing to do with me.

Today I don't have to think about my child being seen as a detriment to my career.

Today I don't have to think about the irony of people thinking I'm lucky because I can park close to the door.

Today I don't have to think about memories of being bullied in high school.

Today I don't have to think about being told to relax, it was just a joke.

Today I don't have to think about whether someone thinks I'm in this country illegally.

Today I don't have to think about those who believe that freedom of religion ends with mine.

Today I don't have to think about how a half-starved 23-year-old being a cultural ideal affects my life.

Today I don't have to think about how much my life is circumscribed by my body.

Today I don't have to think about people wanting me cured of loving who I love.

Today I don't have to think about those who view me an unfit parent because of who I love.

Today I don't have to think about being told my kind don't assimilate.

Today I don't have to think about people blind to the intolerance of their belief lecturing me about my own.

Today I don't have to think about my body as a political football.

Today I don't have to think about how much my own needs wear on those I love.

Today I don't have to think about explaining to others "what happened to me."

Today I don't have to think about politicians saying bigoted things about me to win votes.

Today I don't have to think about those worried that one day people like me will be the majority.

Today I don't have to think about someone using the name of my religion as a slur.

Today I don't have to think about so many of the words for me controlling my own life being negatives.

Today I don't have to think about still not being equal.

Today I don't have to think about what it takes to keep going.

Today I don't have to think about how much I still have to hide.

Today I don't have to think about how much prejudice keeps hold.

Today I don't have to think about how I'm meant to be grateful that people tolerate my kind.

Today I don't have to think about all the things I don't have to think about.

But today I will.

Things I Don't Miss

Jan
15
2010

Apropos of nothing (no, really), here are some things from life which no longer really exist and which I am glad do not.

1. Stupidly expensive long-distance charges. After I left college, I tried to keep in touch with all my friends by phone, and it added up because depending where they were, calling pals could cost up to 40 cents a minute. When my sister briefly lived with me when I was in Fresno, between the two of us we could generate $600 phone bills on a monthly basis, at a time when I was paying $400 a month for an apartment. Yes! I was occasionally paying more for my phone bill than I was for having a place to eat and sleep. Naturally, this was madness.

These days, my long distance phone bill is a flat fee of something like $25; I literally can't think of the last time I had to think about how long I could afford to talk to someone far away on the phone. The phone companies appear to have shifted their Egregious Profit Center from long distance to text messaging, which, as I am not one of Those Damn Kids and rarely text message (and have a $5 add-on to my cell phone account which covers the first 250 texts a month, which is more than I use), suits me just fine.

The real irony here is that I'm rather more likely to e-mail or IM friends than phone them these days, so likely my phone bill would be lower now than back in '91 no matter what. But it's the principle of the thing.

2. Crappy old cars. Which cars qualify as crappy old cars? In my opinion, pretty much all of them. Pre-catalytic converter cars were shoddily-constructed, lead-spewing deathtraps, the first generation of cars running on unleaded were even more shoddily-constructed 70s defeat-mobiles, the 80s were the golden age of Detroit Doesn't Give a Shit, and so on. You have to get to about 1997 before there's a car I would willingly get into these days. As opposed to today, when even the cheap boxy cars meant for first-time buyers have decent mileage, will protect you if you're hit by a semi, and have more gizmos and better living conditions than my first couple of apartments.

Yes, I know. Car lovers scandalized. Well, look. First, go watch that video on YouTube of a 50s-era Chevrolet colliding into a late era car from the same maker. Pay special attention to just how violently the crash test dummy is smeared all over the 50s interior. Which I think makes the point about "deathtraps" I was mentioning earlier.

Second, every time I go back to LA, you know what always surprises me? The mountains. Because when I was kid growing up in LA, you couldn't *see* them. I lived at the foothills of the damned mountains and I still couldn't see them most of the time. Whereas these days first stage smog alerts in LA are a relative rarity, not even bringing into the discussion second stage alerts (in which you could see the air directly in front of you) and third stage alerts (in which you could chew it). And this was in the 70s and 80s, which were substantially better than the 50s and 60s. No, I don't miss crappy old cars one bit.

3. Physical media for music. Audiophiles like to wank on about the warmth of vinyl, and you know, maybe if you take your vinyl and put it into special static free sleeves and then store those sleeves in a purpose-built room filled with inert gases, to be retrieved only when you play that vinyl on your $10,000 turntable which could play a record without skipping through a 7.5 earthquake, ported through your vacuum tube amplifier that sucks down more energy than Philadelphia at night, maybe it *is* warm. Good for you and your warm vinyl.

What I remember about my vinyl was a) it warped, b) it skipped, c) it wore out, d) any sonic benefits of the medium were compromised by my basic turntable and all the dust the damn LPs accumulated. Cassette tapes wore out even more quickly, their sonic reproduction was even worse, and they would get randomly eaten by your Walkman as a sacrifice to the music gods, and it was always your beloved music, not that Poison cassette your great aunt got you because she knows as much about your musical tastes as she knows anything else about you. I would have gladly sacrificed *Look What the Cat Dragged In* to the music gods, in their mercy. But it didn't work that way. It *never* works that way.

Let us not even speak of 8-tracks.

CDs were the best possible physical music medium, for all the crap they get from audiophiles, but even CDs pale against the *awesomeness* that is the intangible digital music file, stored in a tiny, pretty little handheld computer that also plays video and games and lets me read my e-mail. I have three decades of curated personal music, enough to play straight for week without interruption or repetition, with me wherever I go. And while the encoding rate I used to rip "Don't Stop Believin'" might not give me the crystal clarity I could get listening to it on vinyl, on a $10k turntable and through a McIntosh amp, I'll say this: It sounds a hell of a lot better than when I was 12, listening to it on cassette through a mono tape player, or through the transistor radio alarm clock by my bed. Which is to say from a practical point of view it's just groovy, thanks.

4. Smoking allowed everywhere. You know what? It *did* suck to have smokers at the table next to you at a restaurant. It *did* suck to have a movie theater haze up. It *did* suck to be walking in the mall and have some wildly gesticulating smoker randomly and accidentally jam the lit end of his cancer stick into your face. It *did* suck to be trapped in a tube hurling through the sky at 32,000 feet, sucking down recycled air for six hours that had cigarette smoke in it. It *did* suck to have everything everywhere smell vaguely of burnt ash and nicotine addiction.

Now, I'd note that it *also* sucks to be a smoker *today*, as they are exiled to the outdoors in every sort of weather, to huddle together for warmth and companionship in their devotion to the demon weed. They have my sympathy. But given the choice between telling them to go outside and having to suck down their smoke whether I want it or not, I'm good with the current state of affairs.

5. Pull tabs on drink cans. One less bit of ubiquitous trash to be annoyed with. To the dude who invented the stay tab: Bless you, sir.

TODAY'S CANE SHAKING ON THE LAWN: APPS

Jul
23
2010

I don't get apps. Not as in how they work, but why, in fact, they're called "apps." Because you know what? They're *programs*. They are compendiums of code, compiled in a manner that when you execute them in a computing environment, they perform a specific task. Like a program. *Exactly* like a program. Because they *are* programs. So why not call them programs?

Is it because programs is an ungroovy kind of word? Is it for the same reason station wagons are now called "crossover vehicles"? Will the hip young things using Foursquare on their iPhone to let the world know their apartments are unoccupied and ripe for looting be filled with horror if their cute little larceny abettor were called a program? Does the word conjure up intolerable images of a chunky, misshaven nerd, hovering asthmatically over a Commodore 64, waiting the 20 minutes until Omega Race downloads off the cassette by strapping on a feedbag of Cheetos and Mallomars and settling down with the latest copy of *Byte*? Is the word *really* that bad?

I certainly admit that "app" is a nice phoneme of a word, and that "program" doesn't lend itself to such shortening; "There's a prog for that" doesn't quite have the same ring. And I don't really have a problem calling programs "apps" as long as I can tell my brain it's short for "application," which is a specific genus of program, rather than a wholesale replacement of the word. But I don't think that's how people generally use the word, and it just makes me want to shake my cane and *get the kids off my lawn*. Recently I read a piece about what it will mean when we switch over to app-based operating systems, and I was all, what? So the new hotness is a screen on which icons are used to access the programs they represent? Just like the Macintosh in 1984? Somebody get me a chair, the future is *blowing my goddamned mind*.

I like apps. I like the little computers we use to run apps, which fit in my hand and have the same processing and visualizing power a forty pound hulking desktop and a fifty pound CRT screen had a decade ago. I'm not entirely sure why we need a new word to describe these little programs. And while I'm at it, I'm also not sure why you're *still on my lawn*.

Todd Akin

Aug
21
2012

Representative Todd Akin has decided to stay in the Missouri senatorial race, bucking the national GOP, which desperately wants him tossed under the bus for the spectacularly stupid "legitimate rape" thing, and you know what? Good for him. Leaving aside my own love of political *schadenfreude* here, the dude *did* win the Republican primary fair and square, did he not? He is the plurality choice of Missouri's Republican voters, isn't he? He didn't strangle kittens, set them on fire, and insert them into an unmentionable part of some adorable puppy's anatomy, did he?

No; all he really did was say out loud something that an apparently non-trivial number of conservatives seem to believe, i.e., that some rapes are rapier than others, and (probably less common, at least I hope) that at the rapiest level of rape, you probably aren't gonna get knocked up. It's appallingly stupid and wrong, of course. But that doesn't mean he (up until Sunday, anyway) didn't believe it, or that saying something appallingly stupid and wrong but *entirely within the penumbra of conservative thought* should disqualify him from participating in a race he earned the right to be in, through a democratic process. "You stupidly said out loud what many of us actually believe," shouldn't by any rational standard be a reason for his forfeit.

Yes, he's embarrassing the GOP presidential candidate by staying in a race after Romney said he should drop out, and yes, the Democrats will use Akin's comment and his extraordinarily restrictive anti-choice views (reflected, incidentally, in the official GOP platform) like a cudgel on the Republicans every single day that Akin stays in the race. But why is that *Akin's* problem? By all indications, he was not the favored candidate of the national GOP anyway, so no skin off his nose. The national GOP says they're not going to send him money, but if they want to take the Senate, they're not likely to do it without him, so I imagine sooner or later they're going to slip some cash his way regardless. So again, what impetus does Akin have to do anything other than run? For the rest of the GOP, it's about control of the Senate; for Akin, it's whether or not he has a job come next January. He sure as hell doesn't have any reason to quit, and winning, should he win, will be sweet indeed.

And yeah, Democrats binging on schadenfreude, he could win. Even after the "forcible rape" flub, he was still up a point in the polls against Claire McCaskill. He might sink—as I understand it, making an ass of yourself on live TV takes a few days to sink in with the polls—but then again he might not. He apologized for his stupidity, and pitched it in a way that will resonate with evangelicals, for many of whom he is the ideal candidate. Don't kid yourself that he's lost the race already. And of course, that's just one more reason for him to stay in.

I wouldn't vote for Akin; I don't know why anyone would want to vote for someone so heinously ignorant of human biology, which I suspect is indicative of other vasty swaths of ignorance in his mental makeup. I wouldn't encourage anyone in Missouri to vote for him either, as we already have enough appallingly ignorant people in the Senate without adding him to their number. But do I think he should be the GOP senatorial candidate for the state? Absolutely. If Mitt Romney, the national GOP or anyone else has a problem with it, they should bring it up with Missouri's Republican voters. He was their pick for the gig. I think you have to respect that, even if you shake your head that they could choose so poorly.

Tom Becker

Apr
2
2010

Let me tell you about Tom Becker. In 1991, I got my first full-time professional writing gig, as a movie critic for the *Fresno Bee* newspaper. Tom was the Assistant Features Editor there, which is to say he was my boss.

There are many things that are important for a young writer, but the one I want to focus on at the moment is this one: That it helps to have the right editor at the right time. When I started at the *Bee*, I was 22, young enough that I got carded at the first "R"-rated movie I was sent to review, and madly, truly, deeply full of myself, because, hey, I was 22 years old and I spent my time watching movies and interviewing movie stars, so obviously I was doing something *right*, you know? Basically, I was a bit of an ass. Had I been matched with the wrong editor, bad things would have happened.

Tom was, very simply, the right editor for me. I think Tom very quickly sized me up for what I was—a young guy who had the potential to let his ego get in the way of his development as a writer—and also quickly figured out what it was I needed from him, and then set to providing it to me. Tom's method was to be calm and sensible, to give me enough of a lead to try things and then reel me in during the editing process and show me where things needed to be fixed and why. I can't say I always agreed with him—I was a bit of an ass, remember—but *how* he worked with me did the job just as much as *what* he did when he edited. It's a long way of saying that he did his job in a way that didn't set off my ego and insecurities. Over the time I worked with him, I did indeed become a better writer.

That being said, I truly learned to appreciate what Tom did for me not when I was at the *Bee*, but when I left it and took a job at America Online. One of my tasks was to be an editor, and I spent not-inconsiderable time with writers, finding ways to make their writing better, and also finding ways to do it in a way that didn't collapse those writers into tight little balls of neurosis. Once I did my stint as an editor, I went back to look at some of my raw writing from my *Bee* years and was horrified at how *unfinished* it was, and how much it really *had* needed an editor—how much, in point of fact, it needed Tom Becker.

Shortly thereafter I had reason to visit Fresno again, and on a visit to the *Bee* I went over to Tom's desk, to thank him for the help he'd given me, and to apologize to him for being, as previously mentioned, a bit of an ass while I worked with him. Tom was amused, and very gracious, and also, I think, happy to know that his work and patience had been recognized and valued, even if that recognition had been a bit late in coming.

I do recognize it and I do value it. What Tom Becker did for me and for my writing helped make it possible for me to go on to do everything else I have been able to do. He's also responsible for me recognizing that as famously solitary as writers are alleged to be, we really don't work alone. Our words—and our skills as writers—very often do need help, which we get from editors, copy editors, proofers and all the other people between the writer and the audience for our words. Writers are fortunate to have people who strengthen our skills and our work, and it doesn't hurt for us to recognize that fact. I may or may not still be a bit of an ass, but I know how much *more* of an ass I would look like without the help I get from editors and others. I owe that sense of realism, and humility, to Tom.

Tom passed away on Wednesday, at peace and with family and friends by his side, in his home. Tom had known for some time that this was coming and from what friends tell me handled it in the gentle and orderly manner I remember him having. I was fortunate to have been able to say goodbye to him before he left us, and to thank him again for everything he'd done for me. He wrote something to me then which I don't think he would mind me sharing with you:

It makes me happy to know the influence I had on you. I was never sure at the time. You always seemed like a wild horse running free on the plains. All I tried to do was get you to look in the right direction every now and then. Sounds like I did just that. Thanks so much for remembering and absorbing my teachings and editing. I consider my life as a journalist and editor successful and full with the positive influence I had on you and others. And that makes me happy. I always was trying to teach as I went along. I think I did with you. Now you are spreading the word to others, so maybe there will be fewer hurt feelings and more working together between writers and editors in the world thanks to your stories about me. I am honored.

In fact, it is I who am honored, to have worked with Tom and to have been taught by him. And I am honored to be able to tell all of you this little bit about him and about how he was important to me.

If you are a writer, in Tom's honor I would ask you to think about the editors and others who have helped to you to become the writers you wanted to become. Everyone else, think on your teachers and mentors who with patience and humor and possibly even a bit of love looked past your unformed nature, saw what you could be, and helped you be just that.

Your appreciation of their work would be a fine memorial to my friend, teacher and editor Tom Becker. You might not have known him, but I bet you know someone like him. Let that person know that you know what they did for you. You won't regret it.

Twitter

Apr
3
2009

Ben rather crankily wants to know my thoughts on:

Twitter: A revolution in information consumption & dissemination OR I don't give a fuck what you want for breakfast.

What Twitter is, frankly, is a public exhibition of what used to be a private activity. It's phone texting—its character limit is right in line with the character limit on SMS texts—but rather than to just one person it goes out to dozens, or hundreds, or thousands, depending on who you are and how many followers you have. That Twitter has become massively popular is unsurprising because texting is massively popular; indeed, I have a suspicion that if you told most people under the age of 35 that they had to choose between texting or making voice calls, voice communication would drop to next to nothing. For a generation that grew up texting, Twitter isn't a revolution, it's simply an expansion of how they were communicating anyway. And in point of fact, it's even better than blogging for quite a lot of people, because when you're limited to 140 characters, you don't have to feel bad about not having all that much to say.

That most Twitter communication *is* aggressively banal should also not come as a huge surprise. First, news flash: *people* are banal. Yes, all of us, even you (and especially even me). Even the great minds of the world do not spend all their time locked in the contemplation of the mysteries of the universe; about 90% of their thoughts boil down to "I'm hungry," "I'm sleepy," "I need to poo," "Check out the [insert secondary sexual characteristics] on that [insert sex of preference], I'd really like to boink them," "I wonder what Jennifer Aniston is doing right now, John Mayer can no longer tell me on his Twitter feed," and, of course, "Look! Kitty!" That the vast majority of Twitter posts encompass pedestrian thoughts about common subjects like food, music, tech, jobs and cats is entirely unsurprising, because this is what people think about. Hell, even Stephen Fry, patron saint of Twitter, tweets about what fruit he's having and what's going on with his iPhone. And he's more clever than any six of the rest of us will ever be. When Stephen Fry tweets about his goddamn *snack*, you can be forgiven about tweeting that, say, your cat has fur (which, in fact, I have just now done).

Second, phone texting, Twitter's technological and philosophical predecessor, was not known as a place for weighty, meaty thoughts—it was known for "Where R U?" and "IM N claz N IM SO BORED" and other such messages of limited scope and mental appeal. But that's pretty much what texting is for: Short thoughts about not much. That Twitter, shackled as it is to 140 characters per post, is not the Agora Reborn should not come as a huge shock.

However, this is a feature, not a bug. Twitter, along with text messages, IMs and to some extent blog posts (although not this particular blog post) and social networking pages belong what I think is a relatively new category of communication which I call "Intermediary Communication"—which is to say communication that exists between the casual, spontaneous and intimate nature of oral communication (talking to a group of friends, as an example) and the more planned, persistent and broadcasting nature of written communication. Intermediary communication feels spontaneous and intimate, but it exhibits the persistent and broadcast nature of written communication, and this is what often gets people in trouble—the famous "oh crap I talked shit about my job on my blog and my boss read it and now I'M FIRED" thing, exemplified by Heather Armstong.

But while this intermediary communication has its pitfalls, it also has its advantages. Fact is, the reason Twitter is so popular is that people *like* all those banal little messages that skitter across the service. For the people you know—friends, family and co-workers—those "I'm eating fruit now" messages take the place of the little, not-especially-notable interactions you have on a daily basis that add up to a familiar and comfortable sense of the world and your place in it. When in fact you can't see those friends, family, etc on a daily basis, these banal tweets still group them into your daily, unremarkable life, and in doing so make them seem *closer* and therefore more of a part of your world. Twenty years ago you'd maybe make time to call distant members of your tribe once a week, and that sort of punctuated, telegraphed communication would have to do. Twitter (and other intermediary communication like it) puts them quite literally back into the stream of your life. This is not a bad thing.

For the people you *don't* know—the celebrities whose feeds one follows—the banality of Twitter makes you feel closer to them, too. *Hey! Stephen Fry eats fruit! I eat fruit! He's just like me!* And then you send Stephen Fry a reponse tweet about the fruit you had, and bask in your fruit-enjoying fraternity. Does this benefit Stephen Fry somehow? I suspect not; a shared liking for juicy, vitamin-C-bearing foods is probably not a bond that directly translates to Mr. Fry's agent landing him quality roles; likewise, I'm not sure John Mayer's hyperactive tweetery making him look like geek America's spastic younger brother is going to translate into music sales. But I don't think marketing is why Fry or Mayer fiddle about with Twitter; I think they do it for the same reason everyone else does. And in both cases it's probably nice for them to have a halfway "normal" communication channel.

(There are celebs who look at Twitter as just another marketing avenue, mind you. You will know them by the fact their feeds, in addition to being banal, are also *boring*.)

All of which is to say that the banality and silliness and unremarkable pedestrian nature of Twitter is what the service actually has going for it—it's baked into the service's DNA. It's why it's successful and why it (or something very much like it) will continue to be successful going forward.

(This entry: 6,091 characters. Not suitable for Twitter. Which is, you know. Why I keep the blog.)

The Venereal Disease Channel Imaginatizes Greatastically

Mar 17 2009

People have been asking me to weigh in on the whole "SciFi Channel changing its name to Syfy" thing, so here's me weighing in: *Meh*. It seems like pointless fiddling for the sake of pointless fiddling to me, but if it makes them happy, then, you know. Have fun with it, guys. I like a fair amount of the programming, so I'll watch it whatever they call it.

That said, I think they might have picked a better name. Apparently one of the motivating factors to change the name from "scifi" to a phase-changing-vowel-filled homonym was to have a name that was trademarkable and extensible, and it seems no one else in the world actually uses the word "syfy" for anything. Well, except Poland, where the word is used to identify crusty, scabby sexually transmitted diseases, and no, this is not a joke. No one there is going to use the word to associate with their product, any more than someone here might try to market, say, Chlamydia™ brand adhesive bandages.

Note to SciFi Channel: when your new brand identity means "venereal disease" in *any* language, it's the sort of thing that—excuse the term—*gets around.*

You would think NBC Universal's brand people might have caught this (heh) ahead of time. They do have people for this. And maybe they did catch it, but figured, heck, who knows Polish? Aside from 40 million Poles? Problem is, this is one of those things that Those Perverse Internets, and the equally-perverse people involved in them (not coincidentally SciFi Channel's primary viewing demographic) will find out almost immediately and then proceed to have a big ol' jolly field day with. As they did, and are doing.

Look: When your core audience looks at your new branding and exclaims "Hey! It's the Venereal Disease Channel!" from the day you announce it until the day, a few years later, when you finally slink away from it and try to pretend it never happened, you may have chosen your brand identity poorly. Yes, "Syfy" is brand extensible. But then, the Polish "syfy" is extensible too, in its way, although not in a way most people would want. So, yes, this is a problem. Glad it's not my problem.

To be honest, however, the incipient "Syfy" branding doesn't bother me nearly as much as the new brand's tagline: "Imagine Greater." I mean: really? "Imagine Greater"? What, were complete sentences too dear down at the marketing shop? I know there's a *recession* on, but maybe they could have checked in the couch cushions for loose change. Or if they were simply intending to break grammar into pieces, for jazzy, kicky effect, why not go all the way? "Imagine Greater" is settling for the bronze when "Imaginate Greatably" is within one's grasp. And, hey, it's *brand extendable.*

"Syfy" tells me the branding people involved here don't know how to read Polish, and you know what, that's fine. But "Imagine Greater" suggests they don't know how to read English, either, and that's *not.* Seriously, SciFi Channel: you *paid* someone for "Imagine Greater"? Hell. I wouldn't have given that to you for free. Clearly I need either to get into marketing, or run away from it as fast as I possibly can.

What Happens in the Acela Quiet Car Stays in the Acela Quiet Car, Unless Twitter is Involved

Jun 7 2012

Yesterday I traveled from New York City to Philadelphia on the train, specifically Amtrak's Acela high-speed train. The compartment I ended up sitting in was the "Quiet Car," i.e., the one in which you don't use your cell phone to make calls and otherwise keep things down to a murmur. Naturally, I went on Twitter to joke about it:

On the Acela to Philadelphia. In the "quiet car." My airhorn is soon to be a delightful surprise!

But then something strange began to happen:

People are beginning to hum in the quiet car of the Acela. I think that may be against the rules.

And then, my friends, *it got nuts*:

OH MY GOD THE QUIET CAR OF THE ACELA HAS ERUPTED INTO A FULL BLOWN PRODUCTION OF STEPHEN SONDHEIM'S "MERRILY WE ROLL ALONG"

HOLY CRAP NOW THE QUIET CAR ON THE ACELA HAS THE MOST RIGHTEOUS GUITAR SOLO BATTLE SINCE RALPH MACCHIO AND STEVE VAI IN "CROSSROADS"

GEEZ LOUISE NOW EACH OF US IN THE ACELA QUIET CAR HAS BEEN GIVEN A TEN FOOT JAPANESE DRUM AND TOLD TO BEAT IT FOR OUR VERY LIVES

JUMPIN' JIMNEY THEY HAVE BROUGHT OUT THE VUVUZELAS AND DEMANDED A JAZZ FREE FORM VERSION OF "NOVEMBER RAIN"

DEAR LORD IAN MCKELLEN AND PATRICK STEWART HAVE ARRIVED IN THE ACELA QUIET CAR AND ARE NOW PERFORMING A DECLAIM-OFF

Now arriving in Philly. THIS HAS BEEN THE MOST UNSATISFACTORY QUIET CAR EVER AND I WILL COMPLAIN TO AMTRAK.

Seriously.

What I Think About *Atlas Shrugged*

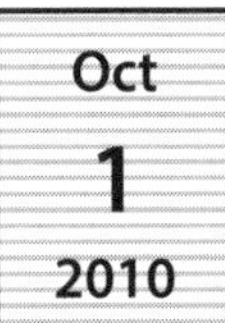

In the wake of a side-swipe comment about the delusional nature of some Ayn Rand fans, I was asked by a friend of mine to share my thoughts on *Atlas Shrugged* with the general public. I suspect this friend then went off to make herself some popcorn in preparation for the presumed inevitable mind-losing that will occur in the comments. That's what I am to you people: cheap entertainment. Well, fine.

I've mentioned it in passing before, but I'll go a little more in detail about it now. I enjoy *Atlas Shrugged* quite a bit, and will re-read it every couple of years when I feel in the mood. It has a propulsively potboilery pace so long as Ayn Rand's not having one of her characters gout forth screeds in a sock-puppety fashion. Even when she does, after the first reading of the book, you can go, "oh, yeah, *screed*," and then just sort of skim forward and get to the parts with the train rides and motor boats and the rough sex and the collapse of civilization as Ayn Rand imagines it, which is all good clean fun. Her characters are cardboard but they're consistent—the good guys are really good in the way Rand defines "good," and everyone else save Eddie Willers and the picturesquely doomed Cherryl Brooks are obnoxious shitheels, so you don't really have to worry about *ambiguity* getting in the way of your zooming through the pages.

Rand is an efficient storyteller that way: You know early on what the rules of her world are, she sticks with those rules, and you as the reader are on a rail all the way through the story. It's not storytelling that works for everyone, and it doesn't work for me with every book I read. But if you're in the mood not to work too much, it's fine to have an author who points dramatically at the things she wants you to look at, and keeps the lights off the things she doesn't. Basically, I find her storytelling restful, which I suppose isn't a word used much to describe her technique, but which fits for how it works for me.

A good way for me to describe how I relate to *Atlas Shrugged* is to note that one time when I was in college in Chicago, the only way for me to get back home to California for the Christmas holidays was to take a Greyhound bus. This meant a 53-hour-long bus ride in the company of felons (no joke; the bus stopped at Joliet and some rather skeevy-looking parolees from the prison got on. One of them decided to sit by me and I was treated to delightful stories of prison rape all the way through Iowa). The way I handled the trip was to take *Atlas Shrugged* along for the ride, and when I was bored, to crack open the book and start reading. The book would put me in a fugue state and when I looked up again from the pages, an entire state would have gone by. It's no exaggeration when I say that *Atlas Shrugged* probably saved my sanity on that bus trip. So well done, Ms. Rand, and thanks.

That said, it's a totally ridiculous book which can be summed up as *Sociopathic idealized nerds collapse society because they don't get enough hugs.* (This is, incidentally, where you can start your popcorn munching.) Indeed, the enduring popularity of *Atlas Shrugged* lies in the fact that it *is* nerd revenge porn—if you're a nerd of an engineering-ish stripe who remembers all too well being slammed into your locker by a bunch of football dickheads, then the idea that *people like you* could make all those dickheads suffer by "going Galt" has a direct line to the pleasure centers of your brain. *I'll show you!* the nerds imagine themselves crying. *I'll show you all!* And then they disappear into a crevasse that Google Maps will not show because *the Google people are our kind of people,* and a year later they come out and everyone who was ever mean to them will have starved. Then these nerds can begin again, presumably with the help of robots, because any child in the post-*Atlas Shrugged* world who can't figure out how to run a smelter within ten minutes of being pushed through the birth canal will be left out for the coyotes. Which if nothing else solves the problem of day care.

All of this is fine, if one recognizes that the idealized world Ayn Rand has created to facilitate her wishful theorizing has no more logical connection to our real one than a world in which an author has imagined humanity ruled by intelligent cups of yogurt. This is most obviously revealed by the fact that in Ayn Rand's world, a man who self-righteously instigates the collapse of society, thereby inevitably killing millions if not billions of people, is portrayed as a messiah figure rather than as a genocidal prick, which is what he'd be anywhere else. Yes, he's a genocidal prick with excellent engineering skills. Good for him. He's still a genocidal prick. Indeed, if John Galt *were* portrayed as an intelligent cup of yogurt rather than poured into human form, this would be obvious. *Oh my god, that cup of yogurt wants to kill most of humanity to make a philosophical point! Somebody eat him quick!* And that would be that.

The fact that apparently a very large number of people don't recognize Galt as the genocidal prick he is suggests a) Rand's skill at stacking the story-telling deck is not to be discounted, and b) as with any audience with a large number of nerds in it, a non-trivial number of *Atlas Shrugged* readers are possibly far enough along the poorly-socialized spectrum that they don't recognize humanity does not in fact easily suss out into Randian capitalist superheroes on one side and craven socialist losers on the other, or that Rand's neatly-stacked deck doesn't mirror the world as it is, or (if one gives it any sort of genuine reflection) model it as it should be.

To be fair to Rand, she's certainly not the only science fiction/fantasy author who has lashed together a universe out of twine and novel but shallow philosophical meanderings (Objectivism: the spongy white bread at the Great Buffet of Human Ideas), and then populated it with characters tuned to exist in that universe and that universe only. She's not even the only author to have enthusiastic nerds confuse that Potemkin universe with a possible one, who then go about annoying the rest of us, who have no desire to be characters in *that* sort of universe, thank you kindly. But on the other hand, Rand did spend a lot of time getting high on her own supply, which most pushers are smart enough not to do, and at the moment, her claque of enthusiastic nerds certainly seems to be the most *energetic*, which doesn't really please me. I wish they could be more like Heinlein nerds, who keep to their own freeholds.

So that's how it susses out for me. As a pulpy, fun read about an unrealistic world that could never happen, I give *Atlas Shrugged* a thumbs up. As a foundational document for a philosophy for living in reality with other actual live human beings, I rank it below *Jonathan Livingston Seagull* and *The Secret*, both of which also have the added value of being shorter.

WHAR IT'S LIKE TO HAVE ME FOR A DAD

Jul
26
2011

My daughter is at ranch camp this week—which is not a camp where everything has been covered in delicious ranch dressing but rather a camp where the campers take care of their own horse for a week—and while the camp does not allow the campers to bring electronic equipment with them, it does allow parents to send e-mails, which they will then print out and deliver to the campers. Here is the e-mail I just sent my child.

> *Hello, sweetheart! I thought I would drop you a note to let you know we love you and are thinking about you and hope you are having fun out there with your horses and new friends and everything.*
>
> *Also, we don't want you to worry if you hear news about super intelligent zombie badgers attacking Western Ohio. It's totally not true. Yes, there are super-intelligent badgers. Yes, they are attacking, with their evil badger guns that shoot mini-badgers that have even smaller guns that shoot even smaller badgers. BUT THEY ARE NOT ZOMBIES, and that's really the most important thing.*
>
> *We are fine, since we (as you know) have been prepared for a super-intelligent badger attack for years. Some of your friends may have been eaten, however. Well, most of them have. In fact, all of them have and the school year has been cancelled and you will instead be tutored by a robot. It will teach you calculus and in return you will teach it how to love, and also to shoot super-intelligent badgers. That's the deal, and I think it's a fair one.*

Oh, and when you come home, don't tell your mother I told you about the badger thing. She doesn't want to speak of it EVER AGAIN. It makes her a little crazy, actually; she runs around the house bellowing "DIE MUSTELID DIE!" until I give her chocolate. So don't mention badgers, unless you have chocolate. But not dark chocolate. You know she doesn't like that.

Anyway, to recap: Hope you're having fun, horses, super-intelligent badgers, robots learning how to love, bellowing mom, chocolate (not dark). I think that covers it.

Oh, except: I love you and miss you, and also I love you.

Dad

And that's what it's like to have me as a dad. In case you were wondering.

Where It Began

Jun
21
2008

You know, as a young teenage boy, I was about as homophobic as any young teenage boy is. Why? Oh, for all the usual reasons, including years of soaking up general anti-gay sentiment without even knowing or understanding it (for example, playing lots of games of "smear the queer" in elementary school), and of course having just hit puberty, being oversaturated by hormones, and thus being turned on by just about *everything*, and wondering *oh my god* what it meant that I found Boy George maybe a little cute. So yeah: Basic gay panic case at 14 years old. What can you do.

Getting over that took the usual things, like actually knowing gay people, learning the history of gays and lesbians, finding out that many of the people I admired culturally were gay or bisexual, sorting out my own sexuality to my satisfaction, and also coming to the conclusion that a lot of the people who didn't like gays and lesbians weren't the sort of people I wanted to hang around with anyway. It took time, and I think I'm fortunate to come to the place where I am at the moment.

That said, and unlike most people, I can tell you exactly when the first time I actually thought about homophobia was, and the first time it seemed like nonsense to me. It was when I saw the video for "Smalltown Boy" by Bronski Beat on the video show of a local UHF channel.

In the video, if you haven't watched it (and won't watch it now), a young gay man (played by BB lead singer Jimmy Sommerville) visits a local gym, where a swimmer seems to come on to him, only to beat the crap out of him with a bunch of friends. Jimmy is taken home by the cops, and this is how his parents find out he's gay. He decides to leave home, and his dad is still so upset that he can't shake his own son's hand goodbye. And off he goes.

I remember being 15 years old, watching the video, and feeling sad for the Jimmy Sommerville character, and also being aware enough to know that the video was almost certainly based on experience; if not Sommerville's directly, then that of someone else in the band, or of someone they knew. I knew the band members were gay—there was a kid at school who got every issue of *Smash Hits*, so we were all caught up on all the Brit bands of the time—so it wasn't hard to connect the dots. And when the dots were connected up, they seemed unfair.

I'm somewhat famous for noting that life isn't fair (ask Athena, after she's tried to use the "unfair" defense to get out of doing something), but at the same time, there's a difference between the fact that the universe is inherently unfair on a cosmic level, and the fact that life is unfair because people are actively making it so. There's not much one can do about the former, but the latter is fixable. What was going on with Jimmy Sommerville's character in that video was unfair in the latter way. There was no reason he shouldn't be loved by his family. There was no reason he ought not find love with someone else.

None of this hit me like a ton of bricks, I should say. I was 15, I wasn't a brilliant critical thinker, and I had other things going on in my mind at the time (mostly involving a girl I had no chance of getting with; another story of messed-up sexuality *entirely*). But I can say the video and the song stuck in my head and I came back to both more than once, trying to figure out why they affected me as much as they did. I did figure it out, eventually.

Now, I like to think that without the video and song, I would have still ended up where I am on this particular subject; I suspect that sooner or later people do become who they are meant to be, no matter how they get there. But this takes nothing away from the fact this was the video and the song that got that ball rolling in my life. It does point to how music can be meaningful, and yes, change lives in its way.

I'm not the only one who thinks this of course, or even thinks this about this particular song and video. A couple of years ago Andrew

Sullivan singled out "Smalltown Boy," as a critical anthem for the gay community: "Even now, it chokes me up," he said. "The video is a record of the beginnings of a revolution. You can feel it coming." I don't doubt he's right that it mattered to any number of gay men, back in the day. For at least one other person, it mattered too.

Who Gets To Be a Geek? Anyone Who Wants To Be

Jul
26
2012

The other day CNN let some dude named Joe Peacock vomit up an embarrassing piece on its Web site, about how how awful it is that geekdom is in the process of being overrun by attractive women dressing up in costumes ("cosplaying," for the uninitiated) when they haven't displayed their geek cred to Mr. Peacock's personal satisfaction. They weren't *real* geeks, Mr. Peacock maintains—he makes a great show of supporting *real* geek women, the definition of which, presumably, are those who have passed his stringent entrance requirements, which I am sure he's posted some place other than the inside of his skull—and because they're not *real* geeks, they offend people like him, who *are* real geeks:

> *They're poachers. They're a pox on our culture. As a guy, I find it repugnant that, due to my interests in comic books, sci-fi, fantasy and role playing games, video games and toys, I am supposed to feel honored that a pretty girl is in my presence. It's insulting...You're just gross.*

For the moment, let's leave aside the problem of a mentality that assumes that the primary reason some woman might find it fun and worthwhile to cosplay as one of her favorite science fiction and fantasy characters is to get the attention of some dudes, to focus on another interesting aspect of this piece: Namely, that Joe Peacock has arrogated to himself the role of Speaker for the Geeks, with the ability to determine whether any particular group of people is worthy of True Geekdom. This on the basis, one presumes, of his resume and his longtime affiliation as a geek.

Well, fine. Hey, Joe: Hi, I'm John Scalzi. I am also a longtime geek. My resume includes three *New York Times* bestselling science fiction books, three books nominated for the Best Novel Hugo, six other Hugo nominations (as well as Nebula, Locus, Sidewise and other award nominations), one novel optioned for a science fiction film, a stint consulting for the *Stargate: Universe* television show, a long history in video games as a player (Atari, yo) and as a writer, including writing for the *Official US Playstation Magazine* for six years and currently writing a game for Industrial Toys. I wrote a column on science fiction film for four years and have two books on the subject. I've been writing this blog for fourteen years and was one of the early adopters of self-publishing one's books online; additionally three books of mine (including one Hugo winner) have been of work originally published online. I was a special guest at this year's ComicCon. I am the toastmaster of this year's Worldcon. I am the sitting president of the Science Fiction and Fantasy Writers of America.

I outrank you as Speaker for the Geeks.

You are *overruled*.

Your entire piece is thrown out as condescending, entitled, oblivious, sexist and obnoxious.

And no, you can't object (well, you *can*, but you'll be summarily overruled). You made the decision based on your life experience as a geek that you could tell other people who is welcome as a geek and who is not. Based on *my* life experience as a geek, I have made the decision that I am qualified to tell you to suck eggs. You want to slap down people who you don't feel qualify for geekdom? Then I get to slap you down for being *wrong*, on the basis of being higher up in the geek hierarchy. You don't like it? Then you shouldn't have played this game to begin with. You played your cards, and I now I've played mine. This round goes to me. I have the conch. And now I will speak.

Who gets to be a geek?

Anyone who wants to be, any way they want to be one.

Geekdom is a nation with open borders. There are many affiliations and many doors into it. There are lit geeks, media geeks, comics geeks, anime and manga geeks. There are LARPers, cosplayers, furries, filkers, crafters, gamers and tabletoppers. There are goths and horror geeks and steampunkers and academics. There are nerd rockers and writers and artists and actors and fans. Some people love only one thing. Some people flit between fandoms. Some people are positively poly in their geek enthusiasms. Some people have been in geekdom since before they knew they were geeks. Some people are n00bs, trying out an aspect of geekdom to see if it fits. If it does, great. If it doesn't then at least they tried it.

Many people believe geekdom is defined by a love of a thing, but I think—and my experience of geekdom bears on this thinking—that the true sign of a geek is a delight in sharing a thing. It's the major difference between a geek and a hipster, you know: When a hipster sees someone else grooving on the thing they love, their reaction is to say "Oh, *crap*, now the *wrong people* like the thing I love." When a geek sees someone else grooving on the thing they love, their reaction is to say "ZOMG YOU LOVE WHAT I LOVE COME WITH ME AND LET US LOVE IT TOGETHER."

Any jerk can love a thing. It's the *sharing* that makes geekdom awesome.

Let's take these women cosplayers, who Mr. Peacock is so hand-flappingly disgusted with and dismissive of. Let's leave aside, for now, the idea that for those of this group attending ComicCon, spending literally hundreds and perhaps even thousands of dollars on ComicCon passes, hotels, transportation, food, not to mention the money and time required to put together an excellent costume, is not in itself a *signal indication* of geek commitment. Let's say that, in fact, the *only* reason the women cosplayers are there is to get their cosplay on, in front of what is likely to be an appreciative audience.

So what?

As in, so what if their only geekdom is cosplay? What if it is? Who does it harm? Who is materially injured by the fact? Who, upon seeing a woman cosplaying without an accompanying *curriculum vitae* posted above her head on a stick, laying out her geek bona fides, says to him or herself "Everything I loved about my geekdom has turned to ashes in my mouth," and then flees from the San Diego Convention Center, weeping? If there is such an unfortunate soul, should the fragile pathology of their own geekdom be the concern of the cosplaying woman? It seems *highly doubtful* that woman spent hundreds if not thousands of dollars to show up in San Diego just to ruin some random, overly-sensitive geek's day. It's rather more likely she came to enjoy herself in a place where *her expression of her own geekiness* would be appreciated.

So what if her geekiness is not your own? So what if she isn't into the geek life as deeply as you believe you are, or that you think she should be? So what if she doesn't have a geek love of the things you have a geek love for? Is the *appropriate* response to those facts to call her gross, and a poacher, and maintain that she's only in it to be slavered over by dudes who (in your unwarranted condescension) you judge to be not nearly as enlightened to the ways of geek women as you? Or would a more appropriate response be to say "great costume," and maybe *welcome* her into the parts of geekdom that you love, so that she might possibly grow to love them too? What do you gain from complaining about her fakey fake fakeness, except a momentary and entirely erroneous feeling of geek superiority, coupled with a permanent record of your sexism against women who you don't see being the right *kind* of geek?

These are your choices. Although actually there's a third choice: Just let her be to do her thing. Because here's a funny fact: *Her geekdom is not about you.* At all. It's about her.

Geekdom is personal. Geekdom varies from person to person. There are as many ways to be a geek as there are people who love a thing and love sharing that thing with others. You don't get to define their geekdom. They don't get to define yours. What you can do is share your expression of geekdom with others. Maybe they will get you, and maybe they won't. If they do, great. If they don't, that's their problem and not yours.

Be your own geek. Love what you love. Share it with anyone who will listen.

One other thing: There is no Speaker for the Geeks. Not Joe Peacock, not me, not anyone. If anyone tells you that there's a right way to be a geek, or that someone else is not a geek, or shouldn't be seen as a geek—or that you are not a geek—you can tell them to fuck right off. They don't get a vote on your geekdom. Go cosplay, or play filk, or read that Doctor Who novel or whatever it is you want to do. Geekdom is flat. There is no hierarchy. There is no leveling up required, or secret handshake, or entrance examination. There's just you.

Anyone can be a geek. Any way they want to. That means you too. Whoever you are.

Anyone who tells you different, you send them to me.

Why I Don't Just Admit I Am a Democrat

Aug
8
2012

Got an e-mail from someone who's apparently been reading my archives to figure out my political views. It was a hostile e-mail, but at the heart of the e-mail is a legitimate question, which I will paraphrase as such:

> *You say you're politically independent but you vote like a Democrat. Why don't you just admit you're a Democrat?*

The answer is: Well, because I'm *not*.

Three points here:

1. Being a Democrat, in the most obvious sense, would mean being a member of the Democratic Party here in the United States. I am not a member of the Democratic Party currently, nor have I ever been, unless you count the five minutes in 2008 when I checked the "Democrat" checkbox so I could vote in the the 2008 Ohio presidential primary. By that standard I may have been a member of the Republican Party as well at one point, since I believe I voted in a GOP primary once in Virginia (I can't remember if that required a statement about my party; suffice to say I think closed primaries are silly). From the first time I could vote, I have registered as an independent.

Reasons for this: One, on a practical level, it cuts way the hell down on the amount of political junk mail I get. I find most political mailings obnoxious and insulting to my intelligence, not to mention a waste of trees, so the less that I have to see, the better. Two, on a philosophical level, I think political parties are a bit of a menace. I don't know if I would actually be happier with our political system if political parties didn't exist and all political candidates had to fend for themselves without a national organization riding herd on them, but I do know that I would be *willing* to live in the universe where that was the case, to see how it worked out.

2. I don't have a party, but I do have political views. If I lived in Canada, Australia, New Zealand, England or most of what used to be called Western Europe, those political views would probably get me tagged as a member of the major local conservative party. Here in the US, they currently align most frequently with the Democratic party, our ostensibly "liberal" major political party. But 40 years ago, they probably would have gotten me tagged as a moderate Republican. This to my mind suggests there is wisdom in not aligning with actual political parties, and instead establishing one's own political ideals and then finding which candidates most closely align one's ideals, and political goals.

3. I have (and do) vote for political candidates other than Democrats, and don't automatically vote for Democratic candidates. I've noted before that when I lived in Virginia's 10th District, I regularly voted for Frank Wolf, a conservative Republican; he had many positions I didn't like (including his abortion stance) but he also was the head of the House's Transportation committee (i.e., nice smooth roads in Northern Virginia), had a principled stance on human rights, and even his positions that I opposed were based on his moral and philosophical beliefs rather than mere political expediency. In the end the positives for me outweighed the negatives, and I could vote for him over his opponents in each cycle.

Here in OH-8, I've not voted for John Boehner, but there have been times when I didn't vote for his Democratic opponent, either, because I didn't like their positions, or thought that the advantages of giving him my vote would outweigh the advantages of keeping Boehner, who is, after all, Speaker of the House, and was House Minority Leader prior to that (this election cycle there's no Democrat running against Boehner, so I don't have the option of voting for a Democrat in any event). Beyond that, in state and local elections, I've voted for Republican candidates in most election cycles, when I believed that they were the most qualified candidates for that position and/or that they were running for a post where the more nutty aspects of the current Republican Party orthodoxy would not be a problem.

So, to recap: Philosophically aligned against political parties in a general sense, never registered for any political party, which party my personal politics align with depends on geography and temporality in any event, and I've never voted a straight ticket in my life, so far as I know. So there you are.

This is not to say, mind you, that I am *neutral* as regards my opinions on the US political parties as they are currently ideologically and practically constituted; I don't think it'll be a huge surprise to anyone that I am not at all a fan of the Republican Party in its most recent iteration. I would be delighted for the party to swing back toward people who have foundations based in a coherent political philosophy, rather than "whatever Obama is for, I am against, and rich people can do no wrong ever," which is what it seems to boil down to these days for the GOP. The Democratic Party is no prize, but it's at the very least not nearly as far down the slope of truculent irrationality. "Not as truculently irrational," however, is not a sterling inducement for me to join the Democratic Party. Or any party, to be honest about it.

Why In Fact Publishing Will *Not* Go Away Anytime Soon: A Deeply Slanted Play in Three Acts

Feb
3
2010

CHARACTERS:

ELTON P. STRAÜMANN, *a modern-thinking man with exciting ideas*
JOHN SCALZI, *a humble writer*
KRISTINE SCALZI, *the wife of a humble writer*

ACT I

SCENE OPENS ON STRAÜMANN and SCALZI, standing.

STRAÜMANN:

The publishing world is changing! In the future, authors will no longer need those fat cat middle men known as "publishers" to get in the way of their art! It will just be the author and his audience!

SCALZI:

Won't I need an editor? Or a copy editor? Or a cover artist? Or a book designer? Or a publicist? Or someone to print the book and get it into stores?

STRAÜMANN
(waves hand, testily):
Yes, yes. But all those things you can do *yourself.*

SCALZI:
And I'm supposed to write the book, too?

STRAÜMANN
(snorts):
As if writing was *hard*. Now go! And write your novel!

SCALZI goes off to write his novel. STRAÜMANN stands, alone, on stage, for several months. Eventually SCALZI returns, with a book.

STRAÜMANN:
You again! What took you so long?

SCALZI:
Well, I had to write the book. Then I had to edit it, copy edit it, do the cover, do the book design, have it printed, act as my own distributor and send out press releases. It cost me thousands of dollars out of my own pocket and the better part of a year. But look! Here's the book!

STRAÜMANN
(pulls out his electronic reader):
I'm sorry, I only read on *this*.

SCALZI sighs, slinks off the stage.

STRAÜMANN
(yelling after SCALZI):
And where's the sequel? *Why aren't you writing more?!?*

ACT II

It is A YEAR LATER. SCENE OPENS on STRAÜMANN and SCALZI, standing.

STRAÜMANN:

I'm still waiting for that sequel, you know.

SCALZI:

I spent all my money last year making that first book. And it didn't sell very well.

STRAÜMANN

(sneers):

Well, what did you expect? The editing was sloppy, the copy editing was *atrocious*, the layout was amateurish and the cover art looked like it was Photoshopped by a *dog*. Who would want to buy *that*?

SCALZI

(dejected):

I know.

STRAÜMANN:

Seriously, what were you *thinking*.

SCALZI:

But that's my point! I want to get professional editing and copy editing and book design and cover art, but I just can't afford it.

STRAÜMANN

(smiles):

Scalzi, you naive fool. Don't you realize that thanks to the current economy we live in, editors and copy editors and artists are desperately looking for work! Surely some of them will work for almost nothing! Scratch that—they'll work for *exactly* nothing!

SCALZI:

Is that ethical? To get work from people without paying them?

STRAÜMANN:

Of *course* it is. They'll profit from the *exposure.*

SCALZI:

I don't think a printer is going to want to be paid in exposure.

STRAÜMANN:

Then release the book electronically to skip on all those printing costs!

SCALZI:

Yes! And then sell it for a reasonable price!

STRAÜMANN

(shrugs):

Well, do what you want. I'll be getting it off a torrent.

SCALZI:

What?

STRAÜMANN

(brandishing his electronic reader):

I paid $300 for this thing! Honestly, how much do you expect me to pay to *fill* it?

SCALZI:

So, pay people nothing to help me create a book I make nothing on, for people who will refuse to pay for it.

STRAÜMANN:

I wouldn't put it *that* way. But yes.

STRAÜMANN and SCALZI stand for a moment, silent.

SCALZI:

I'm trying to remember if you voted for Obama.

STRAÜMANN

(snorts):

As if I'd vote for a *Communist*.

ACT III

SEVERAL MONTHS have passed. SCENE OPENS on STRAÜMANN and SCALZI, standing.

STRAÜMANN:

Dude, where the fuck is that sequel? I'm dying over here.

SCALZI:

Well, I was going to write it, but when I tried to find editors and artists to work on it for free, I kind of hit a road block. The ones who were good wouldn't work for free, and the ones that were free weren't good.

STRAÜMANN
(rolls his eyes):
Well, duh. I could have told you that.

SCALZI:
But…

STRAÜMANN:
But that's not important now. What's *important* is that we get you writing again.

SCALZI:
But I don't have the money to make another book with professional help, and I don't have the time to make another book on my own.

STRAÜMANN:
As it happens, I have a solution for you. And look, here she is.

ENTER KRISTINE SCALZI from STAGE LEFT.

STRAÜMANN:
Mrs. Scalzi, a word, please.

KRISTINE:
Yes?

STRAÜMANN:
As you may know, your husband is a writer. But he is finding it difficult to do writing recently because of issues of cost and time. I know that you are the organized, financially-minded person in your relationship, so allow me to suggest to you that you become his publisher. While he writes, you locate and

pay for an editor, a copy editor, a cover artist, a book designer, a publicist, a printer and a distributor. This will leave him free to focus on his craft, and the sequel I so desire.

KRISTINE:

I see. And you propose I fund these people how?

STRAÜMANN:

Well, I'm sure I don't *know,* Mrs. Scalzi, but I have faith in your ability to do so.

KRISTINE:

So to recap, you want me to quit my full-time job and devote all my time to my husband's career.

STRAÜMANN:

Of course not! I never said for you to *quit your job.* You need the health insurance.

KRISTINE:

Ah. Could you come over here for just a second?

STRAÜMANN

(walks toward KRISTINE):

Yes?

KRISTINE clocks STRAÜMANN in the head, stunning him, then rips off his testicles, stuffs them into his mouth and sets him on fire while he chokes on them. STRAÜMANN dies.

KRISTINE

(to SCALZI):

You. Find a *fucking publisher.*

SCALZI:
Yes, dear.

CURTAIN FALLS.

Why Yes, I Should Write About Politics

Sep 30 2008

Over on his site, writer Paolo Bacigalupi asks the question "Should Fiction Writers Write About Politics?" in the wake of a reader comment after Paolo did, indeed, write about politics. While Paolo answers the question to his own satisfaction (I encourage you to read it), let me state my own, probably unsurprising, opinion here:

Why yes, fiction writers *should* write about politics, if they choose to. And so should doctors and plumbers and garbage collectors and lawyers and teachers and chefs and scientists and truck drivers and stay-at-home parents and the unemployed. In fact, every single adult who has reason enough to sit down and express an opinion through words should feel free to do just that. Having a citizenry that is engaged in the actual working of democracy matters to the democracy, and writing about politics is a fine way to provide evidence that one is actually thinking about these things.

The real question here is, "is it smart for fiction writers to potentially alienate readers by airing their politics?" My response to this, again to absolutely no surprise to anyone, is another question: "why should a fiction writer be obliged to be silent on the life of the state in which he or she lives?" Do readers really think it's wise that writers, of *all* people, stay quiet on the matters that affect their lives and the lives of their families, friends and nation, because some person they don't even *know* might feel slightly discomfited, and doesn't have the wit to separate a work of fiction from the largely unrelated real world concerns of the writer?

As long as we're asking whether fiction writers should write about politics, let's ask: should fiction writers write about sports? Because if I say, oh, that the Georgia Bulldogs *suck* and I hope that Tennessee well and truly kicks their ass on October 11, I'm going to alienate an entire state's worth of people, some of whom might now never get my loathing out of their heads every time they see my name on a book. Should fiction writers write about computers? Because if I express my opinion that Apple computers are merely status bait for anxious beta males, I invite a veritable rain of hate from those same beta males, some of whom will never forgive me for not kneeling at the altar of Steve. Should fiction writers write about sexuality? Because if I admit that during my second year of college I totally went gay for a semester and don't regret a single moment of it, I'm going to alienate the people who believe that scarfing wang is not a thing boys should do. Should fiction writers write about religion? Because if I express my belief that those who believe in consubstantiation rather than transubstantiation are taking the express elevator to Hell, then, whoops, there goes a whole swath of protestants.

Now, as it happens, I don't hold these opinions about consubstantiation, or the Georgia Bulldogs, or Apple computers, nor did I, in fact, spend any time in college in hot, sweaty m4m action. But it doesn't matter; the fact of the matter is that *any* opinion I hold and publicly discuss has the potential to alienate someone, somewhere, perhaps to the detriment of future sales of my fiction. I mean, for Christ's sake, out there in the world is a guy who holds me in spittle-flinging contempt because I think the word "alright" is the incorrect way to say "all right." It seems doubtful he will ever buy any of my books. Should fiction writers write about the *English language?* After all, lots of people seem to think "alright" is a real word. Should we content ourselves merely to pity them in private?

Of course not, just as we should not be obliged to keep to ourselves opinions about sports, sexuality, technology, religion, food, toys, war, science, music and so on. The reader who believes a fiction author should keep his or her opinions to themselves is effectively (if generally unintentionally) saying "You exist only to amuse me. You are not allowed to do anything else." To which the only rational response is: blow me.

I'm not going to hesitate to add my voice to the national dialogue on any subject just because someone somewhere might not be happy with what I have to say. And more to the point, I think it is *bad and dangerous thinking* for people to suggest that fiction writers should have to live in a black box of opinion. The idea that writing fiction somehow obliges or even just encourages a vow of silence on any subject, politics or otherwise, that might offend someone somewhere, is flatly odious.

Indeed: The idea that practicing *any* profession somehow obliges or even encourages a vow of silence on any subject, politics or otherwise, that might offend someone somewhere, is odious. Everyone should be encouraged to say what they wish to say about the important matters of the day. Everyone should feel that participation in the life of their community and their state and nation is a critical act. To do less invites ignorance and ultimately tyranny.

To go back to fiction writers and politics, there's another reason I feel obliged to freely speak my mind: Because so many writers cannot. PEN has a handy list of writers currently imprisoned all over the world because they've written about the world they live in; it also has a list of writers who had been imprisoned and who, while now released, continue to face prosecution and danger should what they write offend the wrong people. Are there fiction writers on these lists? There sure are. These writers chose to speak about their world, despite the certain risk, and were punished for it by prison terms or worse—and I'm supposed to hold my tongue because someone might not *buy my book?* Give me a fucking break. I couldn't do that. I wouldn't *dare.*

And yes, it means that some people won't buy my books. So what. I live in a place where it will never come to this, but if I had to make the choice between selling fiction and speaking my mind about politics, I would speak my mind and not once regret the choice. There are always other ways of making money; my conscience requires I participate in the political life of my country. If not selling another word of fiction were the cost of that participation, I'd be getting off cheap, particularly when you consider the alternatives.

Why New Novelists Are Kinda Old, or, Hey, Publishing is Slow

Jun
24
2009

From the e-mail pile today:

> *Whenever I hear about a "new" novelist, they turn out to be in their 30s. Why is that? It seems like you hear about new musicians and actors and other creative people in when they are in their 20s.*

Excellent question. Leaving aside the mechanics of why it pays to be young in the music and acting industries, here's what's up with those old new novelists:

1. Writing an entire novel is something most people have to work up to. Because you know what? Writing sixty to one hundred thousand words of fiction is not something most people cannonball through, even if they assure you, with the appropriate amount of false modesty, that they're really better at long-form fiction. Maybe they are, but they still had a long walk to get there. *I'm* better at long-form and it took me until I was 28 before I could do it. Meanwhile I'd been writing short for years up to that point, in the form of reviews and columns and humor pieces and (yes) occasional attempts at short fiction that I mostly abandoned after a page or two. Lots of people in their teens and early 20s start novels; rather fewer finish them.

Why? Well, some of them start novels and finish short stories, which is a surprise both for the would-be novelist and the would-be novel. Others (and this included me in my 20s) start writing something that they thought might be a book-length idea, only to find not only did it not qualify as a short story, it was better for everyone involved if the stunted, weird thing was taken behind the tool shed, whacked with a shovel and buried without anyone else knowing it ever existed.

Some others actually finish a whole novel-length pile of words whose best quality, alas, is that it gave its author a chance to exercise his or her fingers. The erstwhile author realizes that making it into a novel would require pulling it apart and starting over, and the thought of doing so fills them with same joy as they might get from sucking down a Dran-O mojito. So the not-actually-a-novel gets stuffed into the proverbial drawer or trunk, never again to see the light of day.

All of this, incidentally, is *perfectly fine*. Craftsmen don't make their masterpiece the first time they approach a potter's wheel (or whatever). Most writers aren't going to write a brilliant or even passable novel the first time they sit down in front of a keyboard and intone (to themselves if no one else) that today is the day they will commit *art*, in a convenient, novel-sized package. They usually have to work up to it, one way or another. That takes time, just as learning any craft takes time.

And when people do finally manage to write something that is actually identifiable to anyone else but the author as a novel, guess what?

2. Most people's first novels well and truly suck. Oh my, yes they *do*. Which again is perfectly fine. Writing anything over 60,000 words that still recognizably tells one single story is a hell of an achievement in itself. Asking that it also be *good* is just being mean to the author, and the novel. It's like watching someone run their first full-length marathon, ever, and criticizing them for not finishing in the top ten. I mean, shit. That can be the goal for the *second* race, right?

Most first novels are no damn good. Second ones are often better, but not always, and often not by much. Third and fourth novels, the same thing. Fact is—and this should not be news at this late date—ask most debut novelists how many novels they wrote before they got one published, and you'll find out the answer is: two, three, four—sometimes more. Debut novels are almost never first novels; they're just the first novels *you* see. And all those other novels you will never know about? They took lots of time to write, too.

Which brings us to the next point:

3. The physical act of writing a novel takes a long time. Yes, we all know of the authors who can crank out a perfectly publishable novel of 60, or 80, or 100,000 words in just under six weeks. But there are two things to note. First, most of those hyperkinetic authors are not newbie novelists; they're people who have been writing long enough that certain aspects of novel writing are encoded into their brain's muscle memory. Second, if you're a would-be novelist, you'll probably never be one of those people anyway.

No, I'm not intending to insult you. Most currently published authors don't write that quickly either. I know successful, working authors who are happy to get 250 words of fiction a day, because that's 90,000 words a year: A full-sized novel. But consider that there are any number of writers who have trouble getting *that* much out a year, because—surprise!—a novel is usually more than just sitting down and cranking out a word count. There are those little things like plot, and character, and pacing, and dialogue and so on and so forth. All of those things take time to develop.

Note also that while you're doing all of this as a budding novelist, you are also most likely doing all the other things in your life that constitute *your life*: A day job, spouse and family, hobbies and friends, reading and television and video games and even (wait for it) sleep. It all adds up—and it all subtracts from the amount of time you have to write.

What all this means is that writing those three or four novels an average writer has to burn through before they write a publishable novel will likely take years.

But hey! A budding novelist has put in the time and the work and the effort and has sacrificed numerous innocent, trusting pizzas to the

Gods of Writing, and has finally got a novel good enough to sell. Good for them. Now it's time for the next point:

4. Selling a novel takes a long time. At this point, like the Game of Life™, there are two paths a would-be novelist can go by. The first path is the path of Finding an Agent. This path takes more time but potentially opens the door to more publishers, because most publishers these days require agented submissions.

Finding an agent is a slog. One has to query the agent, wait to see if the query is accepted, and then if it is sample chapters and an outline go out in the mail. Then more waiting to see if the agent asks for more. If he or she does, it's time to send the whole manuscript and then wait again to see if he or she thinks the writer is worth their time to represent. At any point the agent can say "no," at which point our budding novelist will have to start over again.

But if the agent says "yes," then comes the part where he or she starts schlepping the novel to publishers. Presuming the agent gets a publishing house interested in looking at the manuscript, it could be weeks or even months before there's response, either positive or negative. If it's the latter, it's on to the next publisher.

The second path is the Path of the Slush Pile. This gets the work out there quicker but fewer publishers still accept unagented manuscripts, and as you might guess from the name "slush pile," the rate at which editors work through the slush pile is pretty slow. Baen Books, which accepts unagented manuscripts, lists their response time as nine to twelve months: Yes, you could make a baby (if you *can* make a baby) before our poor theoretical writer here would hear back about their literary child. And if at the end of those nine months to a year Baen (or whomever) says no, the poor writer has to start all over again.

And along either path, there's no assurance that the novel—despite being of publishable quality—will sell (this is where I suggest you do a Web search on Teresa Nielsen Hayden's evergreen "Slushkiller" piece, which details why). This means that at some point the writer may have to give up the ghost on this particular novel and move on to try to sell the next one—which of course, they were busy writing while they were waiting for that other one to sell.

All of this—you are sensing the theme by now—takes lots of time.

But wait! Despite the myriad challenges, a novel has actually been sold! Excellent. Now guess what?

5. Publishing a novel often takes a long time. Once a book has an offer, there's the time it takes to work through the contract. Then the editing process begins—it's very likely the editor working with the writer will want tweaks and edits to the novel. This round of editing takes time, depending both on how much work the book needs and how well the writer takes direction during the editing process. After that comes the copy editing, with the writer required to go through the manuscript, answering copy editor queries and signing off on the edits. And beyond this is all the production stuff the writer is not directly involved with, like cover art, interior and cover design, and so on and so forth. This, yes, takes time.

But even when that's done there's more waiting! That's because the publisher will need to find a spot for the novel on its release schedule, one that allows it to highlight the work and also gives it time to secure publicity and advance reviews and all that good stuff. That spot on the release schedule may be a year or even two in the future. This is the part that really drives writers nuts: Everything's done and yet, no book. It's *madness*, I tell you.

So, let's recap: It takes time for most people to learn how to write to novel-length. It takes time to write well at that length. It takes time to write *to* that length. It takes time to land a publisher and it takes time to get that novel to market. And suddenly, it makes sense why so many debut novelists just happen to be in their thirties.

You want a real world example, you say. Fine, take me. I'll note my own path to publication has some irregularities in it, but overall it works well enough for these purposes. Ready? Here it is. The number at the end of each line tells you how old I was each step of the way:

1969—1997: Time spent learning to write well enough to write a novel (28).

1997: Wrote first complete novel (28)

1997—2001: Life intervenes and keeps me away from fiction (32).

2001: Wrote second novel (32)

2002: Offer made on second novel, now my debut novel (33)

2003: Contract signed for debut novel (33)

2004: Editing and early publicity for debut novel (35)

2005: Debut novel published (35)

2006: Won the John W. Campbell Award for Best New Writer (37)

So, eight years from first completed novel to having a debut novel in the bookstores, and four years between completing the debut novel and it being published in book form. And if you think it's ironic to win a "Best New Writer" award at the ripe old age of 37, consider that 37 is pretty much the average age of the Campbell winners over the last 35 years. "New" does not equal "young."

Having said all of that, it's worth noting that a whole stack of writers have managed to get novels published while they were in their twenties—it's not *that* huge a trick to do so . These debuts are not necessarily any worse (or better) than those of authors who debut in their 30s or later. Some writers are publishable more quickly, some are in the right place at the right time with the right books, and some people are simply unfathomably lucky.

Also, at this point in time there are more authors who are willing to attempt self-publishing—either online or through print-on-demand—thus avoiding the whole "finding a publisher" time suck. We could have a debate on whether this is wise, from the point of view of distribution, publicity, marketing and/or writers debuting before their work is worth *reading*, but that's a debate for another entry. The fact of the matter is that if you self-publish, your debut as a novelist will undoubtedly come sooner.

But for the folks who do it the old-fashioned way—and, currently, the way that still affords them the best chance for notoriety and a chance at a long-term career as a novelist—the combination of writing skill development and the mechanics of contemporary publishing conspires to drive the age of most debut novelists into the thirties. It doesn't seem likely to change anytime soon.

Why Not Feeling Rich is Not Being Poor, and Other Things Financial

Sep 21 2010

My "Being Poor" piece has been getting a workout the last couple of days, because people were linking to it in response to a blog post by Todd Henderson, a law professor at the University of Chicago. Professor Henderson was kvetching about the possibility of Obama raising his taxes (or more accurately, Obama allowing the Bush era tax reductions to sunset) when he was just scraping by on a household income high enough for the president to have an interest in letting his tax cut expire—i.e., above $250,000, which puts his household in the top 1.5% or so of all income earners.

Henderson's lament has since been taken down from its original blog—he appears to have been hurt and confused as to why so many commenters and other bloggers had a distinct lack of sympathy for him as he laid out how the change in the tax regime would affect his gardener and nanny and his children's private schools—but economist Brad De Long rescued the piece from Google Cache, accompanied by some pungent thoughts on Henderson's predicament.

It's pretty clear that Henderson either forgot or didn't know that the problems of the well-off tend to be less than impressive to people whose own problems are not so nearly high-toned. Yes, it's awful that you may have to cut back on your gardener and your housecleaner and your nanny, but do please understand that in airing such a lament, you establish that in fact you *have* a gardener, housecleaner and nanny. Which is an enviable trifecta of domestic hands on deck, to be sure. Such a loadout largely disqualifies you from sympathy from those who do without. Which is most people, many of whom would like to have a job right now, and a side order of health insurance to go along with it.

Or to put it another way, while an Ivy League graduate currently employed as a law professor at one of the most prestigious universities in the world has a perfect right to complain in public about how he and his equally gainfully-employed medical doctor wife might have to make adjustments to their wholly enviable professional lifestyle because their top marginal tax rate might go up a couple of percentage points, he really ought to have the good sense *not* to. You end up looking foolish on the Internet when you do. Which Professor Henderson now appears to realize, and has at least temporarily excused himself from the Internet because of it.

Professor Henderson may have been foolish to write what he did, but in fairness I don't believe he deserved to be bludgeoned with my Being Poor piece in response. When he was kvetching about scraping by, he wasn't suggesting that he was in any way poor—not he, with his gardener and housecleaner and nanny and private schools. It's the wrong tool to employ against him, and I feel reasonably qualified to say so. Professor Henderson's lament isn't saying that he's poor, or even feels poor. His lament is that he isn't *rich,* and certainly doesn't *feel* like he's rich, what with his debts and owes—which aside from his domestic help, also more seriously include the massive school loans that come with law and medical degrees, and a mortgage which Professor Henderson implies but does not say is currently underwater. Not being (or feeling) rich is an entirely different thing than being poor, and I don't think it serves anyone well to confuse the two states.

Now, if you are part of the rabble who populates the lower 98.5% of American income brackets, you may ask: is it really possible to be in the top 1.5% of income earners in the United States and not realize you're rich by most objective standards? Sure, as long as two things are in play: First, that your picture of "rich" is predicated on how billionaires live and act; second, that your financial outlays come reasonably close to your financial intake. So in the first case, if your mental image of being rich includes helicopters and supermodels at your beck and call, in equal and staggering amounts, then making a quarter of a million a year looks rather more like an "average" or "middle-class" income, even when it is manifestly not. When rich folk say they feel middle-class, they're not (always) being disingenuous, it's just their way of saying "I don't own a castle on an island."

Likewise, if you make a quarter of a million a year but send out most of it paying for things, then asking yourself "wait, I'm supposed to be *rich*, here?" doesn't seem horribly unreasonable. When one is poor, the problem you have with money is not having any. When one is well-off, the problem you have with money is managing it. When you have more money, you do more things with it, and that means more opportunities for it to get away from you if you're not paying attention. This is a high-class problem to have, mind you, and generally speaking it's not going to generate a large gout of sympathy from anyone else, especially those with little money to manage. But it's still a problem, especially when it's *your* problem.

But it is *your* problem, and it doesn't mean you're not well off, or even rich by many relevant real-world standards. Because, my dear 1.5% folks: you so very *are*. The median household income in the US is about $46,000 a year. If your household is bringing in five times that on an annual basis, you certainly have the *potential* to be doing reasonably well anywhere in the United States—even in Chicago, and even in Hyde Park—provided you have some sense about how you allocate your income and resources. And as regards the very-likely-soon-to-be-sunset Bush tax cut, if shaving off an extra couple of percent off your income *above* $250,000 will send your family into a dark spiral of money woes, you have *other* issues which you should address. Taxes are not your biggest problem in that case. Accountants are your friends.

So what have we learned today?

1. Don't complain to the Internets about trying to get by on $250,000 a year;
2. Being poor and not feeling rich are not the same thing, don't confuse the two;

3. Even well-off people can have money woes;

4. With great income comes great (financial management) responsibilities.

There, we're done for the day! Let's go get some pie.

Worth Promoting to Its Own Post: Notes on Arguing

Aug 16 2011

Here's a comment I made in a thread, which I am promoting to its own post (with some edits for context) because I think it says something relevant about discussions here, especially (but not limited to) political ones:

1. One is entitled to one's own opinions, but not one's own facts. Commensurately, anecdote may be fact (it happened to you), but anecdote is usually a poor platform for general assertions, since one's own experience is often not a general experience.
2. If you make an assertion that implies a factual basis, it is *entirely proper* that others may ask you to back up these assertions with facts, or at least data, beyond the anecdotal.
3. If you cannot bolster said assertion with facts, or at least data, beyond the anecdotal, you have to accept that others may not find your general argument persuasive.
4. This dynamic of people asking for facts, or at least data, beyond the anecdotal, is in itself non-partisan; implications otherwise are a form of *ad hominem* argument which is generally not relevant to the discussion at hand.
5. If you offer evidence and assert it as fact, you may reasonably expect others to examine such information and to rebut you if they find it wanting and/or find your interpretation incorrect in some manner.

All of which is to say that asserting from anecdote without being able to bolster said assertion with actual facts is likely to get your assertion discounted; if you present facts without rigor, you're likely to see those discounted as well. Again, this is neither here nor there as regards one's personal politics; this is simply about making a robust argument.

People here have a low tolerance for general assertion from personal anecdote because rhetorically speaking *I* have a low tolerance for general assertion from personal anecdote, and over time that rubs off on others who comment here regularly. That low tolerance is in fact non-partisan on my part, as I have called out liberals for bad argument when they have offered one, and I have called out people in non-political threads for the same thing (when one's politics are not in evidence). There are indeed a lot of liberals here; there are also quite a few conservatives as well. Everyone gets dinged when they argue poorly.

In a general sense, if one wants to have one's arguments and assertions taken seriously here, they need to be serious arguments and assertions. There's nothing wrong with making an observation from personal experience; I do it all the time. But I also note the anecdotal nature of the observation; and when I don't, guess what? People here call me on it.

This is all to be noted for future reference.

Writers and Financial Woes: What's Going On

Nov
9
2009

n e-mail:

You talk about money and writing a lot, so let me ask you: What is it with writers and money? Lots of them seem to be in financial hot water these days.

Hmmmm. Well, let's start by pointing out two rather salient points (note this discussion is primarily US-centric, but may have application elsewhere):

1. Things are tough all over. "These days" includes a profound recession, for which employment is a lagging factor, so let's make sure we factor that not-trivial datum into our mindview. On top of this general employment malaise, writers of all sorts are taking an extra set of lumps: Journalism is losing thousands of full-time writers out of newspapers and magazines, writers in corporate settings are no safer than any other white-collar worker and publishing companies are actively trimming their author rosters and slicing advances. I'd hesitate to suggest that writers are having it worst of all recently, but you know what, they're not just skating through this recession, either. They've got it middlin' bad.

On top of this:

2. It's not just writers who make lousy financial choices. There aren't enough writers in the United States to cover all the bad mortgages out there right now, to make one obvious point. It's not just writers who push the average consumer debt above $7,000 per card holder. It's not just writers who save almost none of their income, leaving them vulnerable to sudden, unexpected changes in personal fortune. Writers are often bad with money, but then so are secretaries, and doctors, and teachers, and plumbers, and members of the military and any other group of people you might care to imagine, excepting possibly accountants, and honestly I wouldn't even put it past *them*. So when we're singling out writers for discussion, let's remember they are not alone out there on the far end of the "wow, we really *suck* at finances" spectrum.

Having noted the above, here are some additional reasons why writers seem to so often fall face first, financially. Note that not all of these apply equally to every writer; we're talking in vast generalities, here.

First, some practical issues:

3. Writer pay is generally low and generally inconsistent. And if one writes fiction for some/all of one's writing output, especially so. I've written in detail about writing rates and payment before so it's not necessary to go into detail again right at the moment. But what it means is that if one is a writer, one does a fair amount of work for not a whole lot of money, and then has to wait for that payment to arrive more or less at the pleasure of the person sending the check. Unfortunately, writers like pretty much everyone else have fixed expenses (mortgage/rent, bills etc), and *those* people generally do not wait to be paid at the pleasure of the writer; you pay your electric bill regularly or you don't get electricity. This means writers are often in a situation where despite working prodigiously, they don't have money in hand to pay regular, fixed monthly expenses.

4. Writers often lack what meager social net actually exists in corporate America. Writers are often self-employed, which means they bear the full brunt of the cost of health insurance or go without, and when they do pay for health insurance, they pay a lot because their individual plans don't spread out risk like corporate plans do. Since per point three writers don't get paid a lot (or regularly), very often they go without—as often do their spouses and children, if the spouse does not work for someone who provides health insurance. Which means they are quite susceptible to even incidental medical costs wreaking holy hell with their finances, and my own anecdotal experience with writers is that they are not exactly a hale and hearty group to start.

Self-employed writers don't get 401(k)s and often don't get around to funding IRAs, so their ability to save for retirement is made that much more challenging. They are on the hook for their full amount of Social Security taxes and also have to file taxes quarterly, and the IRS keeps a close eye on them (and all self-employed folks) for fraud and so on. Add it all up, and not being formally on the corporate teat makes it easier for writers to find themselves in a compromised financial situation.

5. Writers, like many people (even presumably educated folks), often have rudimentary financial skills. Which means even when they do have money and a desire to save it intelligently, they often don't know how or have already gotten themselves into a compromised financial situation which makes smart and sane financial practices more difficult. Now, for writers, to some extent we can blame them and their arty-farty educations for this lack. I'm not sure how many MFA or undergrad writing programs out there require a "real world basic finance" class for a degree, but I'm guessing I can count them on one hand and have up to five fingers left over. Likewise, my anecdotal experience with writers suggests that not a whole lot of them have a vibrant love affair with mathematics, even the relatively basic sort that underpins day-to-day financial planning. So there are two strikes against them right there.

But to be fair to writers, once again, it's not just them. I have a philosophy degree; it didn't require a real world financial management class either. I don't believe I actually ever took a class in basic financial planning and management, *ever,* and I'm guessing I'm not the only one there. This leaves basically everyone to get their financial educations from rah-rah financial bestsellers, fatuous talking heads on CNBC and folks like the sort who recently suckered millions of Americans into buying far more home than they could rationally afford on the basis that hey, the real estate market will never ever go down. This is, basically, an appalling state of affairs, and not just for writers.

Having enumerated some practical issues, here are some (for lack of a better term) "lifestyle" reasons why writers often have money problems:

6. Writers are often flaky. Which can mean (pick one or more) that they have short attention spans, which penalize them for things like finances; they get bored quickly and therefore make bad economic decisions because they want to stop thinking about them and get on to interesting stuff; because they are clever with words they think that means that they are smart outside of their specific field (and particularly with money), which is a common mistake people good in one intellectual area make; they trust people they should not with their money and/or their life situations; they go with their guts rather than with their brains; they prioritize immediate wants over long-term needs; and so on.

We could have a nice fun argument about whether flaky people become writers or whether being a writer makes one flaky, but it's a discussion that's not relevant at the moment; the point here is that many authors by their personal nature are not well-composed for the sober, staid and completely *boring* task of dealing with money.

(Note I'm not simply running down other writers here; ask my wife why it was when we met I had all my utilities on third notice, despite the fact I could afford to pay the bills. It will confirm my own "flaky like a pie crust" nature.)

Related to this:

7. Writers are often irrational risk-takers. Because how can you *write* about life without *experiencing* it, etc, which is a convenient rationale for doing stupid things and getting caught in bad situations, up to and including terrible relationships, addictions, impulsive life-changing decisions and so on, all of which end up having a (not in the least) surprising impact on one's financial life. Hell, even a bog-standard nicotine addiction will set you back $9 per pack in NYC and $5 everywhere else (not counting the cost of one's lung cancer treatments later). Whether these sorts of irrational risks actually *do* make one a better writer is of course deeply open to debate, but again, it's a rationale as opposed to a reason.

Note that in the cases of 6 and 7 above, there's another potential correlating issue, which is that writers like many creative types appear to have higher incidence of mental illness than your random sample of, say, grocery store managers or bus drivers. Mental illness—particularly illness that goes untreated/undertreated due to financial constraints—will have corresponding effects on one's financial situation.

8. Writers are often attracted to other creative folks, including other writers. Nothing wrong with this in a general sense, mind you. We all love who we love, and what's not to love about another witty, smart and talented person? The problem *financially speaking*, however, is that other writers very often have the same basic financial issues: low, irregular pay, no benefits, poor finance skills, tendencies toward flakiness and risk-taking, and such. Two incomes are theoretically better than one, but two sporadic incomes accompanied by everything else that comes attached to the writing life isn't necessarily as much better than one would expect. And don't forget: Kids may happen. They often do.

9. Writing can be expensive. The actual act of writing is not expensive, mind you—if one had to one could do it for free off a library computer, although few do—but everything around it adds up. Typewriters, paper, ribbons and correcting fluid have been replaced by computers, printers, printer ink and internet access, so the sunk cost there is roughly the same as it ever was, as are the costs of sending manuscripts and correspondence, at least to the markets which still require paper submissions. Writers who write in coffee shops and cafes pay "rent" in coffee and pastries; it sounds silly, but those things ain't cheap when you check the tab. Writers are gregarious and go to things like workshops and conventions and writers' nights at the local bar;

these aren't required costs but they are desirable activities and they cost money to attend (even if it's just to get an overpriced beer).

Do all these things mean writers are more susceptible than other trades/professions to encounter serious financial issues? Not necessarily; folks in other creative fields (acting, music, art, dance) have the same set of practical and lifestyle challenges, and while the challenges of other lines of work will vary, they're still there—hell, even doctors and lawyers find themselves saddled first with huge amounts of debt and then with some impressive overhead to keep their practices going. Pick a profession—there's lots of ways to get yourself in financial hot water doing it.

However, there is one thing that can make it appear that writers as a class are in more financial trouble than other folks, regardless of whether or not it's true:

10. Writers write about their situations. Because they're *writers,* you see. Writing is what they *do.* And lots of writers feel the need to share their financial situations with an audience, to a greater or lesser degree. Why? Because (again, pick one or more) writing helps writers think through their situation; writing is therapy; writers feel an obligation to share; writers are hoping for sympathy, encouragement and possibly solutions or even help. Whatever their reasons, it shouldn't be very surprising that you'll more than occasionally read an author lay out his or her financial woes, and (yes) do it in an interesting and engaging style that sticks in your head more than, say, a similar blog post by a janitor might. It's an interesting curse, you might say.

So those are some reasons writers might be having a hard time of it right now—and why it might seem they're having a harder time than some others.

Writing: Find the Time or Don't

Sep 16 2010

Over the last couple of months I've gotten a fair number of letters from aspiring writers who want to write but find themselves plagued by the vicissitudes of the day, i.e., they've got jobs, and they're tiring, and when they come home they just want to collapse in front of the TV/spend time with family/blow up anthills in the backyard/whatever. And so they want to know two things: One, how I keep inspired to write; two, how one manages to find the time and/or will to write when the rest of life is so draining. I've addressed these before, but at this point the archives are vast, so I'll go ahead and address them again.

The answer to the first of these is simple and unsatisfying: I keep inspired to write because if I don't then the mortgage company will be inspired to foreclose on my house. And I'd prefer not to have that happen. This answer is simple because it's true—hey, this is my job, I don't have another—and it's unsatisfying because writers, and I suppose particularly authors of fiction, are assumed to have some other, more esoteric inspiration. And, you know. Maybe other authors do. But to the extent that I have to be inspired to write at all on a day-to-day basis (and I really don't; you don't keep a daily blog for twelve years, for example, if you're the sort of person who has to wait for inspiration to get your fingers going across a keyboard), the desire to make money for myself and my family works well enough. Another day, another dollar, etc.

Now, bear in mind here I'm establishing a difference between inspiration for writing on a daily, continuing basis, and inspiration for specific pieces of work; those inspirations aren't necessarily related to getting paid, and can come from any place. But even then, I find the two inspirational motivations work in a complementary fashion. I am inspired to write a particular story or idea in a fanciful way, and then the practical inspiration of getting paid gets my ass in a chair to write the thing. It's a congenial, if somewhat unromantic, way of doing things.

As to the second of these, my basic response here is, Well, look. Either you want to write or you don't, and *thinking* that you want to write really doesn't mean anything. There are lots of things I think I'd *like* to do, and yet if I don't actually make the time and effort to do them, they don't get done. This is why I don't have an acting career, or am a musician—because as much as I'd *like* those, I somehow stubbornly don't actually do the things I need to do in order to achieve them. So I guess in really fundamental way I *don't* want them, otherwise I'd make the time. *C'est la vie.*

(This sort of skips over the question of whether I'd be *good* at either acting or music, but that's neither here nor there. By not trying, I'm not even achieving failure.)

So: Do you want to write or don't you? If your answer is "yes, but," then here's a small editing tip: what you're doing is using six letters and two words to say "no." And that's *fine*. Just don't kid yourself as to what "yes, but" means.

If your answer is "yes," then the question is simply when and how you find the time to do it. If you spend your free time after work watching TV, turn off the TV and write. If you prefer to spend time with your family when you get home, write a bit after the kids are in bed and before you turn in yourself. If your work makes you too tired to think straight when you get home, wake up early and write a little in the morning before you head off. If you can't do that (I'm not a morning person myself) then you have your weekend—weekends being what I used when I wrote *Agent to the Stars*.

And if you can't manage that, then what you're saying is that you were *lying* when you said your answer is "yes." Because if you really wanted to write, you would find a way to make the time, and you would find a way to actually write. Cory Doctorow says that no matter what, he tries for 250 words a day (that's a third of what I've written in this entry to this point), and if you write just 250 words a day—the equivalent to a single, double-spaced page of text—then in a year you have 90,000 words. That's the length of a novel. Off of 250 words a day. Which you could do. On the goddamned *bus*. If you really wanted.

This is why at this point in time I have really very little patience for people who say they want to write but then come up with all sorts of excuses as to why they don't have the time. You know what, today is the day my friend Jay Lake goes into surgery to remove a huge chunk of his liver. After which he goes into chemo. For the third time in two years. Between chemo and everything else, he still does work for his day job. And when I last saw him, he was telling me about the novel he was just finishing up. Let me repeat that for you: Jay Lake has been fighting cancer and has had poison running through his system for two years, still does work for his day job and has written novels. So will you please just shut the fuck up about how hard it is for you to find the time and inspiration to write, and just do it or not.

And to repeat: It's *okay* if you don't. There's nothing wrong with deciding that when it really comes down to it, you want to do things other than writing. It's even okay to start writing, work at it a while, and decide it's not for you. Being a writer isn't some grand, mystical state of being, it just means you put words together to amuse people, most of all yourself. There's no more shame in not being a writer than there is in not being a painter, or a botanist, or a real estate agent—all of which are things I, personally, quite easily do not regret not being.

But if you want to be a writer, then *be* a writer, for god's sake. It's not that hard, and it doesn't require that much effort on a day-to-day basis. Find the time or make the time. Sit down, shut up and put your words together. Work at it and keep working at it. And if you need inspiration, think of yourself on your deathbed saying "well, at least I watched a lot of TV." If saying such a thing as your life ebbs away fills you with existential horror, well, then. I think you know what to do.

You Never Go Full McCain

Sep 14 2012

Here's the thing about Mitt Romney: He's a Republican candidate for president in the unenviable bind of not being able to run on any sort of record at all. He's tried to run on his record as a businessman, but that's been no good. The Democrats have done a pretty effective job painting him as a robber baron lighting cigars with the pensions of little old ladies, whose companies Bain & Company just liquidated for the LOLs. He can't run on his record as a governor, because then the GOP base has its face rubbed in the fact that Romney *gave socialized medicine to gay people who could get married,* and that just won't do. He can't go out there and articulate his economic plan, bolted on as it is by the good graces of his Vice Presidential candidate Paul Ryan, because Ryan's economic plan is frankly insane, the sort of plan you make when you apparently think that the oliganarchy of the Russian 1990s is something to aim for, not run away from.

Constrained as he is, he's got nothing he can actually use to make a case for himself but himself—Mitt Romney, with that genial smile that doesn't quite reach his eyes, that head of hair strategically left to gray at the temples, and that paternal aura of competence that says, *hey, trust me, put me in the job and we'll deal with all those silly fiddly details later.* And you know what? With the economy still farting about and Obama still being as cuddly as a prickly pear, and Romney having a bunch of SuperPACs willing to shovel money until there's not a swing state that's not carpetbombed with ads, this had a reasonably good chance of working. But ultimately it only works if you actually trust Romney—or alternately, have no reason to *distrust* Romney—to make sane, responsible and intelligent decisions.

Which is why Romney blew up his chance to be president this week: He showed, manifestly, that he's indeed capable of making horrible, awful, very bad, no good, terrible choices. First, by deciding that a foreign crisis, generally considered to be off-limits for bald, obvious politicking, would be an excellent time to engage in some bald, obvious politicking. Second, by making a statement slamming the president while the crisis was still in the process of developing and getting worse. Third, by blaming the president for an action he had no hand in (the press release from the under siege embassy) and which his administration had disavowed. Fourth, when after the facts of the events became clear, and it became clear that Romney's statement had some serious factual holes in it, for doubling down at a press conference on assertions everyone knew by that time *weren't correct*.

How appalling was Romney's decision-making process in attacking Obama on the embassy attacks? So appalling that it took *three whole days* for the GOP to find a way to get its messaging to support Romney's position (sort of). And in the meantime, everyone in the world was treated to diplomats, politicians and commentators on both sides of the aisle saying the somewhat more articulate equivalent of "What is this I don't *even*" to Romney's antics.

Was there a legitimate criticism to be made of the administration's handling of the embassy attacks? Sure, although it would have been smarter not to release it on September 11. Did Romney make it? No. When presented with a fine opportunity to recraft and restate his criticism, did Romney take advantage of it? Quite the opposite, in fact. Has Romney's refusal to walk back his initial screw-up compromised legitimate criticism about how the embassy attacks have been handled? Oh, my, *yes*. It's amazing, actually. It's as if at every turn in the crisis Romney had an opportunity to do something that *wouldn't* make him look like a cat with a bag on its head navigating through a room full of bar stool legs, and chose instead the opposing course. It's impressive in its way, but it's a not a good way to be impressive.

What Romney has done here is in fact similar to something his predecessor John McCain did in 2008: Seize a moment in a crisis to take a bold step, without checking to see if one is in fact stepping into the abyss. McCain's moment came when the economy started collapsing in on itself, and McCain decided to suspend his campaign, postpone the debates and generally attempt to make it look like he was already president. This didn't go over particularly well, as you may recall. It certainly puzzled me. For me it signaled the point at which Obama began pulling away with the election, because it made McCain look panicky and befuddled rather than decisive and in charge. As I wrote at the time:

> *I wish that this sudden, overwhelming concern wasn't such a transparent attempt to continue the McCain presidential strategy of attempting to win the White House without being required to articulate coherently to the public or the press why he's presidential material. McCain has missed more Senate votes this year than any senator not recovering from a massive stroke, so an active presence in the Senate is not something he's put much of a premium on since beginning his campaign. He isn't rushing to Washington to help, he's running away from everything else. He is the Sir Robin of the 2008 presidential election.*

Fast-forward to 2012. Here is another crisis, of a different sort. Here's another candidate, attempting to look bold and decisive, ending up looking like he has no idea what he's doing and in the process stripping away the one item he has to base his campaign on: The illusion that he can be trusted to do the right thing. Here's another place where there's an excellent chance we'll one day look back and say: This is where the GOP lost the presidency this time around.

Romney went Full McCain on this one. We see how well it worked for McCain. I suspect it'll work just as well for Romney.

Right Here, Right Now

Nov
24
2011

There's no way to note this without appearing just the tiniest bit morbid, so I'll come right out and say it: One day, I will be dead. Indeed, if you are reading this in the future (and one day, you may just be!) I may already be dead. In which case: Uh, hello, future. I hope you're enjoying your personal rocket packs, which I never got, you lucky bastards. But that's okay, because so far, when I lived and where I lived was not bad for me in the slightest. In fact, for someone like me, it was (and to get back to the current time, *is*) a pretty good time to be alive.

It has its problems. Right now the US is in a severe money crunch and something that we're being told isn't an actual depression but is about as close to one as anyone under the age of eighty has ever experienced. Class divisions are as stark as they have been in the history of our country. We're in an extraordinarily partisan political environment that's paralyzing our governments, federal and state, and we're about to gear up for an election year that promises to rival the presidential elections of the early 1800s in terms of sheer nastiness. And then there's the rest of the world. Oy.

It's a mess. But it's never not a mess. This is not to discount the problems we have now—please, let's *not*—but it is a reminder that every time and every generation has its crises and its troubles. In my own lifetime of 42 years to date, troubles in the United States have included the Vietnam War, Watergate, oil embargos, stagflation, recessions, the cold war, the rise of the national debt, climate change, 9/11, the Iraq and Afghanistan wars and banking crisis. That's nothing compared to the

40 years before I was born, mind you. But it's enough to make the point that whenever you live, one's world and one's nation will be beset by challenges. We're humans. This is what we do.

I note this to acknowledge the fact this time and place are not perfect. I do what I can to help it become what I see as more perfect, while knowing it'll never get there in my lifetime or (judging from the history of the world) in the lifetimes of probably the next hundred generations to come. Perfection is probably not the point for humans anyway; the working toward it is. It's like the speed of light: something you'll never reach no matter how much energy you put into it, but still worth getting as close to as possible because of the things you'll learn by doing so.

So: not a perfect time. But is it the *right* time for me? I think so. Part of this is entirely practical: this is the time of three "A"s: Air conditioning, antibiotics and anesthesia, all of which make life longer and more pleasant. It's also the time when I walk around with a computer that fits into the palm of my hand that lets me access information from the entire span of human history, more books, music and moving entertainment that I could read, listen and see if I had seven more lifetimes, and which allows me to communicate, instantly and cheaply, with friends on the other side of the planet almost as easily as if they were in the room with me. I live in a time where I can make a living, sitting in a room in my house, typing.

Part of this is transitional: I live in a time where human rights, while being contested as they always are, are more widely spread than at any other point in history. Technology is making these rights all but unavoidable, even as it equally offers up new challenges to issues like privacy and government intrusion. I am living in a time where I get to see people who were denied their right to care for each other like any others gain those rights, and in that struggle help the rest of us become better people ourselves. I live in a time where we're finally becoming serious about weaning ourselves from oil and all the attendant political and social baggage that dependency has required from us. I mean, holy crap, General Motors offers an electric car—for *real* this time. It's not to say that transitions solve problems—every change brings up new issues and challenges. But I like that these changes are happening now, and am happy to accept the idea that change does not equal "and now we never have to think about any of this ever again."

Part of it is personal: I like the *people* I know now. Living in any other time and any other place would mean different people in my life. I don't doubt that I would be able to find good people with whom to live my life—but it wouldn't be *these* people, and my life would be different, and to a non-trivial extent, I would therefore be different as well. I'm grateful that living now has led me to my wife, and has resulted in my child, both of whom I cannot imagine my life being improved without, no matter who else could theoretically replace their roles. I can't imagine wanting to be without the other people that I love, who live here and now. These are the right people for me. They exist now and only now, here and only here.

Living now means I won't live later, which is more than a little annoying for a science fiction writer, who spends so much of his time imagining people, places and times in the future. It's also a little depressing for someone who likes being alive, and conscious, and engaged in a world with so many interesting things about it. I like everyone once held out the hope that before I shuffled off that they'd find a way to make people live forever. They have not, but this is not necessarily a bad thing. I probably wouldn't turn down the opportunity to live longer (and healthier, and better, and with more hair and less saggy chin, please); I don't really expect to live forever, nor do I ultimately see the wisdom of cursing this planet with the same static seven billion people. There's also the pertinent point my friend Mykal Burns brought up several years ago when I asked him if he wanted to live forever: "Why would I want to live forever? I get bored *now*."

I won't live forever. I will die one day, and there will be many things many people will experience—both good and bad—which I never will. That's the deal. It is biologically speaking the reason you have kids, so that part of you goes on even if you don't. Socially speaking, it's why you make an effort to raise your children to be intelligent and active people, engaged in the world, so that their world, for the time they are in it, is one they are happy to be in. It's why we as humans continue to try to make the world better, so that humans, whether specifically our children or not, will continue on. By the activity in our own lives, we implicitly accept that *we* will not last.

I will not last. But right now I *am* here, and I am thankful that I get to be here, now. To you people of the future, who might read this after I'm gone, I envy you the things that you get to see and do that I will not, the people you will know and the places that you will go, both here and—who knows? I *am* a science fiction writer—elsewhere. But know this: By not being here where I am, when I am, you missed out on a lot, too. These were and are exciting times to live through, with some of the best people you could hope to meet.

I wish you could have known them, the times and the people, as I do. I am sorry that you will not. But I hope that in your time, in your place and with the people you know and hopefully love, that you are as thankful for them I am with mine. If you are, then that is something we can share, no matter what else separates us. I hope you feel it.